THE
UNCOMMON GOURMET

ELLEN HELMAN

TEN SPEED PRESS
P. O. Box 7123
Berkeley, California 94707

Cover and text design by Purney Design, Boston
Typeset by Font & Center, Weston, Massachusetts

Library of Congress Cataloging-in-Publication Data

Helman, Ellen.
    The uncommon gourmet / Ellen Helman.
        p.   cm.
    Includes index.
    ISBN 0-89815-519-3
    1. Cookery   I. Title.
TX714.H44   1993
641.5--dc20   92-32082
                                                            CIP

Printed in the United States of America

  2 3 4 5 — 97 96 95 94

With heartfelt thanks to:

Bobby, Lee and Jen
For their constant love and support.

Ilene and Suzin
For making it all happen.

Odette
For her invaluable help and guidance.

TABLE OF

CONTENTS

PREFACE

The taller the toque, the more accomplished the chef!

The essence of cooking is an art, and therefore, every cook is an artist. All artists create to excite the senses; the culinary artist also strives to awaken and stimulate the senses. The look, smell, taste, and texture are all part of food's appeal. The recipes in this book aim to illustrate this idea.

Recently there has been a renaissance in the culinary arts. People's tastes have taken on new directions and new dimensions. This has been typified by a growing awareness of fresh, natural foods, free of additives and preservatives, and by an interest in their preparation and presentation. Chefs and cooks alike are striving for tantalizing dishes with delicate tastes and subtle flavors.

There has been a mushrooming revolution in what is considered "chic" foods. Such offerings as pesto, sun-dried tomatoes, goat cheese, salsas and relishes, fruity vinegars, pastas, and ethnic foods are high on the list. One of my favorites is pasta because of its versatility as well as its wholesomeness. With this in mind, a key emphasis in *The Uncommon Gourmet* is on flavorful dishes using fresh ingredients with a concentration on seafood, poultry, vegetables, salads, and pasta.

As a form of self-expression, both men and women have become enthusiastically involved in cooking. They display a certain life style that includes sophisticated tastes. Unlike most other artists, the "gourmet" artist receives instant gratification, and is rewarded by seeing people enjoy and derive pleasure from his creation.

Cooking is a challenging, creative hobby. One must participate in order to experience the pride and satisfaction that cooking can offer—so indulge yourself! Remember, eating is a necessary and vital part of living, and you can make this a pleasurable experience by adding interest and color to the food. Let those most important to you savor the genius of your creations, as the finished product reflects the thought, time, and effort you have invested. As every artist has his own color palette, so each cook reaches for his or her unique palette of seasonings—his signature—his favorite herbs, spices, and condiments that distinguishes his recipes from all others. Some of my most favored ingredients tend to have Mediterranean influences. I keep my pantry stocked with these specialties: garlic, roasted red peppers, sun-dried tomatoes, Dijon mustard, balsamic vinegar, pine nuts, basil, Parmesan cheese, and pesto.

In this book, I have attempted to help the adventurous cook achieve interesting ways of seasoning and saucing foods without undo fuss. Many recipes can be prepared in advance, especially those dishes needing extra attention. It does not require special talents to prepare a delicious meal, just a little patience and a lot of love.

Good eating and happy times!

Ellen Helman

Most people find the toque, or chef's hat, intriguing. Little seems to be written about its origins. However, references say the cap was modeled after the black hat worn by priests in ancient Byzantine monasteries. During the Middle Ages it seems that many cooks took refuge in the monasteries from harsh rulers. To separate the cooks from the monks, the chefs donned distinguished tall white hats instead of the usual black ones worn by the priests.

The hat has remained white as it is the symbol of cleanliness. The height allows for more air to circulate around the chef's head in hot kitchens. The very high hat indicates the chief chef; the sous-chiefs, or assistants, wear shorter versions. The tall toque is a definite sign of accomplishment in haute cuisine.

BASICS

There are several points of information and advice that are helpful in the understanding and use of the recipes in this book. Keep them in mind when creating a masterpiece:

1. Presentation and eye appeal are of crucial importance. Always make the food look attractive—use interesting containers to house the food—baskets and hollowed-out breads for raw vegetables; decorate the food with garnishes—parsley, greenery, a flower, chopped nuts. Remember, if the food looks appealing, people will want to eat it!

2. When baking, always preheat the oven for 10 minutes.

3. When baking, always use the middle rack in the oven.

4. When eggs are called for in a recipe, use extra-large ones.

5. Butter may be replaced by margarine in a recipe.

6. When oil is used in a recipe, pure vegetable oil is preferable, unless olive oil is specified.

7. About salt—to salt or not? I salt very sparingly when cooking, just enough to bring out the flavors and enhance the food. In most recipes I have suggested using salt to taste; in certain recipes I have noted specific amounts, and unless on a salt-restricted diet, follow the amount indicated.

8. If fresh herbs are readily available, by all means substitute them in any recipe. Use 3X the amount of fresh for the dried amount (1 teaspoon dried = 1 tablespoon fresh).

9. The basic recipes that are included in this section are essential tools for the cook.

PIE CRUST

This recipe makes enough dough for a 9-inch deep-dish crust. It is especially good for quiche.

1¹/₂ cups all-purpose flour
¹/₂ teaspoon salt
4 tablespoons unsalted butter
4 tablespoons margarine
4 tablespoons ice water

1. Sift the flour and salt into a mixing bowl. Add the cold butter and margarine. Using a pastry blender, cut the shortening into the dry ingredients until the texture of coarse cornmeal.

2. Sprinkle with the ice water, a tablespoon at a time, while stirring with a fork. When all the water has been added, work the dough with your hands to form a ball. Wrap the dough in plastic wrap and chill for 1 hour.

3. Roll the dough out on a floured board to ¹/₈-inch thick. Line a 9-inch deep-dish pie pan. Crimp the edges.

4. Before prebaking, prick the bottom of the shell with a fork. Line the dough with a foil pie plate filled with beans or rice. Bake in a 425° oven for 8 minutes. Remove the bean-filled foil pan. Return to the oven for 4 minutes more. Cool the shell and adorn with your favorite quiche or pie filling.

One deep-dish 9-inch pie crust

HOMEMADE PASTA

There's nothing quite like the taste and texture of freshly made pasta. Store bought pasta pales by comparison. Some specialty shops have taken to selling their own homemade pasta which is quite good, but for those who enjoy creating, this is wholesome eating.

2 cups flour
3 large eggs
1/2 teaspoon salt

1. Using the steel blade in your food processor, place all of the ingredients in the processor bowl. Pulse only until the dough comes together and forms a ball. Remove the dough and divide it into 2 to 3 portions for rolling. Refrigerate 1 to 2 hours, until the dough is cold.

2. With a hand pasta rolling machine, start feeding a flattened portion of the dough through the kneading rollers on the number six setting. Repeat passing the dough through the number six setting 2 more times; flour the dough lightly, then lower the gauge from six to four, and finally to the number two setting, feeding the dough through the rollers until you achieve the desired thinness. (The thinner the pasta, the less cooking time.) Then pass the pasta through the appropriate cutting roller to get the desired shape. Hang the pasta to dry for 2 hours. You may now boil it for 2 to 3 minutes, or flour it lightly, and freeze it for later use.

6 portions

Note—To increase the recipe, use 1 to 2 more eggs than each additional cup of flour. (With 4 cups of flour, use 5 to 6 eggs.)

HOT MUSTARD

Beware, this mustard is quite strong if used straight as a spread in sandwiches. It is delicious when used to coat meat, lamb, chicken, and fish before cooking; mixed with butter as a sauce for vegetables; and incorporated into salad dressings. It's a staple in our pantry!

> 4 ounce tin Colman's dry mustard
> 1 cup sugar
> 1/8 teaspoon cayenne pepper
> 1 cup cider vinegar

1. In a saucepan, mix the mustard, sugar, and pepper. Add the vinegar, stirring well. Let the mixture sit for 4 hours.

2. Heat the mustard over medium-high heat, stirring constantly until the mixture comes to a boil.

3. Remove from the heat and pour into a well-sealed jar or container. Cover and let cool completely before refrigerating. Note—the mustard will keep 2 months in the refrigerator.

About 2 cups

BASIC VINAIGRETTE

A classic olive oil and red wine vinegar dressing with enchanting variations. Use the finest grade olive oil—extra virgin—for exquisite flavor.

2 tablespoons red wine vinegar
1/4 teaspoon salt (or to taste)
lots of freshly ground black pepper to taste
1/3 cup olive oil

1. In a bowl combine the vinegar, salt, and pepper.
2. Whisk in the olive oil until completely incorporated.

For a Dijon Vinaigrette, simply add:
1 clove garlic, smashed
1 teaspoon Dijon mustard

For an Herbal Vinaigrette, add:
1 clove garlic, smashed
1 teaspoon Dijon mustard
1/2 to 1 teaspoon of your favorite dried herb—basil, oregano, tarragon, or thyme, or in combination

Enough dressing to serve 6

HOLLANDAISE SAUCE

An easy blender version of this classic butter sauce. This is excellent over cold chicken, poached salmon, broccoli, asparagus, and artichokes.

3 egg yolks
2 tablespoons lemon juice
pinch salt
generous pinch cayenne pepper
1/2 cup melted butter

1. In a blender or food processor, combine the egg yolks, lemon juice, salt, and cayenne, pulsing to mix.

2. While the machine is running, add the hot butter in a slow, steady stream. Turn the machine off when all the butter has been incorporated. Use at once or refrigerate for later use. Return to room temperature before serving.

3/4 cup sauce

BEARNAISE SAUCE

My own simple rendition of the classic butter-based tarragon sauce prepared in a food processor. It is a wonderful sauce for roasted beef, chicken, shrimp, and lobster. Also try it over your favorite green vegetables—or not so favorite—and you'll soon discover how good they can be.

3 egg yolks
1/2 tablespoon lemon juice
1/2 tablespoon tarragon vinegar
pinch salt
freshly ground pepper to taste
pinch cayenne pepper
1 teaspoon dried tarragon
1 tablespoon snipped chives
1/2 cup lightly salted butter, melted

1. Put the egg yolks, lemon juice, vinegar, salt, peppers, tarragon, and chives in the bowl of a food processor or blender.

2. Turn the machine on, and slowly add the melted butter in a steady stream. Continue to process a few seconds after all the butter has been added, making sure all the ingredients are well blended.

3. Serve the sauce immediately, or let cool slightly and refrigerate for later use. Bring to room temperature before serving. Note—the sauce thickens upon standing.

1 cup sauce

ARTICHOKE-MUSTARD SAUCE

A creamy mustard-based sauce featuring chopped artichoke hearts. I use this sauce to adorn any cooked meats—steak, lamb, pork—chicken or turkey, or to dress a piece of grilled fish.

> *1/4 cup Dijon mustard*
> *6 tablespoons boiling water*
> *3/4 cup olive oil*
> *freshly ground pepper to taste*
> *2 teaspoons lemon juice*
> *14 ounce can artichoke hearts, drained and coarsely chopped*

1. Place the mustard in a bowl. Gradually add the water, beating constantly, until all the water has been incorporated.

2. In a slow, steady stream, add the oil, whisking constantly until all the oil has been added and the sauce is creamy.

3. Stir in the pepper and lemon juice, mixing well.

4. Add the chopped artichoke hearts and stir to blend. Serve the sauce as is, or refrigerate for later use. If you choose to prepare the sauce in advance (may be done up to 8 hours ahead), bring the sauce to room temperature before serving.

Approximately 2 cups sauce

LIQUID MEASURES

1 pinch	less than $1/8$ teaspoon
1 teaspoon	$1/3$ tablespoon
$1\frac{1}{2}$ teaspoons	$1/2$ tablespoon
3 teaspoons	1 tablespoon
2 tablespoons	$1/8$ cup
4 tablespoons	$1/4$ cup
8 tablespoons	$1/2$ cup
16 tablespoons	1 cup ($1/2$ pint)
32 tablespoons	2 cups (1 pint)
64 tablespoons	4 cups (1 quart)

EQUIVALENTS

Butter:	1 stick	$1/2$ cup = 4 ounces = $1/4$ pound
	4 sticks	2 cups = 16 ounces = 1 pound
Cheese:		
Hard cheese, grated	4 ounces = 1 cup	
Chocolate:		
Chips	6 ounces = 1 cup	
Unsweetened	1 square = 1 ounce	
Coconut:		
Flaked	$3\frac{1}{2}$ ounces = $1\frac{1}{3}$ cups	
Egg Whites:	7 large whites = 1 cup	
Flour:		
All-Purpose	1 pound = $4\frac{1}{4}$ cups unsifted	
Herbs:	1 tablespoon fresh = 1 teaspoon dried	
Lemon:		
Juice	1 medium lemon = 2 to 3 tablespoons juice	
Rind	1 medium lemon = 1 tablespoon grated zest	
Rice:	1 cup raw = 3 cups cooked	
Sugar:		
Granulated	1 pound = $2\frac{1}{4}$ to $2\frac{1}{2}$ cups	
Brown, firmly packed	1 pound = $2\frac{1}{4}$ cups	
Confectioners'	1 pound = $4\frac{1}{2}$ cups sifted	
Walnuts:		
Nutmeats	1 pound = 4 cups	

GOOD BEGINNINGS

Appetizers and hors d'oeuvres are meal openers. They welcome your guests and should tantilize the palate and whet the appetite for what is to follow.

Hors d'oeuvres are best when they are bite-size or finger foods to accompany cocktails. Appetizers are often more formal and served at the dinner table as a first course.

Make the food look beautiful. Present it with style and flair. Use various foods in place of bowls for interesting ways of serving many hors d'oeuvres—mushrooms stuffed with Boursin, a hollowed-out red cabbage to house a dip, a scooped-out round of bread to house pâté, smoked salmon mousse mounded on cucumber rounds. Try to make the food colorful and appealing. Decorate it with garnishes and serve it in unusual containers. Fill baskets with cheese wafers and spiced nuts; fill a large brandy goblet with marinated vegetables; serve gravlax on a bed of uncooked, dried spinach pasta; or marinated shrimp heaped into a mold, garnished with a single peony or dahlia. Try a straw hat filled with a bounty of crudités.

Let your creativity flow, making good beginnings a visual experience!

DIPS AND SPREADS

CURRY GARLIC DIP

I will be forever grateful to Aunt Shirley for introducing us to this recipe. A mayonnaise base is seasoned with curry, garlic, and Worcestershire sauce which blend together for an unusual flavor. This dip is always a smashing success. It's also fabulous as a sauce for cold steak, pork, or lamb, and divine with cold, poached shrimp!

> 1 pint mayonnaise
> 3 tablespoons chili sauce
> 1 tablespoon curry powder
> 1 tablespoon garlic powder
> 1/4 teaspoon salt
> 1/4 teaspoon pepper
> 1 tablespoon grated onion
> 1 tablespoon Worcestershire sauce

1. Combine all ingredients in a large bowl and mix well. Cover and refrigerate for at least 24 hours, allowing the flavors to blend together. (This dip will keep refrigerated for 2 to 3 weeks.)

2. Present with an assortment of lightly blanched and raw vegetables.

About 2 cups of dip

SOME FAVORITE CRUDITES

- Artichoke hearts
- Asparagus
- Broccoli
- Carrots
- Cauliflower
- Celery
- Cherry tomatoes
- Cucumber
- Mushrooms
- Green, red, yellow, and orange peppers
- Radishes
- Snow peas
- Zucchini

TAPENADE

My version of the Italian olive spread—a smooth and creamy tuna, anchovy, and black olive purée. Serve this appetizer with toasted French bread slices, raw vegetables, or cooked tortellini. It also makes a delectable sauce for grilled veal chops, chicken, or turkey breasts.

6¹/2 ounce can tuna, drained
2 ounce can anchovies, rinsed in warm water and drained
1 tablespoon Dijon mustard
2 tablespoons lemon juice
1/4 cup chopped fresh parsley
1 tablespoon capers
1/2 cup canned pitted ripe black olives
freshly ground black pepper to taste
2/3 cup olive oil

1. Place all of the ingredients except the olive oil in the bowl of a food processor. Purée until smooth.

2. In a slow, steady stream, add the oil and continue to process until completely incorporated and the sauce is creamy.

3. The sauce may be prepared 24 hours in advance and kept refrigerated. Return to room temperature to serve.

8 to 10 portions

SPICY BEAN DIP

Legumes, of which the kidney bean is one, have become a fashionable item in gastronomy—very chic and also very nutritious. In this dip, the humble red kidney bean is puréed with "hot" chili seasonings for a real Southwestern treat. A well-received, easy to prepare dish for gatherings and casual munching; great served with nacho chips or vegetables.

19 ounce can red kidney beans, rinsed and drained
1 to 2 cloves garlic, crushed
1 tablespoon chili powder
1/2 teaspoon celery seed
1/4 teaspoon cayenne pepper
salt to taste
1/8 teaspoon black pepper
2 tablespoons chopped fresh parsley
2 tablespoons lemon juice
1/2 cup olive oil

1. Put all of the ingredients except the olive oil in the bowl of a food processor. Purée until pasty.

2. In a slow, steady stream, add the oil while continuing to process, until thick and creamy. (May be prepared 1 to 2 days in advance and refrigerated until needed. Return to room temperature to serve.)

6 portions

HUMMUS

The cumin gives this Middle-Eastern spread a distinctive flavor. Best served with wedges of pita bread.

20 ounce can chick peas, drained
1/2 cup olive oil
1/4 cup lemon juice
2 to 3 cloves garlic, crushed
1/4 teaspoon cumin
1 teaspoon chopped fresh parsley
salt and freshly ground pepper to taste
pita bread

1. Place the chick peas in a colander and rinse with cold water. Drain well.

2. Combine the drained chick peas, oil, lemon juice, and seasonings in the bowl of a food processor or blender. Purée the mixture until smooth.

3. Transfer the hummus to a bowl and chill until needed. It will keep refrigerated 2 to 3 days.

4 to 6 portions

CHEDDAR SPREAD

A creamy cheddar pâté piquantly seasoned.

1/2 cup butter
8 ounces cream cheese
1/2 pound sharp cheddar cheese, grated
1 tablespoon Worcestershire sauce
1/4 teaspoon black pepper
1/2 teaspoon dry mustard
3 tablespoons chopped fresh parsley
generous pinch cayenne pepper

1. Combine all the ingredients in a food processor and blend until smooth.

2. Scrape into a bowl. Cover and refrigerate until needed. When ready to serve, return to room temperature. Serve with crackers, slices of French bread, and cucumber rounds.

6 to 8 portions

CHICKEN LIVER PATE

A creamy textured pâté delicately flavored with apple and seasoned with garlic and ginger. In addition to its use as a spread, the pâté makes a tasty stuffing for mushroom caps.

4 tablespoons butter
1 medium onion, finely chopped
1 clove garlic, crushed
1 large Granny Smith apple, peeled, cored, and sliced
1 pound chicken livers
1 tablespoon dry white wine
4 ounces cream cheese
2 tablespoons mayonnaise
salt to taste
1/8 teaspoon pepper
1/8 teaspoon ground ginger
1 tablespoon chopped fresh parsley

1. Melt the butter in a large skillet. Add the onion, garlic, and apple, and sauté over medium heat until the onion is golden.

2. Add the chicken livers. When they begin to lose their redness, add the white wine. Cook for 5 minutes until the liver is well done.

3. Remove the skillet from the heat. Transfer the liver mixture to the bowl of a food processor, along with the cream cheese, mayonnaise, salt, pepper, ginger, and parsley. Process until smooth and creamy.

4. Scrape the purée into a serving bowl. Cover and chill 2 to 3 hours. Let the pâté return to room temperature before serving. Surround the pâté with slices of crusty French bread.

8 or more portions

FRESH FRUITS WITH LIME-COCONUT CREAM

A colorful, refreshing beginning to a meal—cut up fruits with a creamy coconut dip.

1 pint sour cream
1/2 cup sweetened shredded coconut
1/4 cup freshly squeezed lime juice and pulp
1 tablespoon finely grated lime peel
1 tablespoon honey
2 kiwi
1 cantaloupe
1/2 honeydew melon
1 medium pineapple
1 pint strawberries
2 medium bananas

1. Combine the sour cream, coconut, lime juice, peel, and honey; blend well. Refrigerate at least 2 hours until ready to use.

2. Peel the kiwi, and slice into rounds. Cut the melons and pineapple into 1-inch chunks. Wash and hull the strawberries. Pile the fruit in a large glass bowl, and refrigerate until needed. When ready to serve, slice the bananas and add to the bowl. Present the fruit accompanied by the coconut dip.

6 to 8 portions

FAVORITE SUMMER MELONS

- Cantaloupe
- Casaba
- Cranshaw
- Honeydew
- Persian
- Watermelon

Wedges of melon are delicious plain, with a squeeze of lime, or draped with thin slices of prosciutto or smoked salmon.

BAKED BRIE PRALINE

This always brings rave reviews. It is the stuff of which dreams are made! Warmed Brie cheese encrusted with a chopped pecan and brown sugar topping. For a change of pace, try this as a dessert cheese with a sliced pear accompaniment.

1 baby Brie or wedges of Brie cheese, total weight of 2¹/2 lbs.
³/4 cup chopped pecans
¹/3 cup dark brown sugar, firmly packed

1. Preheat the oven to 350°. Grease a 10-inch quiche or pie pan.

2. Remove the white rind from the Brie. Place the Brie in the prepared pan. If you are using several wedges rather than a baby Brie, it will be necessary to alternate the directions of the pieces to fit them in the pan.

3. Stud the Brie with the pecans, pressing the nuts into the cheese. Sprinkle the brown sugar over the top.

4. Set in the oven for 15 minutes until warm and melted or heat in a microwave. Place under the broiler very briefly to carmelize the sugar, being careful not to burn the nuts or the sugar. Serve immediately with table water crackers or French bread.

10 to 12 portions

TANTALIZING TIDBITS

For a simple, yet always successful presentation, arrange fresh fruit, cheeses, and nuts as a meal opener.

• Roquefort, sliced Granny Smith apples, and walnuts.
• Brie, figs, and pecans.
• Jarlsberg, purple grapes, and cashews.
• Chèvre, pears, and almonds.

As wonderful as a beginning, it is just as superb to cap a splendid meal!

FINGER FOODS

SPICED WALNUTS

Light and crispy! Cheese and wine accompaniment round out these tidbits.

> 3 cups walnuts
> 2/3 cup sugar
> 1 tablespoon orange juice
> 1 teaspoon cinnamon
> 1/2 teaspoon nutmeg
> 1/2 teaspoon ground cloves
> 1 teaspoon grated orange peel
> 1 egg white from an extra-large egg

1. Preheat the oven to 300°. Grease a cookie sheet.

2. Pile the walnuts in a large mixing bowl.

3. Combine the sugar, orange juice, spices, and egg white and blend thoroughly. Pour the spice mixture over the walnuts and toss well.

4. Spread the nuts out in a single layer on the prepared cookie sheet. Bake for 30 minutes, stirring every 10 minutes. Transfer the nuts to a plate to cool. The nuts will keep in an air tight container for 2 weeks.

Enough for 6 to 8 portions

OLIVES A LA GRECQUE

A mélange of olive varieties—the longer these marinate, the better they are! Of Mediterranean origin, olives have been a staple of Italy for centuries. Olives are characteristically salty, and add piquancy to otherwise bland food.

2 cups stuffed Spanish green olives
2 cups oil cured black Italian olives
2 cups colossal ripe black olives
³/₄ cup olive oil
¹/₄ cup red wine vinegar
2 large cloves garlic, smashed
¹/₄ cup chopped fresh parsley
¹/₂ teaspoon Dijon mustard
freshly ground pepper to taste

1. Drain all the olives well, and pile them in a glass bowl.

2. Whisk together the oil, vinegar, garlic, parsley, mustard, and pepper. Pour the dressing over the olives, and toss well.

3. Cover and refrigerate the mélange overnight. After 24 hours, remove the garlic, toss again, and serve. This will keep refrigerated for 3 weeks.

8 or more portions

MARINATED MUSHROOMS

Whole mushrooms are marinated in a delicate-herbed Dijon vinaigrette.

> 1 pound mushrooms
> 2 tablespoons Dijon mustard
> 2 tablespoons lemon juice
> 6 tablespoons olive oil
> salt to taste
> 1/8 teaspoon pepper
> 1/2 teaspoon dried oregano
> 1/2 teaspoon dried tarragon
> 2 tablespoons chopped fresh parsley

1. Clean the mushrooms and heap them into a glass bowl.

2. Whisk together the mustard, lemon juice, oil, salt, pepper, and herbs. Pour the vinaigrette over the mushrooms and toss. Cover and refrigerate at least 6 hours.

3. Toss again before serving.

6 portions

MUSHROOMS BOURSIN

Mushrooms stuffed with herbed Boursin cheese and spinach for a truly delicious sensation!

1 pint medium-size mushrooms
5 ounce package Boursin cheese
$^1/_2$ cup cooked, chopped spinach
$^1/_2$ cup chopped fresh parsley

1. Preheat the oven to 450°.

2. Clean the mushrooms and remove the stems. Mix together the Boursin and spinach. Stuff each cap with a spoonful of the cheese mixture. Coat the cheese with the chopped parsley.

3. Arrange the stuffed caps on a baking sheet and set in the oven for 10 minutes. Serve piping hot!

6 portions

IDEAS FOR STUFFED MUSHROOMS

- Stuff caps with pâté, brush with melted butter, heat and serve.
- Fill caps with a mixture of sour cream, chives, and Parmesan. Place in the oven and enjoy piping hot.
- Stuff caps with chopped prosciutto and grated mozzarella; run under broiler.
- Stuff caps with a mixture of chopped, smoked salmon, cream cheese, dill, and freshly ground pepper.
- Fill caps with cooked, chopped spinach mixed with ricotta and Romano. Drizzle with butter and bake.
- Fill caps with Roquefort and grated apple and warm in oven.

ARTICHOKE HEARTS AND PROSCIUTTO

An easy to prepare and elegant finger food! Artichoke hearts are wrapped in paper thin slices of prosciutto and then marinated in an orange-thyme imbued olive oil. The salt-cured Italian ham complements the bland flavor of the artichoke hearts.

> *14 ounce can artichoke hearts, drained and cut in half*
> *1/3 pound prosciutto, sliced paper thin*
> *1/4 cup olive oil*
> *1/2 teaspoon dried thyme*
> *1/2 teaspoon finely grated orange peel*
> *freshly ground pepper to taste*

1. Wrap each artichoke heart in a slice of prosciutto and secure with a toothpick.

2. In a separate bowl, whisk together the olive oil, thyme, orange peel, and pepper. Pour the dressing over the roll-ups and let marinate 1 to 2 hours or as much as overnight.

3. Serve at room temperature.

12 to 16 roll-ups

ASPARAGUS WITH SMOKED SALMON

Poached asparagus spears are wrapped with slices of smoked salmon. A colorful combination—the pink of the salmon set against the vivid green of the asparagus.

24 mature asparagus spears, peeled and steamed 7 to 8 minutes
3 slices smoked salmon, cut in half lengthwise
freshly ground pepper
2 tablespoons finest quality extra virgin olive oil

1. Wrap 4 asparagus spears with a slice of smoked salmon forming a bundle. Place seam side down on a salad plate. Repeat the process with the remainder of the spears.

2. Season the bundles generously with freshly ground pepper, and drizzle with the olive oil.

3. Present the asparagus wraps at room temperature.

6 portions

GREEN BEANS POMMEROY

Steamed green beans are dressed with a dill-mustard sauce and punctuated with toasted pine nuts. This makes a lovely presentation as a first course, and can also double as a salad or side accompaniment.

1 pound green beans, trimmed
¹/4 cup pine nuts, toasted (see page 273)

Dill-Mustard Sauce:
2 tablespoons Pommeroy mustard (A grainy French mustard, available
    in fine food shops)
2 tablespoons raspberry vinegar
¹/3 cup olive oil
salt and pepper to taste
1 teaspoon dried dill

1. Steam or poach the green beans for 5 minutes until tender crisp. Drain and plunge them into ice water for 5 minutes—this retards further cooking of the beans and brings out their brilliant green color. Drain well and place in a serving dish.

2. Sprinkle pine nuts over the beans.

3. In a small bowl, whisk together the mustard, vinegar, oil, and seasonings until thick and creamy. Pour the mustard sauce over the beans and let marinate 1 to 2 hours, or refrigerate overnight. Return to room temperature before serving.

4. To serve, portion equal amounts of the green bean-nut mixture on each plate, drizzle with the marinade, and present.

6 portions

MARINATED POACHED CARROTS

Carrots are delicately poached before marinating in a garlic-flavored olive oil. Simple, yet absolutely delicious!

2 pounds carrots
1/2 cup extra virgin olive oil
2 large cloves garlic, minced

1. Peel the carrots and cut on the diagonal into 3-inch lengths.

2. Poach the carrots in a pot of boiling salted water for 7 to 8 minutes—until they are barely tender.

3. Remove the carrots from the water, drain well, and arrange in a serving dish.

4. Drizzle the oil over the carrots, season with the minced garlic, and toss well.

5. Cover and refrigerate overnight, or as much as 2 days, as the marinating improves the flavor.

6. When ready to serve, bring the carrots to room temperature. Remove them from the oil, and present them to your guests.

6 to 8 portions

SNOW PEAS AND CARROT ROUNDS

A gift for the Gods!—blanched carrots and snow peas in an herbed marinade, served cold. This may be served for casual nibbling, or presented as individual portions for more formal occasions.

> 1/2 pound carrots, peeled
> 1/2 pound snow peas, stems removed
> 1/4 cup oil
> 1 tablespoon white vinegar
> salt and freshly ground pepper to taste
> 1/2 tablespoon chopped fresh dill or 1/2 teaspoon dried
> 1/4 cup chopped fresh parsley
> 2 tablespoons snipped chives

1. Slice the carrots into 1/4-inch thick rounds.

2. Plunge the carrot rounds into a large pot of boiling water and blanch for 3 minutes. Remove the carrots and place in a bowl of ice water for 3 minutes. Drain well and transfer carrots to a serving bowl. Repeat the procedure with the snow peas, blanching them for 1 minute only, and setting them in ice water for 1 minute. Add the blanched snow peas to the carrots.

3. Whisk together the oil, vinegar, salt, pepper, and herbs.

4. Pour the herbed vinaigrette over the vegetables and toss. Cover and place in the refrigerator to marinate for 1 to 2 hours, or as much as overnight. When ready to serve, toss again and present, spooning any extra dressing over each portion.

4 to 6 portions

CRISPY SKINS

Baked potato skins seasoned with garlic and Parmesan cheese. They are better than potato chips!

6 large baking potatoes
salt and freshly ground pepper to taste
4 tablespoons butter, softened
2 tablespoons olive oil
1 large clove garlic, crushed
1/2 cup Parmesan cheese
1/2 tablespoon chopped fresh parsley
1 tablespoon snipped chives

1. Preheat the oven to 375°.

2. Scrub the potatoes well. Pierce the top of each potato. Bake for 1 to 1 1/2 hours, until tender.

3. Let the potatoes cool. Cut each in half lengthwise and scoop out the pulp, leaving a hollowed-out shell. Season the skins with salt and pepper.

4. Mix together the butter, oil, garlic, Parmesan, parsley, and chives to form a paste. Spread the seasoned butter equally over the inside of the potato shells.

5. Bake in a 400° oven until the potatoes are browned and crisp. Serve immediately.

6 portions

IDEAS FOR STUFFED POTATO SKINS

Fill the hollowed-out baked skins with one of the following combinations; then heat and enjoy.
- Caviar, sour cream, and chopped onion—best served at room temperature.
- Cooked, chopped bacon and cheddar cheese.
- Herbed butter—dill, garlic, tarragon, or cajun.
- Ratatouille.
- Cooked, chopped spinach, feta, and dill.
- Boursin and snipped chives.
- Pâté and grated apple.
- Pesto and crumbled goat cheese—chèvre.
- Chopped plum tomatoes, grated mozzarella, and fresh basil.

CARAWAY CHEESE ROUNDS

These are tangy, buttery cheese wafers generously seasoned with caraway seeds.

1 cup butter
2 cups flour
2 cups sour cream
7 ounces Romano cheese, grated
1 to 2 tablespoons caraway seeds (amount depends on taste)

1. Cream the butter. Add the flour, sour cream, cheese, and caraway seeds; blend thoroughly. Shape the dough into a log about 2 inches in diameter. Cover and refrigerate at least 6 hours, or overnight.

2. When ready to serve, preheat the oven to 350°. Grease two cookie sheets.

3. Remove the dough from the refrigerator and slice 1/4-inch thick. (Return unused dough to the refrigerator while the first batch is baking.) Arrange the caraway cookies on the prepared baking sheets, 2 inches apart.

4. Set in the oven for 20 to 25 minutes until golden. Serve immediately or cool to room temperature. We prefer them hot from the oven.

4 dozen cookies

HERBED GOAT CHEESE TOASTS

The heady flavor and creamy texture of the warmed chèvre or Montrachet is heightened by an array of aromatic spices and punctuated with scallions. Almost like a mini pizza with a rich flavor.

6 ounce goat cheese—chèvre or Montrachet, cut into 8 slices
1/2 teaspoon dried thyme
1/2 teaspoon dried marjoram
1/4 teaspoon dried savory
2 tablespoons chopped fresh parsley
1/4 teaspoon freshly ground black pepper
salt to taste
2 tablespoons chopped scallions
1/4 cup olive oil
1 medium red onion, sliced into 16 thin rings
loaf French bread

1. Lay the cheese slices in a shallow pan. Combine the herbs, scallions, and oil and pour this sauce over the cheese. Marinate 2 to 3 hours or as much as overnight.

2. Cut the French bread into 16 slices, each 3/4-inch thick. Cover each bread round with an onion slice.

3. Cut each cheese slice in half and spread a piece of cheese on top of each slice of onion. Drizzle with the herbed olive oil.

4. Bake in a preheated 400° oven for 10 minutes until warm and melted.

16 cheese toasts

CHICKEN NUGGETS

Crispy chicken pieces coated with pumpernickel bread crumbs, served with horseradish cream sauce. My family favors this style of chicken so much that I oftentimes prepare it as a main course.

> *1 pound boneless chicken (breasts or thighs)*
> *salt and freshly ground pepper to taste*
> *2 tablespoons flour*
> *1 egg beaten with 1 tablespoon water*
> *2 cups fresh pumpernickel bread crumbs*
> *4 tablespoons butter or vegetable oil*
> *Horseradish Sauce (recipe follows)*

1. Cut the chicken into 1-inch cubes.

2. Season the chicken pieces with salt and pepper, and dredge in flour.

3. Dip each piece of chicken in the egg mixture and roll in the bread crumbs, coating generously. As each piece is breaded, transfer it to a platter. After all pieces have been coated, refrigerate for 30 minutes to help the crumbs adhere.

4. When ready to cook, melt the butter in a large non-stick skillet over high heat until sizzling. Add the chicken and cook 2 to 3 minutes to brown. Turn the pieces over and cook 1 to 2 minutes more to brown on the other side.

5. Transfer the crisp nuggets to a platter and serve with the horseradish sauce. These may be prepared in advance and reheated in a 350° oven for 10 to 15 minutes.

4 to 6 portions as an hors d'oeuvre

Horseradish Sauce:
1/2 cup sour cream
1 1/2 tablespoons white horseradish

In a bowl, blend together the sour cream and horseradish. Refrigerate until needed.

About 1/2 cup sauce

CHICKEN WINGS CAESAR

Chicken wings marinated in a zesty Caesar dressing and baked until golden.

1 tablespoon white vinegar
1 tablespoon white wine
2 tablespoons Dijon mustard
1 large clove garlic, crushed
1 bay leaf, crushed
1 teaspoon dried thyme
pinch cayenne pepper
salt to taste
$1/2$ teaspoon black pepper
2 to 3 tablespoons Parmesan cheese
$1/2$ cup oil
2 pounds chicken wings (about 12 wings)

1. Whisk together the vinegar, wine, Dijon, garlic, bay leaf, thyme, cayenne, salt, pepper, and Parmesan cheese. Continue to beat, drizzling in the oil in a slow stream, until all the oil is incorporated.

2. Place the chicken in a large pyrex baking dish. Pour the dressing over the wings and marinate 3 to 4 hours, turning occasionally.

3. When ready to serve, preheat the oven to 350°.

4. Remove the chicken from the marinade and arrange the wings on cookie sheets, skin side up. Pour the extra marinade over the chicken.

5. Bake for 1 hour until golden brown. Serve hot out of the oven; they're also delicious cooled to room temperature for picnic fare.

4 to 5 portions, allowing 2 to 3 wings per person

YAKITORI

A delicate and delightful Japanese-inspired dish. Thin strips of chicken and scallion pieces are alternately skewered and marinated in a honey-soy sauce before being grilled.

1/4 cup honey
1/4 cup mirin (a sweetened rice wine, available in Oriental markets)
1/4 cup dark soy sauce
2 pounds boneless, skinless chicken breasts
2 bunches scallions, cut into 2-inch lengths

1. Combine the honey, mirin, and soy in a small saucepan. Bring to a boil and simmer for 5 minutes. Cool to room temperature. (This sauce may be made 4 to 5 days in advance and refrigerated until needed.)

2. Split the chicken breasts in half down the center. Cut each half into 1-inch wide horizontal strips.

3. Alternately skewer the chicken and scallion pieces. Pour the marinade over all and let sit for 20 to 30 minutes. When ready to serve, grill over hot coals 4 inches from heat source, 3 minutes per side, basting with any extra marinade.

6 to 8 appetizer portions; 4 main-course portions

QUICHES AND FILLED PASTRIES

ARTICHOKE FRITTATA

A crustless, quiche-like tart of Italian inspiration—eggs, artichoke hearts, roasted peppers, and scallions are accented with Parmesan cheese.

2 tablespoons olive oil
4 scallions, chopped
8 eggs, beaten
14 ounce can artichoke hearts, drained and coarsely chopped
3/4 cup Parmesan cheese
1 large red pepper, roasted (see page 243), and cut into 1/2-inch strips
1 large green pepper, roasted (see page 243), and cut into 1/2-inch strips
1 clove garlic, crushed
salt and freshly ground pepper to taste

1. Preheat the oven to 350°. Grease a 9-inch deep-dish pie pan.

2. Heat the oil in a skillet. Add the scallions and sauté until softened. Transfer the sautéed vegetable to a large mixing bowl.

3. Add the eggs, artichoke hearts, Parmesan, red and green peppers, garlic, and salt and pepper to taste; blend thoroughly.

4. Pour the mixture into the prepared pan.

5. Bake for 35 minutes until puffed and golden. Serve piping hot.

6 portions

DEEP-DISH MUSHROOM PIE

The French egg and cheese pie still holds a place of importance in American cuisine. Here's a deep-dish quiche combining the winning combination of cheddar and mushrooms.

> 9-inch deep-dish pie shell, prebaked (see page 7)
> 2 tablespoons butter
> 1 pound mushrooms, sliced
> 2 tablespoons minced onion
> 1 cup grated sharp cheddar cheese
> 3 large eggs
> 1 cup heavy cream
> 1/4 cup milk
> salt and freshly ground pepper to taste
> 1/2 teaspoon Worcestershire sauce

1. Allow the pie shell to cool slightly before filling.

2. Preheat the oven to 375°.

3. Heat the butter in a skillet until sizzling. Add the mushrooms and sauté over high heat until golden brown, and all the liquid has evaporated. Cool the mushrooms and place over the cooled pie crust.

4. Sprinkle the minced onion and grated cheese over the mushrooms.

5. Whisk together the eggs, cream, and milk until well blended. Season with salt, pepper, and Worcestershire sauce. Spoon the custard over the mushroom filling.

6. Bake for 35 to 40 minutes until browned and the center is firm. Let the quiche stand for 10 minutes before slicing.

6 to 8 portions

HAM AND CHEESE QUICHE

This quiche boasts a flavorful filling of bacon, imported ham, scallions, and Romano cheese. A fresh mixed garden salad and crusty French bread turn this into delightful luncheon fare.

> *9-inch deep-dish pie crust, prebaked (see page 7)*
> *5 slices cooked bacon, coarsely chopped*
> *2 ounces imported ham, chopped (Prosciutto is a particularly*
>   *tasty choice.)*
> *1/4 cup chopped scallions*
> *3 large eggs*
> *1 pint medium cream*
> *1/2 cup grated Romano cheese*
> *1 teaspoon Dijon mustard*
> *freshly ground pepper to taste*

1. Allow the pie shell to cool.

2. Preheat the oven to 375°.

3. Sprinkle the bacon, chopped ham, and scallions over the pie crust.

4. Whisk together the eggs, cream, and cheese thoroughly. Add the Dijon and pepper to taste. Pour the custard over the bacon and ham filling.

5. Set the quiche in the oven for 30 minutes, or until a knife inserted in the center of the pie comes out clean. Serve immediately.

6 to 8 portions

QUICHE ROCHELLE

A tart filled with spinach, apple, raisins, and pine nuts baked in a rich custard.

9-inch deep-dish pie crust, prebaked (see page 7)
1/2 cup raisins
5 ounces frozen chopped spinach, thawed
1 large crisp apple, peeled and coarsely grated
1/3 cup pine nuts
1 cup grated Gruyère cheese
1 1/2 cups heavy cream
3 large eggs
salt and freshly ground pepper to taste
pinch nutmeg

1. Allow the pie shell to cool before filling.

2. Preheat the oven to 375°.

3. Plump the raisins by covering them with boiling water for 20 minutes. Drain well.

4. Drain the spinach and squeeze out any excess liquid.

5. Toss the spinach, plumped raisins, apples, pine nuts, and Gruyère together in a large bowl.

6. Beat together the cream and the eggs until well blended. Season with salt and pepper to taste and a pinch of nutmeg. Pour the custard into the spinach mixture; mix thoroughly. Pile the filling into the pie shell.

7. Bake for 35 to 40 minutes or until set. Allow the quiche to sit for 10 minutes before slicing.

6 to 8 portions

CHEESE EN CROUTE

A mouth-watering nibble. A cheese puff surrounded by bacon and baked until golden.

1 pound loaf sliced white bread
1 pound cheddar cheese
3/4 pound bacon

1. Trim the crusts from the bread. Flatten the slices with a rolling pin.

2. Cut the cheese into fingers 1/2-inch thick and 3-inches long.

3. Lay a slice of cheese at the edge of a square of bread and roll up. Slice the roll into thirds.

4. Cut each slice of bacon into thirds. Wrap a piece of bacon around each cheese roll. Place seam side down on a baking sheet. (Up to this point may be prepared 4 to 6 hours in advance. Return to room temperature before baking.)

5. Preheat the oven to 450°. Bake for 20 to 25 minutes until the bacon is golden and crisp. Serve immediately.

Approximately 50 rolls; 10 or more portions

SPINACH AND PROSCIUTTO EN CROUTE

A pastry turnover encasing a spinach, cheese, olive, and prosciutto filling, baked until golden. This hors d'oeuvre gets a 5-star rating in our home—it's my husband's favorite!

2 tablespoons olive oil
1 small clove garlic, crushed
1/4 teaspoon black pepper
1 tablespoon Parmesan cheese
1 pound frozen puff pastry, thawed
10 ounce package frozen chopped spinach, thawed
1/2 pound coarsely grated Swiss cheese
1/4 pound prosciutto, thinly sliced
1 cup ripe black olives, sliced
1 egg yolk
1 tablespoon cold water

1. Mix together the oil, garlic, black pepper, and Parmesan. Cover and marinate for 2 to 3 hours.

2. Roll out the puff pastry on a floured board to form a rectangle 12 x 20-inches. (Pinch any seams together so that you essentially have one large piece of dough.) Chill for 30 minutes.

3. Squeeze the spinach of all its liquid. Spread the spinach down the center of the length of the dough forming a layer 4 inches wide and extending to within 1-inch of either end.

4. Cover the spinach with half of the Swiss cheese. Blanket the cheese with even layers of prosciutto. Spoon the marinade over the ham.

5. Sprinkle the remainder of the Swiss cheese over the prosciutto. Top everything with black olives.

6. Fold the dough like a turnover, overlapping the sides. Crimp the ends together firmly to seal. Place seam side down on an ungreased baking sheet. (Up to this point may be prepared 2 to 4 hours in advance and refrigerated. Return to room temperature to bake.)

7. Beat the egg and water together. Brush the pastry with the egg wash. This gives the loaf a golden glaze when baked.

8. Bake in a preheated 350° oven for 30 minutes. Transfer to a platter, cut into 1 1/2-inch wide slices, and serve immediately.

6 portions

TORTA RUSTICA

A colorful and mouth-watering layered loaf using my favorite pantry ingredients—roasted peppers, sun-dried tomatoes, pesto, artichoke hearts, and Italian cheeses, encased in a bread round.

> *1 round sour dough or boule, 7 to 8 inches in circumference*
> *2 large red peppers, roasted (see page 243), and sliced into 2-inch widths*
> *2 large green peppers, roasted (see page 243), and sliced into 2-inch widths*
> *6 ounces provolone cheese, sliced*
> *12 sun-dried tomatoes, sliced in half*
> *4 ounces mozzarella cheese, sliced*
> *14 ounce can artichoke hearts, drained and cut in half*
> *1/4 cup pesto (see page 128)*

1. Slice off 1/4 from the top of the bread round. Hollow out the bottom, leaving a 1/2-inch thick shell.

2. Assemble the torta. Layer the ingredients in the bread shell in the following order:

> roasted peppers
> 3 ounces provolone cheese
> sun-dried tomatoes
> mozzarella cheese
> artichoke hearts
> pesto
> 3 ounces provolone cheese

Cover with the bread cap. (Up to this point may be prepared 2 to 4 hours in advance and refrigerated. Return to room temperature before baking.)

3. Wrap the torta in silver foil and bake in a preheated 350° oven for 30 to 40 minutes, until the cheeses are melted. Uncover, slice into wedges, and serve.

6 portions

SANDWICH STUFFERS

When looking for a satisfying, easy to put together, meal on the run, try an enticing sandwich combination.

1. Lettuce, tomato, bacon, avocado, and Roquefort.

2. Roast beef, Boursin, and Swiss on French bread.

3. Tuna, hard-cooked egg, and capers with mustard mayonnaise.

4. Smoked turkey, Gruyère, and mustard mayonnaise on cisel bread.

5. Dilled cream cheese, smoked salmon, and cucumber slices on pumpernickel.

6. Chicken and lettuce with curry mayonnaise on raisin pumpernickel.

7. Roasted pork with horseradish on pumpernickel.

8. Chicken, prosciutto, and Brie on a croissant.

9. Lettuce, tomato, feta, shrimp, olive oil, and lemon juice in pita bread.

10. Bacon, turkey, Swiss, tomato, and spinach on rye.

11. Crabmeat, hard-cooked egg, tomato, and avocado on whole wheat.

12. Imported ham and Swiss, with hot mustard, dipped in egg, and fried in butter.

SPINACH PHYLLO

The flaky phyllo dough is filled with a stuffing of spinach, cheeses, and eggs, and seasoned with dill for a taste tantalizer, reminiscent of the Greek spanakopita.

2 (10 ounce) packages frozen chopped spinach, thawed
1 medium onion, finely chopped
1/4 cup olive oil
1/2 pound feta cheese, crumbled
6 ounces farmer's cheese, grated
3 eggs, well beaten
1 teaspoon dried dill
1/4 cup fresh bread crumbs
1/2 pound phyllo dough, defrosted
1/2 cup butter, melted

1. Preheat the oven to 425°. Grease a 9 x 13-inch baking dish.

2. Drain the spinach and squeeze out the remaining moisture.

3. Sauté the onion in olive oil for 5 minutes until soft. Add the spinach and simmer over a low flame, stirring occasionally until most of the moisture has evaporated. Remove the skillet from the stove and transfer the mixture to a bowl. Let cool.

4. In a separate bowl, combine the feta, farmer's cheese, eggs, and dill and mix well.

5. Add the bread crumbs and cheese mixture to the spinach; blend thoroughly.

6. Place the phyllo in a damp towel; keep it covered this way while you are working with the pastry.

7. Remove a sheet of dough and place it in the baking dish. Brush it generously with melted butter. Stack a second sheet on top and butter again. Repeat this layering until you have used 10 sheets of dough.

8. Spread the spinach filling evenly over the phyllo. Cover the filling with 10 more sheets of phyllo dough, buttering each layer as before. Brush the leftover butter over the top of the pie.

9. Bake for 20 minutes. Cut into 2-inch squares and serve immediately.

20 squares

SEAFOOD DELIGHTS

ALMOND CRAB SPREAD

A creamy, piquant crabmeat spread generously topped with almonds, served piping hot.

8 ounces cream cheese, at room temperature
2 tablespoons milk
1/2 pound canned crabmeat, drained
1 tablespoon snipped chives
1 tablespoon white horseradish
1 teaspoon Worcestershire sauce
dash Tabasco sauce
1 teaspoon lemon juice
1/3 cup sliced almonds

1. Preheat the oven to 375°.

2. Beat the cream cheese with the milk until softened. Add the crabmeat, chives, horseradish, Worcestershire, Tabasco, and lemon juice. Blend well.

3. Spoon the crabmeat mixture into a serving dish. Sprinkle the sliced almonds over the top.

4. Bake for 25 minutes. Serve at once accompanied by slices of French bread and vegetables for dipping.

4 to 6 portions

CRAB PUFFS

Tasty pop-in-the-mouth cheddar-crab morsels, broiled until puffed and golden. These can be made in advance and stored in the freezer for later use.

1/2 cup butter, at room temperature
1 cup grated extra sharp cheddar cheese
2 tablespoons Parmesan cheese
1/4 cup mayonnaise
5 drops Tabasco sauce
8 ounces canned crabmeat, drained
1 package (6) English muffins, split

1. Cream the butter and cheeses. Mix in the mayonnaise, Tabasco, and crabmeat.

2. Divide the crab mixture into 12 equal portions and spread a portion on each muffin half.

3. Cut each muffin half into eighth's. Spread out the pieces on a cookie sheet and freeze for 1 hour. Store in a plastic bag in the freezer.

4. When ready to serve, take the puffs directly from the freezer and broil 4 inches from heat source for 3 to 5 minutes until browned and bubbly. (Keep a watchful eye on them, so they don't burn.) Serve at once.

96 pieces

DEVILED CRAB

A piquant blend of crabmeat, diced vegetables, seasonings, and cracker crumbs that are baked in individual scallop shells.

2 tablespoons thinly sliced scallions
1/4 cup diced celery
1 small green pepper, diced
1 small red pepper, diced
1 teaspoon dry mustard
1/2 teaspoon lemon juice
generous pinch cayenne pepper
salt and freshly ground pepper to taste
1/2 cup cracker crumbs (I use Ritz crackers)
1/2 pound crabmeat, canned or fresh
1/2 cup medium cream
2 tablespoons chopped fresh parsley for garnish
2 tablespoons melted butter

1. In a bowl combine the scallions, celery, green and red pepper. Season with the mustard, lemon juice, cayenne pepper, and salt and pepper to taste.

2. Add 1/4 cup of the cracker crumbs and the crabmeat. Pour in the cream and stir until thoroughly blended.

3. Pile the mixture into 6 scallop baking shells. Sprinkle the remainder of the cracker crumbs over the filling. Garnish with the parsley and drizzle with melted butter. Refrigerate until needed.

4. When ready to serve, preheat the oven to 350°.

5. Return the crabmeat to room temperature, and place in the oven for 25 minutes until browned and bubbly.

6 appetizer portions; 3 to 4 main-dish portions

ZUCCHINI STUFFED WITH CRAB AND FETA

After sampling a similar appetizer at Another Season Restaurant, I was inspired to duplicate this delectable sensation. Poached zucchini shells stuffed with a divine filling of crabmeat, feta cheese, and mint. Feta cheese, the Greek goat's milk cheese, adds a distinctive tang to this composition. This makes a wonderful beginning to a summer meal, served with a glass of chilled white wine.

3 medium-size zucchini
12 ounces crabmeat
8 ounces feta cheese
1 teaspoon dried mint
1 clove garlic, crushed
2 tablespoons olive oil
freshly ground pepper to taste

1. Scrub the zucchini. Trim off the stems. Place the zucchini in a pot of boiling water and poach for 3 minutes. Lift the squash out of the water and let cool slightly.

2. Slice the zucchini in half lengthwise, and scoop out the pulp, leaving 1/4-inch thick shell. Let the hollowed-out shell drain.

3. Mix together the crabmeat, feta, mint, garlic, oil, and pepper to taste.

4. Mound the filling into the zucchini shells. Slice each boat on the diagonal into 1 1/2-inch wide chunks. Refrigerate until needed. Bring to room temperature before serving.

About 15 pieces; 6 portions

MUSSELS MARINIERE

Mussels—those illustrious shellfish—are braised in a buttery wine and garlic broth. Serve with lots of crusty French bread to mop up the delectable sauce.

2 quarts mussels
freshly ground pepper to taste
6 tablespoons melted butter
2 tablespoons lemon juice
2 cloves garlic, crushed
1 teaspoon Dijon mustard
2 tablespoons chopped fresh parsley
1 cup dry white wine

1. Scrub the mussels thoroughly and debeard them. Rinse them under cold running water to make sure they are free of sand. Heap them in a deep stainless or enamel saucepan. Season with several grinds of pepper.

2. Combine the butter, lemon juice, garlic, Dijon, parsley, and wine in a bowl. Pour the wine sauce over the mussels. Cover, bring to a boil, and simmer gently just until the musels open, about 10 minutes.

3. Heap the mussels in a large bowl, discarding any unopened ones. Spoon the buttery broth over the shellfish, and serve at once.

4 appetizer portions; 2 main-course portions

SALMON ROLL

A pâté of salmon that is generously decorated with chopped nuts and parsley.

1 pound poached salmon
5 ounces Boursin cheese
1 tablespoon lemon juice
2 teaspoons finely chopped onion
1 teaspoon horseradish
1/2 cup chopped pistachio nuts
3 tablespoons chopped fresh parsley

1. Combine the salmon, Boursin, lemon juice, onion, and horseradish in a food processor. Purée the mixture until smooth.

2. Scrape the purée into a bowl and chill at least 6 hours or overnight.

3. When ready to serve, combine the chopped nuts and parsley. Spread the mixture on a sheet of wax paper.

4. Remove the salmon purée from the refrigerator and form it into a log. Roll the log in the nut mixture to coat completely. Transfer to a platter and serve with black bread, cucumber rounds, or plain crackers.

8 portions

MELON WITH SMOKED SALMON

A very colorful and tantalizing meal opener. The soft green wedges of honeydew melon are wrapped with the coral slices of smoked salmon.

1 medium honeydew melon, cut into 12 wedges, rind removed
12 thin slices of smoked salmon
1 lime
freshly ground pepper

1. Wrap a slice of smoked salmon around each wedge of melon.
2. Drizzle with a squeeze of lime juice, and sprinkle with freshly ground pepper.
3. Present on well-chilled plates.

6 portions

SMOKED SALMON MOUSSE

A smooth smoked salmon mousse enhanced by the delicate flavors of lemon and dill. Best served on cucumber rounds or black bread.

1 envelope unflavored gelatin
2 tablespoons lemon juice
2 tablespoons cold water
1/2 cup boiling water
10 ounces smoked salmon
1/2 cup sour cream
1 teaspoon dried dill
2 tablespoons snipped chives
freshly ground white pepper to taste
1 cup heavy cream

1. Lightly coat a 6-cup mold with vegetable oil.

2. Place the lemon juice and cold water in a small bowl. Sprinkle the gelatin over the water and let sit for 10 minutes. Whisk in the boiling water until the gelatin dissolves and let cool to room temperature.

3. Place the smoked salmon in a food processor and purée until smooth.

4. Add the cooled gelatin to the food processor, along with the sour cream and seasonings; blend briefly.

5. While the processor is running, add the cream in a slow, steady stream. Process just to homogenize the mixture.

6. Pour into the prepared mold. Cover and chill at least 4 hours until set.

7. To serve, unmold onto a bed of Boston lettuce, surround with black bread and cucumber rounds.

10 to 12 portions

GRAVLAX

This is delicately cured salmon, served paper thin, accompanied by a dill-mustard mayonnaise. Dill-mustard is the quintessential seasoning enhancement for salmon.

> 2 pounds salmon filets, cut in half across the center
> 3 tablespoons coarse salt
> $1/4$ cup sugar
> $1/2$ tablespoon coarsely ground black peppercorns
> 1 large bunch fresh dill
> Mustard Mayonnaise (recipe follows)

1. Place one half of the salmon filet, skin side down, on a plate.

2. Mix the salt, sugar, and peppercorns together. Remove the coarse stems from the dill. Spread half of the seasoning mixture evenly over the filet. Cover with the dill. Spread the remaining seasoning on the second piece of salmon and flip it over on to the dill, forming a sandwich.

3. Place the fish "sandwich" in a plastic bag and seal it tightly. Put the package in a glass dish and cover it with a 5 pound weight. (I use a brick.) Refrigerate for 3 to 4 days, turning the salmon over every day.

4. When the salmon is cured, remove the filets from the marinade. Scrape away the dill and seasonings. Thinly slice the salmon on the diagonal.

5. When ready to serve, present the salmon with slices of black bread and mustard mayonnaise.

8 portions

Mustard Mayonnaise:
1 cup mayonnaise
2 tablespoons Hot Mustard (see page 9)
$1^1/2$ tablespoons chopped fresh dill

Mix the mayonnaise, mustard, and dill together. Store in the refrigerator until needed.

About 1 cup of sauce

SCALLOPS EN BROCHETTE

Scallops are wrapped in bacon, skewered, and broiled with a brown sugar glaze. These are always a sensation!

1/2 pound bacon
1 pound bay scallops
dark brown sugar

1. Cut the bacon slices into thirds.

2. Wrap each scallop with a piece of bacon and secure with a toothpick. Roll each kebob in the brown sugar, coating each piece generously.

3. Place under a hot broiler 4 inches from the heat source 5 to 6 minutes per side until cooked and browned. Serve immediately.

4 portions

SEVICHE

A Latin American dish of raw scallops that "cook" in a citrus juice marinade, colorfully presented with chopped vegetables.

2 pounds bay scallops
juice of 1 lemon
juice of 1 lime
3 tablespoons orange juice
3 tablespoons olive oil
1 medium green pepper, diced
1 medium red pepper, diced
1 cup coarsely chopped plum tomatoes
1 tablespoon chopped fresh parsley
1 tablespoon snipped chives
generous pinch cayenne pepper
salt and freshly ground pepper to taste

1. Place the scallops in a glass or porcelain dish. Pour the lemon, lime, and orange juices over the seafood. Cover and refrigerate at least 3 hours, allowing the scallops to cook in the citrus juices.

2. Whisk together the oil, green and red peppers, tomato, herbs, spices, and seasonings. Add the dressing to the scallops and toss gently. Transfer to individual plates and serve.

6 to 8 portions

PICKLED SHRIMP

Shrimp are marinated in an herbed vinaigrette, flavored with the tang of dill pickles.

1 pound large-size shrimp, poached
1/2 cup white wine vinegar
1/4 cup oil
salt to taste
1 large clove garlic, crushed
dash of Tabasco
4 tablespoons snipped chives
2 tablespoons chopped dill pickles
4 tablespoons chopped fresh parsley for garnish

1. Pile the shrimp in a serving bowl.

2. In a small bowl, whisk together the vinegar, oil, salt, garlic, Tabasco, chives, and chopped pickles. Pour the marinade over the shrimp and toss well.

3. Cover and refrigerate for 24 hours, stirring occasionally. When ready to serve, toss again, and sprinkle with chopped parsley.

6 portions

MARINATED SHRIMP AND ARTICHOKE HEARTS

Shrimp and artichoke hearts laced with a tarragon-mustard sauce—
best made a day in advance so flavors can mellow.

2 pounds large-size shrimp, cooked
2 (14 ounce) cans artichoke hearts, drained and cut in half

Mustard Vinaigrette:
1/4 cup Dijon mustard
1/2 cup tarragon wine vinegar
1/4 cup chopped fresh parsley
1 teaspoon dried tarragon
freshly ground pepper to taste
1 cup olive oil

1. Pile the shrimp and artichoke hearts into a large glass bowl.

2. In a small bowl, whisk together the Dijon, vinegar, parsley, tarragon and pepper. Add the oil, beating constantly, until thick and creamy. Pour the dressing over the shrimp mixture and toss well.

3. Cover and refrigerate overnight.

4. When ready to serve, bring to room temperature, and mix before presenting.

10 to 12 portions

THE SOUP TUREEN

In general, soups are economical, pleasing, flavorful, and appeal to one's sense of all that is good and simple in life. Soups are very versatile, having a wide range of presentations from robust, hot soups served up on a cold winter's night, to light and refreshing cold summer soups. They adapt to both formal and casual occasions. They are great as luncheon fare, as elegant first courses, or as entrées teamed up with a salad and a loaf of peasant bread. They are both filling and satisfying, being real comfort food. Soups can be altered to suit one's mood by adding more vegetables, seasoning with fresh garden herbs, or garnishing with seafood. Render your stockpot full with a bounty of offerings—soups on!

PIPING
HOT SOUPS

CARROT SOUP

Purée of carrot enhanced by tomato and curry.

4 tablespoons butter
2 medium onions, chopped
6 cups chicken stock
2 pounds carrots, peeled and coarsely chopped
1 cup tomato purée
1/2 to 1 teaspoon curry powder
salt and freshly ground pepper to taste

1. Melt the butter in a large saucepan. When the butter is hot, add the chopped onion, and sauté until soft and translucent.

2. Add the chicken stock and carrots to the pot. Cover and simmer for 20 minutes until the carrots are tender. When the carrots are done, let the broth cool.

3. When cooled, place the cooked carrots, onions, and 1 cup stock in the bowl of a food processor and purée the mixture. Transfer the purée back to the saucepan, mixing with the reserved stock.

4. Stir in the tomato purée, curry, and season with salt and pepper. Set on the heat and serve the soup piping hot. (This may be refrigerated for up to 24 hours in advance of serving.)

8 portions

CREOLE CORN SOUP

A great way to use up leftover corn. The soup showcases the typical Creole flavors of onion, celery, peppers, and tomatoes, blended with sweet corn and fiery cayenne pepper.

2 tablespoons vegetable oil
1 medium-size onion, chopped
2 stalks celery, chopped
1/2 medium-size red pepper, chopped
1/2 medium-size green pepper, chopped
1 large tomato, peeled and chopped
1 clove garlic, crushed
1/8 teaspoon cayenne pepper or to taste
salt and freshly ground black pepper to taste
1 bay leaf
4 cups chicken broth
4 cups corn niblets, cooked

1. In a large saucepan over medium heat, sauté the onion, celery, peppers, tomato, and garlic in the oil until the vegetables are softened.

2. Add the cayenne pepper, salt, pepper, and bay leaf and stir well.

3. Pour in the chicken broth; add the corn. Cover and simmer the soup for 5 minutes until piping hot. Discard the bay leaf before serving.

6 to 8 portions

TOMATO BISQUE

A thick and creamy tomato purée delicately seasoned with herbs and a hint of orange zest. For warm weather fare, this presents itself just as successfully as a cold soup.

> 8 ounce can stewed tomatoes
> 2 cups tomato juice
> 1/4 cup mayonnaise
> juice of a lemon
> 2 tablespoons sugar
> salt and freshly ground pepper to taste
> dash Worcestershire sauce
> 1 tablespoon chopped fresh parsley
> 2 tablespoons snipped chives
> 1 teaspoon finely grated orange peel

1. Place all of the ingredients in a blender or food processor and blend gently to combine. (Up to this point may be prepared in advance and refrigerated until serving time.) Remove the soup to a saucepan and heat on a low light until piping hot.

2. Ladle the hot soup into individual bowls and serve at once.

4 portions

Note—this recipe may be doubled very easily.

CREAM OF POTATO SOUP

A chunky potato and leek soup. The sautéed leeks impart a richness to this delectable soup that is presented hot.

> 2 cups sliced leeks (white part only)
> 4 tablespoons butter
> 1 clove garlic, crushed
> 4 cups chicken stock
> 3 cups unpeeled, diced potatoes (cut into $1/2$-inch cubes)
> $1/2$ teaspoon dried thyme
> salt and freshly ground pepper to taste
> 1 cup light cream
> 3 tablespoons snipped chives

1. To clean the leeks, trim the green stalks from the leeks and discard. Coarsely slice the leeks. Soak the white part in water to remove all of the sand. Drain well.

2. Melt the butter in a large saucepan or stockpot. When the butter is hot, add the garlic and leeks and sauté until the leeks are golden.

3. Add the chicken broth, diced potatoes, thyme, salt, and pepper. Cover and simmer until the potatoes are very tender about 10 to 15 minutes.

4. Stir in the cream and chives and reheat; serve immediately. (If you wish, you may refrigerate for up to 24 hours in advance of serving.)

6 to 8 portions

HEARTY CREAM OF VEGETABLE SOUP

A mélange of fresh vegetables in a light cream stock.

4 cups chicken broth
1 cup broccoli flowerettes
1 cup sliced leeks, white part only (see page 80—how to clean leeks)
1 cup sliced shiitake mushrooms
1 cup sliced celery
1 cup zucchini, sliced and quartered
1 cup summer squash, sliced and quartered
1 cup sliced carrots
4 tablespoons butter
salt to taste
1/2 teaspoon pepper
1 tablespoon chopped fresh parsley
1/2 teaspoon dried dill
dash of Worcestershire sauce
2 cups light cream

1. Heat the chicken broth in a large stock pot. Add the vegetables, cover, and bring to a boil.

2. Lower the heat and simmer for 10 minutes until the vegetables are tender.

3. Add the butter and seasonings.

4. Stir in the cream, and heat gently over a low light until piping hot.

5. To serve, stir the soup and ladle into individual bowls.

8 portions

ONION SOUP AU GRATIN

A crock of golden rich onion soup generously topped with bubbling Swiss and Parmesan cheeses. For Sunday night supper or après ski, team this up with a large garden salad and a bottle of wine for a complete comfort meal.

6 tablespoons butter
2½ pounds Spanish onions, sliced (use Vadalia onions when in season)
1 teaspoon sugar
freshly ground pepper to taste
2 tablespoons flour
6 cups canned beef consommé
1 cup dry white wine
French bread cut into 1-inch thick slices
½ cup Parmesan cheese
1 cup shredded Swiss cheese

1. Melt the butter in a large saucepan. When hot, add the onions, sprinkle with the sugar and pepper and sauté for 20 minutes, until the onions are golden brown, stirring occassionally.

2. When the onions are browned, stir in the flour. Sauté for 2 minutes more.

3. Pour in the consommé and wine. Bring to a boil, lower the heat, and simmer uncovered for 20 minutes. The soup may be served now or refrigerated for later use.

4. To serve, ladle the soup into 6 individual crocks. Float a slice of French bread in each bowl.

5. Combine the Swiss and Parmesan cheeses. Heap a generous sprinkling of the cheese mixture atop each bread round.

6. Bake the crocks in a 350° oven for 15 minutes. Run the crocks under a hot broiler until the cheese is bubbly and golden brown. Serve at once.

6 portions

VIVIAN'S FISH CHOWDER

This is my mother's tried-and-true recipe for a thick and creamy chowder of haddock, potatoes, onions, and bacon. During the summer when clams are in season, I substitute a bucket of steamers for the haddock for a dazzling clam chowder.

> *4 to 5 slices bacon*
> *3 medium onions, sliced*
> *2 large potatoes, diced into $1/2$-inch cubes*
> *2 cups dry white wine*
> *salt and freshly ground pepper to taste*
> *pinch dried thyme*
> *2 pounds haddock, cut into 2-inch chunks*
> *1 pint heavy cream*
> *1 cup milk*
> *2 tablespoons butter*

1. In a large saucepan, fry the bacon until it is light golden brown and crisp. Remove the bacon from the pan with a slotted utensil and chop it coarsely. Set aside.

2. In the bacon fat, sauté the onions until golden.

3. Add the potatoes to the saucepan along with the bacon and white wine. Season with the salt, pepper, and thyme. Cook the potatoes until tender about 5 to 10 minutes.

4. Add the haddock chunks to the saucepan and enough water to cover. Bring to a boil. Lower the heat and simmer gently until the fish is no longer translucent, about 5 to 10 minutes.

5. Stir in the cream, milk, and butter and heat gently until piping hot. To serve, ladle spoonfuls of hot chowder into bowls and present at once.

6 main-dish portions

CIOPPINO

A fisherman's stew consisting of a spicy tomato base teeming with shellfish—lobster, shrimp, clams, mussels, and scallops. This dish is special party fare, as it is a relatively costly one to prepare and makes a very colorful presentation.

1/4 cup olive oil
2 large cloves garlic, crushed
2 medium onions, chopped
1 medium green pepper, diced
1 pound 12 ounce can crushed tomatoes in purée
6 ounce can tomato paste
1 cup water
2 cups dry white wine
1/4 cup Drambuie
juice of one lemon
1 cup chopped fresh parsley (1/2 cup is for garnish)
1 teaspoon dried basil
1 teaspoon dried oregano
salt and freshly ground black pepper to taste
2 (1 1/2 pound) live lobsters in their shell, cut into serving-size pieces
1 pound medium-size raw shrimp, peeled
12 clams, scrubbed
24 mussels, cleaned and debearded
1 pound cape scallops
slices of crusty French bread

1. Heat the oil in your largest stockpot. Add the garlic, onion, and green pepper and sauté over medium heat for 10 minutes until the vegetables are soft.

2. Stir in the tomatoes, tomato paste, water, wine, Drambuie, lemon juice, 1/2 cup parsley, basil, oregano, salt, and pepper. Cover, bring to a boil, lower the heat, and simmer for 30 minutes. (This part may be prepared several hours in advance or as much as 24 hours ahead.)

3. Add the shellfish in their shells to the simmering tomato base. Cover and continue to simmer for 10 minutes, or until the mussels and clams have opened and the fish is done.

4. To serve, stir the cioppino, and ladle into large bowls lined with two slices of French bread. Garnish with the remainder of the chopped parsley, and serve at once.

6 to 8 hearty main-course portions

MINESTRONE

A slow simmering Italian soup laden with garden vegetables, punctuated with red kidney beans, chick peas, and tortellini, and enhanced by aromatic herbs. It's great fare for a kitchen party, accompanied by a variety of peasant breads.

1/4 cup olive oil
1 large clove garlic, crushed
1 large Spanish onion, chopped
4 large carrots, peeled and sliced
4 stalks celery, sliced
1 large green pepper, cut into 3/4-inch squares
1 large red pepper, cut into 3/4-inch squares
1/2 pound green beans, snapped in half
1 small head cabbage, chopped
8 cups chicken broth
35 ounce can Italian plum tomatoes
salt and freshly ground pepper to taste
1 tablespoon dried basil
1/2 cup chopped Italian parsley
3 medium-size zucchini, diced
1 medium-size summer squash, diced
19 ounce can red kidney beans, drained
19 ounce can chick peas, drained
1 pound cheese tortellini
Parmesan cheese for garnish

1. Heat the oil in a large stockpot. Add the garlic, onion, carrots, celery, and peppers, and sauté over medium heat for 10 minutes, stirring occasionally.

2. Add the beans and cabbage, and sauté for 5 minutes more, mixing often.

3. Add the broth, tomatoes with their juice, and seasonings. Bring to a boil, then reduce the heat and simmer, covered, over low heat for 35 minutes.

4. Add the zucchini, summer squash, kidney beans, chick peas, and tortellini. Raise the heat to high and simmer 10 minutes; stir occasionally.

5. To serve, present large bowls of piping hot minestrone, garnished with lots of freshly grated Parmesan.

10 to 12 portions

COLD SOUPS

COLD AVOCADO SOUP

A must for guacamole fans—avocado purée seasoned with onion, garlic, lemon juice, and sour cream.

2 ripe avocados
3 tablespoons lemon juice
2 tablespoons minced onion
2 cups chicken broth
1/2 cup sour cream
1 clove garlic, mashed
1/8 teaspoon cayenne pepper
salt and freshly ground pepper to taste
1 large tomato, thinly sliced (for garnish)

1. Peel the avocados. Cut them into chunks, removing the pits.

2. Put the avocado chunks in a food processor or blender, and purée the fruit until smooth.

3. Add the lemon juice, onion, chicken broth, sour cream, and seasonings, and process until blended. Remove the soup to a tureen, cover, and chill for several hours or overnight.

4. When ready to serve, spoon the chilled soup into individual bowls. Garnish each portion with two thin slices of tomato.

4 portions

CHILLED CANTALOUPE SOUP

A purée of cantaloupe flavored with orange juice, white wine, and Grand Marnier.

>1 large ripe cantaloupe
>1/2 cup dry white wine
>1 cup orange juice
>2 tablespoons honey
>1 teaspoon finely grated orange peel
>2 tablespoons Grand Marnier
>1/2 cup sour cream

1. Remove the rind from the cantaloupe and cut the flesh into chunks. Place the melon in a food processor or blender, and purée.

2. Combine the white wine, orange juice, honey, orange peel, and Grand Marnier. While the processor is still running, gradually add the orange mixture.

3. Add the sour cream and process briefly to blend.

4. Refrigerate the soup for at least 6 hours, and up to 48 hours in advance of serving.

5. Serve the soup cold, ladled into chilled bowls.

6 cups

ICED HONEYDEW SOUP

A light and ever so refreshing soup enhanced by a splash of Midori.

6 cups ripe honeydew melon, cut into chunks
3 tablespoons lemon juice
1/2 cup sugar
1 cup orange juice
1/2 cup dry white wine
2 tablespoons Midori (melon-flavored liqueur)
1 lemon, thinly sliced (for garnish)

1. Place the honeydew in a food processor or blender, and purée the melon. Remove the purée to a large serving bowl or tureen.

2. Stir in the lemon juice, sugar, orange juice, white wine, and Midori. Cover and chill for at least 6 hours.

3. To serve, stir the soup and ladle into chilled cups. Garnish each portion with a slice of lemon.

6 portions

PEACH SOUP WITH FRESH RASPBERRIES

A take-off on the classic peach melba dessert—a delicate blend of cold peach purée, white wine, lemon juice, and apricot brandy, garnished with fresh raspberries and a sprinkling of toasted almonds.

> 8 large, ripe peaches
> 1/2 cup sugar
> 1/3 cup lemon juice
> 1/2 cup white wine
> 1 cup orange juice
> 3 tablespoons apricot brandy
> 1/2 teaspoon finely grated lemon peel
> 1/2 pint raspberries
> 2 tablespoons sliced almonds, toasted (see page 273)

1. Skin the peaches by dropping them into a large pot of boiling water for 1 minute. Remove the fruit from the water and slip off the skins. Cut the peaches into chunks, removing the pits.

2. Place the peach chunks in the bowl of a food processor or blender and purée.

3. Add the sugar, lemon juice, white wine, orange juice, apricot brandy, and lemon peel to the peach purée and process to blend.

4. Place the soup in a tureen or serving bowl and refrigerate until serving time—for at least 2 hours, and up to 48 hours.

5. When ready to serve, ladle the cold soup into well-chilled bowls and garnish each portion with a spoonful of fresh raspberries and a dusting of almonds.

8 portions

GAZPACHO

A cold, chunky tomato-based soup of Spanish origin. Puréed onion, red and green peppers, and cucumber are garnished with chopped vegetables and poached shrimp. This is great warm weather fare teamed up with grilled burgers; also totes well to picnics.

1 small red onion
1 large green pepper
1 large red pepper
1 medium-size pickling cucumber, peeled
1 pound 12 ounce can Italian plum tomatoes
2 tablespoons olive oil
2 tablespoons red wine vinegar
1 clove garlic, crushed
1/4 teaspoon salt
1/4 teaspoon pepper
dash Tabasco sauce
1 cup tomato juice

Garnishes:
1 1/2 cups croutons
1 medium-size green pepper, diced
1 medium-size pickling cucumber, peeled and diced
3 scallions cut into 1-inch lengths
5 ounces small shrimp, poached

1. Coarsely chop the red onion, green and red peppers, and cucumber.

2. Place the chopped vegetables in a blender or food processor.

3. Add the canned tomatoes, olive oil, vinegar, garlic, salt, pepper, and Tabasco to the food processor. Pulse only to blend—do not purée, as the mixture should be slightly chunky. Remove the soup to a tureen.

4. Stir in the tomato juice. Cover and chill the soup for at least 2 hours and up to 24 hours.

5. When ready to serve, stir the gazpacho, and ladle the well-chilled soup into individual bowls.

6. Arrange the croutons, diced green pepper, diced cucumber, sliced scallions, and shrimp in mounds on a platter. Pass the array of garnishes around to your guests.

6 portions

RED PEPPER SOUP

A cold soup rich with the flavor of roasted red peppers, highlighted by ground almonds and garlic. It's also delicious served piping hot on a cold winter's night.

1/2 cup blanched almonds, lightly toasted (see page 273)
1 large clove garlic, crushed
3 large red peppers, roasted (see page 243)
4 cups chicken broth
salt and freshly ground pepper to taste
pinch cayenne pepper
1/2 teaspoon paprika
3 tablespoons sliced almonds, toasted (for garnish) (see page 273)

1. Finely grind the almonds in a blender or food processor. Add the garlic, peppers, and 1 cup of the broth. Purée until smooth.

2. Pour the puréed mixture into a tureen. Stir in the remaining chicken broth and seasonings and chill.

3. When ready to serve, garnish each bowl with a spoonful of toasted sliced almonds.

6 portions

ORANGE-BEET SOUP

Cold grated beets in a refreshing orange-based soup.

2 pounds medium-size beets, scrubbed clean
3 cups liquid from cooked beets
salt and freshly ground pepper to taste
1 cup orange juice
1 tablespoon grated onion
sour cream (for garnish)
1 orange, sliced (for garnish)

1. Place the beets in a medium-size saucepan and cover completely with 1 quart of water. Cover and bring to a boil. Reduce heat and simmer until the beets are tender about 45 minutes to 1 hour. Remove the beets from the cooking liquid with a slotted spoon. Strain the cooking liquid through cheese cloth and reserve.

2. Let the beets cool. Then slip the skins off of the beets, and coarsely grate them.

3. In a large bowl or tureen, combine the grated beets, 3 cups of the reserved liquid, salt, pepper, orange juice, and onion. Cover and refrigerate for 24 hours, letting the flavors mellow.

4. When ready to serve, stir the soup and ladle into chilled bowls. Garnish each with a dollop of sour cream and an orange slice.

4 portions

DILLED SHRIMP SOUP

Cold shrimp and cucumber in a buttermilk-based soup that's delicately blended and seasoned with dill. Great soup for the calorie conscious, even though it doesn't taste skinny!

3 large pickling cucumbers
1 pound medium-size shrimp, cooked
1 quart buttermilk
2 scallions, sliced into 1/4-inch thick rounds
3 tablespoons chopped fresh dill
salt and freshly ground pepper to taste

1. Peel, seed, and coarsely grate the cucumbers.

2. Combine all of the ingredients in a large casserole, stirring to blend well.

3. Cover the soup and refrigerate for 6 to 8 hours, allowing the flavors to mellow.

4. To serve, ladle the chilled soup into cups.

4 generous portions

CREAM OF ZUCCHINI SOUP

A subtle blending of puréed zucchini, buttermilk, sour cream, garlic, and mint, served cold, and garnished with chunks of lobster.

2 medium-size zucchini, sliced into rounds
1 quart buttermilk
1/2 pint sour cream
1 teaspoon dried mint
1 clove garlic, crushed
1 tablespoon snipped chives
1/4 cup chopped fresh parsley
salt and freshly ground pepper to taste
1 cooked lobster tail cut into 1/2-inch chunks

1. Steam the zucchini until tender, about 10 minutes. Drain well. Purée the zucchini in a food processor.

2. In a large tureen or bowl, combine the zucchini, buttermilk, sour cream, and seasonings, mixing well. Cover and refrigerate for at least 6 hours or overnight to allow the flavors to mellow.

3. When ready to serve, stir the soup, and ladle into well-chilled bowls. Garnish each serving with several chunks of lobster meat.

6 portions

BREAKFAST BREADS

Nothing can compare to the robust smell of bread baking. Enjoyed warm, straight from the oven, its wholesome goodness is most apparent. Sweet breads and muffins are especially delicious served with cream cheese, butter, or jam and mugs of hot coffee or tea.

It is well worth noting that all the breads and muffins freeze well. At harvest time, select your favorite fruits and bake up a batch of breads to keep your freezer well stocked. Remember that the recipes call for extra-large eggs.

A special note: when preparing muffins and quick breads, do not over mix the batter—just combine the ingredients until evenly incorporated. Overmixing results in disastrous, tough muffins and breads!

BLUEBERRY MUFFINS

These sinfully delicious muffins are rich with blueberries, and encrusted with a cinnamon-crumb topping. Reminiscent of the famous Jordan Marsh big blues.

2 cups plus 1 tablespoon all-purpose flour
2 teaspoons baking powder
1/2 teaspoon salt
1/2 cup butter
1 cup sugar
2 eggs, beaten
1 1/2 teaspoons vanilla
1/2 cup milk
2 1/2 cups blueberries

Topping:
2 tablespoons self-rising flour
1 tablespoon butter
2 tablespoons sugar
1/2 teaspoon cinnamon

1. Preheat the oven to 375°. Line a 12-cup muffin tin with paper liners.

2. Sift together the dry ingredients—2 cups of flour, baking powder, and salt.

3. Cream the butter and sugar until fluffy. Add the eggs and vanilla and mix until well blended.

4. Add the sifted dry ingredients alternately with the milk to the batter.

5. Mash 1/2 cup of the blueberries, and stir them into the batter.

6. Dust the rest of the blueberries lightly with 1 tablespoon of flour, and gently fold them into the batter.

7. Pile the batter high in each muffin cup. Mix the topping ingredients together until the texture of coarse cornmeal. Sprinkle over the tops of the muffins.

8. Bake for 25 to 30 minutes. Let the muffins cool in the tins for 5 minutes before removing them to racks to cool completely.

12 large muffins

RAISIN BRAN MUFFINS

These dark, moist, muffins studded with fruit add a treat to any breakfast table. They are also rich in fiber which is good for the diet.

2 cups bran cereal flakes
1^1/3 cups milk
^{1}/2 cup butter
^{1}/2 cup dark brown sugar
^{1}/4 cup molasses
1 egg
1^1/2 teaspoons vanilla
1 cup all-purpose flour
^{1}/2 teaspoon salt
1 teaspoon baking soda
^{3}/4 cup raisins

1. Preheat the oven to 400°. Line a large muffin pan with paper cups.

2. Combine the cereal and milk in a bowl and let stand until the liquid is absorbed (at least 5 minutes).

3. In a separate bowl, cream the butter and brown sugar. Add the molasses, egg, and vanilla, and mix until the batter is smooth.

4. Sift together the flour, salt, and baking soda. Add the dry ingredients alternately with the bran to the batter.

5. Gently fold in the raisins.

6. Spoon the batter into the muffin pans. Bake for 20 to 25 minutes. Remove the muffins to racks to cool completely.

12 muffins

MAPLE WALNUT MUFFINS

Use pure maple syrup for a truly delicious maple-flavored muffin.

>   2 cups all-purpose flour
>   1 tablespoon baking powder
>   1 teaspoon salt
>   1/2 cup butter
>   1/2 cup dark brown sugar
>   1/2 cup maple syrup
>   2 eggs, beaten
>   3/4 cup milk
>   1/2 cup finely chopped walnuts
>   1/2 cup chopped dates

1. Preheat the oven to 375°. Line a 12-cup muffin pan with paper baking cups.

2. Sift together the flour, baking powder, and salt.

3. In a large mixing bowl, cream the butter and sugar, beating until fluffy. Add the maple syrup and eggs, beating until well mixed.

4. Add the sifted dry ingredients, alternately with the milk, until all is blended. Gently fold in the walnuts and dates.

5. Spoon the batter into the muffin tins, filling each cup. Bake for 20 minutes, or until a tester inserted in the center comes out clean. Remove the muffins from the pan to a wire rack to cool completely.

12 muffins

CORN BREAD

This corn bread is moist, tasty, and almost cake-like, especially with the sweet, rich flavor of pecans. It makes a wholesome addition to the breakfast table, picnic basket, or bread basket.

1¼ cups sifted all-purpose flour
¾ cup corn meal
⅓ cup sugar
½ teaspoon salt
2 teaspoons baking powder
generous ⅓ cup finely chopped pecans
1 cup milk
1 egg, slightly beaten
½ teaspoon vanilla
¼ cup vegetable oil

1. Preheat the oven to 400°. Grease an 8-inch square baking pan.

2. In a large bowl, combine all of the dry ingredients and nuts.

3. Add the milk, egg, vanilla, and oil, stirring only until evenly moistened. Do not over mix!

4. Pour the batter into the prepared pan and bake for 20 minutes. Delicious served warm with butter and jam.

9 squares

APPLE TEA BREAD

We go apple-picking every fall, and ear-mark a basket of the fruit solely for breads. Some might prefer to serve this bread with cheddar cheese; others might like it unadorned, as it is almost cake-like.

> 1 cup butter
> 2¹/₄ cups sugar
> 3 eggs, beaten
> 1¹/₂ teaspoons vanilla extract
> 3 cups all-purpose flour
> ¹/₂ teaspoon baking powder
> 1 teaspoon baking soda
> 1 teaspoon salt
> 1 tablespoon cinnamon
> dash nutmeg
> 2¹/₂ cups peeled and coarsely grated apples (2 to 3 apples)
> ¹/₂ cup raisins, dusted with 1 teaspoon flour

1. Preheat the oven to 350°. Grease three 8 x 4 x 2-inch loaf pans.

2. Cream the butter, and add the sugar gradually, continuing to work together until light and fluffy. Add the eggs and vanilla beating until well mixed.

3. Sift together the flour, baking powder, baking soda, salt, cinnamon, and nutmeg.

4. Add the dry ingredients in two portions, mixing only until the flour is well incorporated.

5. Fold in the fruits—the apples and raisins.

6. Turn the mixture into the loaf pans, making sure the batter is evenly distributed.

7. Bake the breads 45 to 50 minutes, or until a cake tester inserted in the middle comes out clean.

8. Remove from the oven to cool in the pans for 10 minutes. Then remove the breads from the pans to racks to cool completely.

3 mini loaves

APRICOT DATE LOAF

The combination of apricots and dates make this bread rich, dark, and fruity.

1/2 pound dates, coarsely chopped
1/2 pound dried apricots, coarsely chopped
2 teaspoons baking soda
11/2 cups sugar
1/2 cup butter
13/4 cups boiling water
21/2 cups flour
2 eggs, beaten

1. Preheat the over to 350°. Grease a 9 x 5 x 3-inch loaf pan.

2. Put the dates, apricots, baking soda, sugar, and butter into a large bowl. Pour the boiling water over the ingredients and stir well. Let the fruit soak, and the mixture cool.

3. Sift the flour.

4. When the fruit mixture is cool, add the flour and the eggs, stirring only until the flour is incorporated.

5. Turn the batter into the loaf pan, and bake for 60 to 70 minutes until a cake tester inserted in the middle comes out clean.

6. Remove the bread from the oven. Cool in the pan for 25 minutes, then remove the bread to a wire rack to cool completely.

1 loaf

BANANA TEA LOAF

This is an all-time favorite with my son. The blacker the bananas, the better the bread, as riper fruit imparts a much sweeter flavor. The loaf is encrusted with a sugary topping.

1/2 cup butter
1 cup plus 2 tablespoons sugar
2 eggs
1 teaspoon vanilla
2 cups all-purpose flour
1 teaspoon baking soda
1 teaspoon baking powder
1/4 teaspoon salt
3 medium-size very ripe bananas, mashed

1. Preheat the oven to 350°. Grease a 9 x 5 x 3-inch loaf pan.

2. Cream the butter and 1 cup sugar, and work together until light and fluffy. Add the eggs and vanilla, beating well.

3. Sift the flour, baking soda, baking powder, and salt together.

4. Add the sifted dry ingredients to the creamed mixture, stirring until well combined.

5. Fold in the mashed bananas.

6. Pour the batter into the greased pan. Sprinkle 2 tablespoons sugar over the top of the loaf. Bake 60 to 70 minutes until a cake tester inserted into the center comes out clean. Cool in the pan for 20 minutes, then remove the bread to a rack to cool completely.

1 loaf

CRANBERRY ORANGE BREAD

This holiday bread is special because it is chock full of cranberries and pecans, aromatically spiced, and accented with a splash of Grand Marnier. It is wise to bake up a batch of breads for holiday gift giving and celebrating!

^{1}/$_2$ cup butter
1 cup sugar
2 eggs
1 tablespoon vanilla
2 teaspoons finely grated orange peel
2 cups plus 1 tablespoon all-purpose flour
1^1/$_2$ teaspoons baking powder
^{1}/$_2$ teaspoon baking soda
1 teaspoon salt
1^1/$_2$ teaspoons nutmeg
1 teaspoon cinnamon
^{1}/$_2$ teaspoon ground ginger
^{1}/$_2$ cup orange juice
^{1}/$_4$ cup Grand Marnier
1^1/$_2$ cups cranberries
1 cup chopped pecans

1. Preheat the oven to 350°. Grease a 9 x 5 x 3-inch loaf pan.

2. Cream the butter and sugar until fluffy. Stir in the eggs, vanilla, and orange peel.

3. Sift together the 2 cups flour, baking powder, baking soda, salt, nutmeg, cinnamon, and ginger.

4. Mix the orange juice and Grand Marnier. Add the sifted dry ingredients alternately to the batter with the orange juice mixture.

5. Dust the cranberries and pecans with 1 tablespoon of flour and gently fold them into the batter.

6. Turn the batter into the prepared pan. Bake 50 to 60 minutes. Cool in the pan for 10 minutes, then turn out onto a rack to cool completely.

1 loaf

PUMPKIN BREAD

This bread is always popular at the Thanksgiving and Christmas holidays. It is especially delicious served with a spread made of cream cheese, dates, and walnuts!

> 1 cup butter
> 2^1/2 cups sugar
> 3 eggs
> 3 cups all-purpose flour
> 1 teaspoon baking powder
> ^{1}/2 teaspoon baking soda
> 2 teaspoons cinnamon
> ^{1}/2 teaspoon allspice
> ^{1}/2 teaspoon ground ginger
> 1 teaspoon salt
> 15 ounce can pumpkin

1. Preheat the oven to 350°. Grease three 8 x 4-inch loaf pans.

2. Cream the butter and sugar until light and fluffy. Add the eggs and mix well.

3. Sift together the flour, baking powder, baking soda, cinnamon, allspice, ginger, and salt. Add the dry ingredients to the batter.

4. Stir the pumpkin into the batter.

5. Pour the batter into the loaf pans, dividing it evenly, and bake for 50 to 60 minutes, or until a cake tester inserted into the center comes out clean.

6. Let the breads cool in the pans for 15 to 20 minutes, then remove them to a rack to cool completely.

3 mini loaves

ZUCCHINI PECAN BREAD

When you're overcome with a plethora of zucchini in the summer, this recipe puts the fruit to good use. Zucchini, pecans, raisins, and spices combine to make a moist aromatic bread.

3 eggs, beaten
1 cup oil
$2^1/4$ cups sugar
$1^1/2$ teaspoons vanilla extract
3 cups unpeeled zucchini, coarsely grated
3 cups plus 1 tablespoon all-purpose flour
$1/2$ teaspoon baking powder
1 teaspoon baking soda
1 teaspoon salt
1 tablespoon cinnamon
pinch cloves
pinch nutmeg
1 cup chopped pecans
$1/2$ cup raisins

1. Preheat the oven to 350°. Grease and flour three 8 x 4-inch loaf pans.

2. Beat the eggs, oil, sugar, and vanilla together until thick. Add the zucchini and stir well.

3. Sift together the 3 cups flour, baking powder, baking soda, salt, cinnamon, cloves, and nutmeg.

4. Gradually add the sifted dry ingredients to the zucchini mixture stirring only until the batter is blended.

5. Dust the nuts and raisins with 1 tablespoon of flour and gently fold them into the batter.

6. Pour the batter into the prepared loaf pans, dividing it evenly.

7. Bake for 50 to 60 minutes, or until a cake tester inserted in the middle comes out clean.

8. Let the breads cool in the pans for 20 minutes. Then remove the breads from the pans to racks to continue cooling.

3 mini loaves

PASTA PLEASURES

Pasta, a staple of the past, is a wholesome ingredient of all future cuisine. Pasta is considered a basic pantry item, and is no longer limited to Italian cuisine. Its versatility combined with its nutritional value makes it a highly desirable food choice. High in complex carbohydrates, pasta provides the body with energy.

Pasta is available in varied forms:

1. Flavored pastas—egg pasta, green or spinach pasta, red pepper pasta, and tomato pasta.

2. Cheese and meat filled pastas—tortellini and ravioli.

3. Multi-shaped pastas—shells, ziti (tubular), fusilli (corkscrew), bows, elbows, linguine (long strands), to name just a few.

Fresh pasta is outstanding and available in most markets and specialty food shops. It exceeds dried, packaged pasta both in its taste and texture, being more delicate and flavorful, and cooks in just a few minutes. If you have the time, homemade pasta is a treat worth tasting.

Ways of presenting pasta are limited only by your imagination. No longer do we think of spaghetti and meatballs when we talk about pasta. Such exotic and tantalizing dishes as pasta with ratatouille, fettuccini with chicken livers, and cannelloni with salmon and spinach come to mind. Serve it hot or cold, or anywhere in between. Sauce it with meat, chicken, fish, cheese, or vegetables for inspiring combinations. Use it as a first course to whet your appetite, as an entrée, accompaniment, luncheon dish, in a salad, or as a snack. Pasta combines well with most other foods and therefore should find its way to almost any meal!

PASTA COMBINATIONS

For a quick, nutritious meal, toss freshly cooked linguine with any one of the following mixtures:

1. Assorted mushrooms—cultivated white, shiitake, and oysters—sautéed in butter, drizzled with lemon juice, and coated with Parmesan.

2. Sautéed imported ham, snow peas, and fresh peas, mixed with cream, and seasoned with dill.

3. Chopped onions, leeks, garlic, and scallions sautéed in butter, dressed with heavy cream, and adorned with snipped chives.

4. Artichoke hearts sautéed in garlic and oil with scrambled eggs and cream, finished with Romano.

5. Assorted peppers—red, green, and yellow—sautéed in garlic and oil with julienne slices of salami, all tossed with Parmesan.

6. Chunks of crabmeat and steamed asparagus covered with Hollandaise sauce.

7. Broccoli flowerettes and pine nuts sautéed in garlic and oil.

8. For an Oriental flavor—red pepper, scallions, water chestnuts, beansprouts, and shredded cabbage sautéed in oil and seasoned with soy sauce, ginger, and sesame seeds.

9. Sautéed scallops, shrimp, and lobster tossed with pesto.

10. Crumbled goat cheese (Montrachet or chèvre) marinated in a garlic and herb vinaigrette.

11. Chopped tomatoes, sun-dried tomatoes, sliced black olives, toasted pine nuts, olive oil, and chopped fresh basil.

FETTUCCINE WITH FRESH TOMATOES AND MOZZARELLA

Freshly cooked pasta is teamed up with a sauce of fresh plum tomatoes, mozzarella cheese, and fresh basil leaves. A truly Southern Italian marriage of ingredients.

  2 pounds plum tomatoes, coarsely chopped
  1 cup coarsely grated mozzarella cheese
  6 tablespoons olive oil
  1 large clove garlic, crushed
  3 tablespoons chopped fresh basil
  1/4 cup chopped fresh parsley
  salt and freshly ground pepper to taste
  1 pound fettuccine

1. Combine the tomatoes and mozzarella in a medium-size bowl. Add the oil, garlic, and seasonings and stir well. Up to this point may be prepared in advance and refrigerated until needed. When ready to use, return to room temperature.

2. In a large pot of boiling water, cook the fettuccine according to the package directions. Drain well and place the pasta on a platter.

3. Adorn the fettuccine with the fresh tomato sauce and serve at once.

6 side portions

PASTA WITH SAUCE BOLOGNESE

Having sampled the authentic version when traveling in Italy, I have tried to duplicate this earthy flavored pasta sauce. A slowly simmered typically Italian tomato-meat sauce, lightly flavored with diced onion, carrot, and celery, and finished with cream. Notice there is no salt in the list of ingredients—the vegetables provide the natural salt for the sauce.

> 2 tablespoons olive oil
> 1 small onion, finely diced
> 1 carrot, finely diced
> 1 stalk celery, finely diced
> 1 pound chopped sirloin
> 1 cup dry white wine
> $1/8$ teaspoon nutmeg
> 2 cups peeled and chopped plum tomatoes
> $1/2$ cup medium cream
> 1 pound fettuccine

1. Heat the oil in a saucepan. Add the onion, carrot, and celery, and sauté until the vegetables are limp and golden.

2. Add the chopped sirloin, stirring to break up any chunks. Continue to fry until the meat is well browned.

3. Add the white wine, and simmer for 5 to 10 minutes, allowing the alcohol to evaporate. Add the nutmeg and tomatoes; bring the sauce to a boil, cover, and lower the heat. Simmer the sauce for $1^{1}/2$ hours.

4. After the sauce has cooked and is thickened, stir in the cream and heat through.

5. Cook the fettuccine according to package directions. Drain well and divide among 6 bowls.

6. Ladle spoonfuls of the sauce over the freshly cooked fettuccine and serve at once.

6 portions

PASTA, TOMATOES, AND ARTICHOKE HEARTS PROVENCAL

NOTATIONS

A subtle marriage of flavors—tomatoes seasoned with thyme, fennel, and orange zest, enhanced by artichoke hearts—which combine to form a delectable red pasta sauce.

1/4 cup olive oil
1 large onion, coarsely chopped
28 ounce can Italian plum tomatoes
6 sun-dried tomatoes, chopped (see page 251)
1/2 cup coarsely chopped Italian parsley
1 teaspoon dried thyme
1/2 teaspoon fennel seeds
1 teaspoon dried grated orange peel (Durkee's)
salt and freshly ground pepper to taste
14 ounce can artichoke hearts, drained and cut in half
12 ounces linguine

1. In a large saucepan, heat the olive oil. When hot, add the onion and cook until softened. Add the canned tomatoes, juice and all, breaking up the tomatoes slightly.

2. Add the sun-dried tomatoes and seasonings, lower the heat, and simmer gently for 30 minutes.

3. Add the artichoke hearts and simmer 10 minutes more.

4. While the sauce is cooking, prepare the pasta according to package directions. Drain well.

5. Spoon the sauce over the freshly cooked pasta and serve at once.

4 portions

PASTA WITH PEPPERONI AND SUN-DRIED TOMATOES

A simple, zesty, and somewhat spicy pasta topping—linguine is covered with sautéed sun-dried tomatoes, pepperoni, and mushrooms, and then finished with a sprinkling of Romano cheese.

1/3 cup olive oil
1 large clove garlic, crushed
1 pound mushrooms, thickly sliced
1 1/2 ounces pepperoni, thinly sliced and cut into matchstick pieces
1/2 cup coarsely chopped sun-dried tomatoes (see page 251)
10 ounces linguine
1/4 cup grated Romano cheese

1. In a large fry pan, heat the oil over medium-high heat. When hot, add the garlic and mushrooms and sauté until golden brown.

2. Add the pepperoni and tomatoes, stirring and cooking for 2 minutes. Set aside.

3. Cook the linguine according to the package directions. Drain well.

4. Pour the sauce over the freshly cooked pasta. Sprinkle with the Romano cheese, toss, and serve.

6 side portions

PASTA WITH RATATOUILLE

An herbed tomato-based sauce of classic Mediterranean proportions—
a host of garden vegetables—eggplant, zucchini, red and green
peppers, and onions are ornamented with capers and black olives.

> 2 medium-size zucchini
> 1 medium eggplant
> salt
> 4 tablespoons olive oil
> 1 large red pepper, sliced
> 1 large green pepper, sliced
> 1 large Bermuda onion, sliced
> 2 cloves garlic, minced
> 1/4 cup chopped fresh parsley
> 1 teaspoon dried basil
> salt and freshly ground pepper to taste
> 1 pound plum tomatoes, peeled and chopped
> 1 tablespoon capers
> 1/2 cup sliced black olives
> 1 pound ziti

1. Slice the zucchini into 1/2-inch thick rounds, and cut each round in
half. Peel the eggplant and cut it into 1/2-inch cubes. Place the vegetable
pieces in a colander and sprinkle generously with salt. Let this stand for
30 minutes; then rinse well and pat dry.

2. Heat the oil in a large skillet, and sauté the eggplant and zucchini,
browning lightly. Remove the vegetables and set aside.

3. If necessary, add 1 to 2 more tablespoons of oil to the pan, and
sauté the peppers and onion until soft.

4. Sprinkle with the garlic, parsley, basil, salt, and pepper.

5. Add the tomatoes to the sauce and simmer for 5 minutes.

6. Return the sautéed eggplant to the pan; cover and simmer over
medium heat for 20 minutes. Add the zucchini, capers, and black olives
and simmer uncovered for 15 minutes more.

7. While the sauce is simmering, boil the pasta according to package
directions and drain well. Place the cooked pasta in a large serving
bowl and toss with the ratatouille. Serve hot or cool to room
temperature and present.

6 main-course portions

PASTA WITH GRILLED VEGETABLES

A colorful mélange of grilled vegetables, served over pasta, dressed in a balsamic vinaigrette. It captures the essence of barbecued flavor in a light and tasty composition.

> 1 large head radicchio, sliced in half through the core
> 2 baby eggplants, sliced in half lengthwise
> 1 medium zucchini, sliced in half lengthwise
> 1 medium summer squash, sliced in half lengthwise
> 1 large Spanish or Bermuda onion, thickly sliced
> 1/2 pound mushrooms, skewered
> 1 red pepper, cut in quarters
> 1 green pepper, cut in quarters
> 1/4 to 1/3 cup olive oil
> salt and pepper to taste

Vinaigrette:
> 1 1/2 tablespoons balsamic vinegar
> 1/4 cup extra virgin olive oil
> 12 ounces fettuccine

1. Lightly brush the vegetables with the 1/4 to 1/3 cup olive oil. Season with salt and pepper.

2. Place vegetables over hot coals 4 inches from the heat source and grill 5 minutes per side, until browned and cooked.

3. Remove the vegetables from the grill and heap the mushrooms and onion rings into a large bowl. Slice the remaining vegetables into bite-size chunks and add to the bowl.

4. Whisk together the balsamic vinegar and olive oil and pour the vinaigrette over the grilled vegetable mélange, tossing to coat evenly.

5. Cook the pasta according to package directions. Drain well. Add the pasta to the vegetable dish, toss, and serve. (May be refrigerated for later use; return to room temperature to present.)

8 to 10 side portions; 6 main-course portions

PASTA MONTRACHET

A delicate dish that incorporates julienned vegetables sautéed in dill butter with roasted garlic, tossed with linguine, and garnished with Montrachet.

> 2 leeks, each at least 1¹/2 inches in diameter (see page 80—how to
>   clean leeks)
> 1 medium zucchini, seeded
> 2 large carrots, peeled
> 6 tablespoons butter
> 2 large cloves roasted garlic, crushed (see page 239)
> ¹/4 pound sliced shiitake mushrooms
> salt and freshly ground pepper to taste
> ¹/2 teaspoon dried dill
> 1 pound linguine
> 4 ounces Montrachet or chèvre, crumbled

1. Remove the stems and green leaves from the leeks. Cut the white part into 3 x ¹/8-inch slivers.

2. Cut the zucchini and carrots into matchstick pieces, 3 x ¹/8-inch thick.

3. Melt the butter in a large skillet. Add the crushed garlic, swirling it around in the pan to flavor the butter.

4. When the butter is hot, add the vegetables. Sprinkle with the seasonings, and stir-fry over high heat for 3 to 4 minutes.

5. While the vegetables are cooking, boil the pasta according to package directions. Drain well, and place in a large serving bowl.

6. Cover the freshly cooked pasta with the sautéed vegetables. Garnish with the Montrachet, toss gently, and serve at once.

6 to 8 side portions; 4 main-course portions

SESAME NOODLES

Cold strands of pasta are coated with an Oriental soy and sesame sauce, bespeckled with scallions and sesame seeds.

1 pound linguine or Japanese Udon noodles
$1/4$ cup Oriental sesame oil (available in Oriental markets)
$1/4$ cup soy sauce
$1^1/2$ teaspoons sugar
$1/4$ teaspoon black pepper
1 large clove garlic, smashed
$1/4$ cup chopped scallions
2 tablespoons sesame seeds, toasted

1. Boil the pasta according to package directions. Drain well.

2. In a small bowl, combine the sesame oil, soy, sugar, pepper, garlic, scallions, and sesame seeds.

3. Pour the sauce over the cooked pasta and toss well. Serve at once or refrigerate for later use. Return to room temperature to serve.

6 to 8 side portions

PAN FRIED NOODLES

A typical Thai noodle dish—thin strands of pasta stir-fried with eggs, shrimp, bean sprouts, and ground peanuts in a slightly sweet-flavored fish sauce. This makes a wonderful accompaniment to any meal. It also stands alone most gloriously!

8 ounces cappellini noodles or angel hair pasta
2 eggs
5 tablespoons oil
1 teaspoon lemon juice
2 tablespoons fish sauce (available in Oriental markets; soy sauce may be substituted)
2 teaspoons sugar
1/4 pound medium-size raw shrimp, peeled
5 tablespoons coarsely chopped unsalted peanuts
6 cups beansprouts
4 scallions, cut into 2-inch lengths

1. Cook the pasta in a large pot of boiling water for 2 minutes. Drain well.

2. Beat the eggs until frothy. Heat 2 tablespoons of oil in a small skillet until hot. Add the beaten eggs, stirring gently until well scrambled. Remove from heat.

3. In a small bowl, mix together the lemon juice, fish sauce, and sugar. Set aside.

4. In a wok or large fry pan, heat 3 tablespoons of oil over high heat. When hot, add the shrimp, scrambled eggs, 3 tablespoons ground peanuts, 4 cups beansprouts, and scallions. Stir-fry until the shrimps turn pink. Add the cooked noodles, and mix well. Add the sauce; stir thoroughly.

5. Transfer to a serving dish. Garnish the top with 2 tablespoons ground peanuts and surround the noodles with 2 cups of raw sprouts. Serve at once.

6 to 8 side-dish portions; 3 to 4 main-dish portions

FETTUCCINE WITH CHICKEN LIVERS MARSALA

A Marsala wine sauce teeming with sautéed chicken livers, mushrooms, and imported ham. A different and quick-to-fix pasta sauce.

> 6 tablespoons butter
> 1 clove garlic, smashed
> 1 shallot, finely chopped
> 1/2 pound mushrooms, sliced
> 1 pound chicken livers, divided in half, sinews removed
> 1/8 pound imported sliced ham, cut into 1-inch squares
> salt and freshly ground pepper to taste
> 1/4 cup chopped fresh parsley
> 1/2 cup Marsala wine
> 1 pound fettuccine

1. Melt the butter in a large frying pan. When the butter is hot, add the garlic, shallot, and sliced mushrooms and sauté until the mushrooms are browned.

2. Add the chicken livers and ham. Sprinkle with salt and pepper, cooking the mixture over medium-high heat until the livers lose their pinkness, about 5 to 10 minutes.

3. Sprinkle with the parsley and add the Marsala; lower the heat and simmer 5 minutes.

4. While the sauce is cooking, boil the fettuccine according to package directions. Place the freshly cooked pasta on a deep platter, spoon over the chicken liver sauce, and serve at once.

4 to 6 main-course portions

Note—Chicken livers are perishable, and therefore, any extra should be kept no longer than 1 to 2 days in the refrigerator.

LASAGNA

A slightly different rendition on an all-time favorite. Layers of pasta alternating with a cheese and spinach filling, and a wild mushroom-tomato sauce, all topped with grated mozzarella—a vegetarian specialty.

2 tablespoons olive oil
1 large onion, chopped
2 cloves garlic, crushed
3/4 pound cremini mushrooms, sliced
1/2 pound shiitake mushrooms, sliced
salt and freshly ground pepper to taste
5 tablespoons chopped fresh parsley
1 1/2 teaspoons dried basil
2 bay leaves
1/2 cup dry red wine
1 pound 12 ounce can tomatoes
3 tablespoons tomato paste
1 pound ricotta cheese
1/3 cup Parmesan cheese
2 eggs, beaten
10 ounce package frozen chopped spinach, defrosted and drained
1 pound lasagna noodles
1 pound grated mozzarella cheese

1. Heat the oil in a large saucepan. When hot, add the onion, garlic, and mushrooms and sauté until the onion is soft and the mushrooms are golden.

2. Add salt and pepper to taste, 3 tablespoons parsley, basil, bay leaves, red wine, tomatoes, and tomato paste, and stir well. When the sauce begins to simmer, lower the heat and continue simmering uncovered for 1 hour.

3. While the tomato sauce is simmering, prepare the cheese sauce. In a large bowl, combine the ricotta cheese, Parmesan cheese, eggs, 2 tablespoons parsley, and thawed spinach, and mix well. Set aside.

4. In a large pot of boiling, salted water, cook the lasagna noodles according to the package directions. Place in a colander and drain well.

5. Now assemble the lasagna. In a 9 x 13-inch baking dish, spread a thin layer of the tomato sauce. Cover with a double layer of lasagna. Spread 1/3 of the cheese sauce over the pasta. Cover the cheese sauce with a thick layer of tomato sauce. Sprinkle 1/3 of the mozzarella over all. Cover with a second double layer of noodles. Repeat the layering, ending with the tomato sauce and mozzarella to cover. (You may have extra tomato sauce—this may be frozen for later use.)

6. Bake in a 350° oven for 35 to 40 minutes. Serve at once. Any unused pasta may be refrigerated and reheated at another time.

6 to 8 hearty portions

RIGATONI WITH GRILLED CHICKEN, PROSCIUTTO, AND MUSHROOMS

Tubular pasta with a Drambuie-laced tomato sauce composed of grilled chicken and mushrooms, and accented with prosciutto.

2 tablespoons olive oil
1 large shallot, diced
12 ounces mushrooms, sliced
2 cups ground, peeled canned Italian plum tomatoes
1 teaspoon dried basil
salt and pepper to taste
2 tablespoons chopped fresh parsley
2 cups dry white wine
1/4 cup Drambuie
1 1/2 pounds boneless, skinless chicken breasts, split in half
vegetable oil
1/8 pound prosciutto, cut into 1-inch squares
1 pound rigatoni

1. Prepare the sauce. Heat the olive oil in a large skillet and when hot, add the shallot and mushrooms and sauté until soft. Add the tomatoes, basil, salt, pepper, parsley, wine, and Drambuie. Simmer 20 minutes until thickened.

2. Prepare the chicken. Brush the breasts with oil, and season with salt and pepper. Grill over hot coals 4 inches from heat source, 3 to 4 minutes per side—the chicken should be undercooked. Remove and cut the chicken into finger-size pieces. Add the chicken and prosciutto to the tomato sauce and simmer 2 to 3 minutes.

3. Prepare the pasta according to package directions. Drain well, and mound on a platter. Pour the sauce over the freshly cooked pasta and serve at once.

6 portions

LINGUINE WITH WHITE CLAM SAUCE

Clams, garlic, wine, and pine nuts team for an exquisite accompaniment to pasta.

3 dozen raw clams in their shells
1/2 cup reserved clam juice
4 tablespoons butter
2 tablespoons virgin olive oil
2 cloves garlic, crushed
1 shallot, finely diced
1/8 teaspoon pepper
1/2 cup pine nuts
2/3 cup dry white wine
1/4 cup chopped fresh parsley
1 pound linguine

1. Steam the clams in water to cover, until the shells open. Reserve 1/2 cup of the juice, and shell the clams.

2. In a saucepan, melt the butter and heat the oil. Add the garlic, shallot, pepper, and pine nuts, and sauté for 5 minutes, being careful not to brown.

3. Add the clams, broth, wine, and parsley, and simmer for 5 minutes more.

4. While the sauce is finishing, boil the linguine according to package directions and drain well. Place the pasta in a large serving bowl. Pour the clam sauce over the hot pasta and toss well. Serve at once.

6 to 8 side-dish portions; 4 main-course portions

LINGUINE AND SHRIMP PESTO

Long strands of pasta are dotted with poached shrimp and tossed in the rich Italian basil-flavored, ground pine nut sauce known as pesto.

1 pound linguine
1 cup pine nuts
2 large cloves garlic
2 cups fresh basil, well packed
1/4 cup Parmesan cheese
1 to 1 1/4 cups olive oil
1 pound large-size shrimp, poached

1. Cook the linguine according to package directions. Drain well.

2. In a food processor, place the pine nuts and garlic and grind to a fine paste.

3. Add the basil and Parmesan and process until the mixture is puréed.

4. In a slow, steady stream, add the oil until the mixture thickens like mayonnaise—then you have added enough oil.

5. To serve, spoon the pesto over the freshly cooked linguine and shrimp and toss. Any unused pesto may be stored in the refrigerator for up to 1 week.

6 portions
This makes approximately 2 1/2 cups of pesto—enough to sauce 2 1/2 pounds of pasta.

PESTO

Pesto, the Genoese basil sauce, has taken American cuisine by storm. In its purest form, it's made with fresh basil and garlic, tempered by olive oil and cheese, and ground in a mortar and "pestle"—thus the name pesto. Pesto is an extremely versatile sauce, adding sparkle to many foods. Try it on sautéed chicken breasts; on grilled fish steaks or veal chops; over baked potatoes; as a stuffing for lamb chops; on toasted rounds of French bread; mixed into mayonnaise as a dip for vegetables; or as a sauce for poached shellfish—shrimp, scallops, crab, and lobster.

PASTA AND SHRIMP SORRENTINO

Linguine tossed with shrimp in a red pepper sauce, finished with feta cheese.

> 2 tablespoons olive oil
> 1 large clove garlic, roasted and crushed (see page 239)
> 3 large red peppers, roasted, skinned, seeded, and puréed (see page 243)
> 1 tablespoon tomato paste
> salt and freshly ground pepper to taste
> 1 tablespoon chopped fresh basil or 1/2 teaspoon dried basil
> 1 cup dry white wine
> 1 1/2 pounds large-size shrimp, cooked
> 1 pound linguine
> 1/3 pound feta cheese, coarsely crumbled

1. Heat the oil in a saucepan. Add the garlic, puréed peppers, tomato paste, salt, pepper, and basil. Simmer for 5 minutes.

2. Pour in the wine and continue to simmer for 10 to 15 minutes.

3. While the sauce is simmering, cook the linguine according to the package directions. Drain the pasta well, and place it on a deep platter.

4. Add the shrimp to the sauce and heat for 1 to 2 minutes.

5. Pour the shrimp sauce over the bed of linguine. Garnish with the crumbled feta cheese and serve at once.

6 portions

LOBSTER, CAVIAR, AND PASTA

This dish is so elegant it makes an outstanding addition to a brunch or luncheon.

> 1 cup cooked lobster meat, cut into 1/2-inch chunks
> 1/2 pint sour cream
> 2 ounces salmon or red lumpfish caviar
> 2 tablespoons snipped chives
> 1 tablespoon lemon juice
> freshly ground black pepper to taste
> 1/2 pound linguine

1. In a bowl, combine the lobster, sour cream, caviar, chives, lemon juice, and pepper, blending gently.

2. Boil the linguine according to package directions and drain well. Spoon the lobster sauce over the hot cooked pasta; toss well and serve immediately, or refrigerate for later use. Return to room temperature to serve.

4 to 6 side-dish portions; 2 to 3 main-dish portions

PASTA WITH ASPARAGUS AND SMOKED SALMON

A vibrant dish—the salmony pink of the fish coupled with the spring green of the asparagus, all lightly dressed in a mustard-wine sauce.

> 2 tablespoons butter
> 1 pound asparagus, peeled, cut into 1½-inch lengths,
>   and steamed 2 minutes
> 6 ounces smoked salmon, cut into ½-inch wide pieces
> lots of freshly ground black pepper
> ⅓ cup Dijon mustard
> ½ cup dry white wine
> 1 teaspoon dried thyme
> 12 ounces fettuccine

1. Melt the butter in a medium-size pan over medium heat. Add the asparagus and smoked salmon; heat and stir for 1 minute. Season with pepper.

2. In a bowl, combine the mustard, wine, and thyme. Pour the sauce over the asparagus and salmon and simmer 5 minutes.

3. While the sauce is simmering, cook the pasta according to package directions. Drain well.

4. Pour the sauce over the freshly cooked pasta, toss, and present at once.

6 to 8 side portions; 4 main-course portions

LINGUINE WITH SMOKED SALMON CREAM

This elegant dish boasts the richness of smoked salmon laced with cream, and subtly flavored with dill and chives.

1¹/₂ cups heavy cream
4 tablespoons unsalted butter
generous pinch of cayenne pepper
3 tablespoons snipped chives
1 teaspoon dried dill
6 ounces smoked salmon, cut into ¹/₂-inch strips
1 pound linguine

1. Put the cream, butter, and cayenne pepper in a saucepan, bring to a boil, and simmer until the sauce is reduced by about one-third.

2. Stir in the chives and dill.

3. Add the smoked salmon, mixing gently, and heat through.

4. Boil the linguine according to package directions and drain well. Pour the salmon sauce over the cooked pasta. Toss and serve immediately.

6 to 8 side-dish portions; 4 main-course portions

SALMON, SPINACH, AND CANNELLONI

Rolls of stuffed pasta filled with a mixture of spinach, cheese, and poached salmon, and laced with a heavenly tomato-cream sauce. A definite special occasion dish.

> *10 ounce package frozen, chopped spinach, thawed and drained*
> *1 pound ricotta cheese*
> *2 cups poached, flaked salmon*
> *salt and freshly ground pepper to taste*
> *4 tablespoons butter*
> *2 cups heavy cream*
> *1/4 cup tomato paste*
> *5 ounce package cannelloni (12 pieces) or better yet, homemade pasta cut into 6-inch squares (see page 8)*
> *3 tablespoons Parmesan cheese*

1. Make the filling. In a large bowl, combine the spinach, ricotta, salmon, salt, and pepper. Set aside.

2. Make the tomato-cream sauce. In a medium saucepan, combine the butter, cream, and tomato paste. Bring the mixture to a boil, and let simmer until the cream is reduced by one-third.

3. Cook the pasta according to the package directions, and drain well.

4. Place 1/3 to 1/2 cup of the filling in each cannelloni. (If using homemade pasta, place the filling in the middle of each square of pasta. Fold over the sides towards the middle, overlapping them.) Place seam side down in a pyrex baking dish.

5. Pour the tomato-cream sauce over the cannelloni.

6. Sprinkle with the Parmesan cheese. (Up to this point may be prepared several hours in advance and refrigerated. Return to room temperature before baking.)

7. Bake in a 350° oven for 20 to 25 minutes. Serve at once.

12 rolls—8 generous portions

VIVIAN'S NOODLE PUDDING

A sweet baked custard of noodles, eggs, cottage cheese, and sour cream; great for luncheon, vegetable, snack, or dessert. This makes a special dish for a large party, as it can be prepared in the morning and then reheated in the oven when the guests arrive.

1 pound wide egg noodles
4 eggs, beaten
2 cups milk
1 teaspoon vanilla extract
$3/4$ cup sugar
$1/2$ cup melted butter
$3/4$ cup sour cream
1 pound cottage cheese
1 teaspoon salt
cinnamon-sugar mixture for topping

1. Preheat the oven to 375°. Grease a 9 x 13-inch pan.

2. Boil the noodles 5 to 6 minutes in salted water. Drain well and set aside.

3. In a large bowl, beat the eggs, milk, and vanilla.

4. Add the sugar, butter, sour cream, cottage cheese, and salt to the egg mixture and blend.

5. Combine the noodles with the custard and stir until the custard mixture is evenly distributed amongst the noodles.

6. Pour the pudding into the prepared pan. (Up to this point may be prepared 4 to 6 hours in advance and refrigerated. Return to room temperature before baking.)

7. Bake for 1 to $1^{1}/4$ hours until set and golden. After 30 minutes, sprinkle the top with cinnamon-sugar to coat lightly. This may be served hot, warm, or at room temperature—whatever your preference. I recommend it hot out of the oven. Any unused pudding may be refrigerated and reheated at a later time.

15 or more portions

GRAND PRESENTATIONS

Whatever form the main course takes, be it meat, fish, or fowl, make it grand. The entrée should be the focus of the meal with complementary garnishes and vegetable accompaniments. Titilate your palate with unusual dishes, boasting intriguing spices and delicate sauces.

SUCCULENT MEATS

People's concern about cholesterol and interest in light meals have made them shy away from meats. Red meat in particular, no longer has the appeal and widespread popularity it once did. However, meats are still a good source of protein, are relatively inexpensive, and can be prepared with ease. Always purchase the best cuts of meat available to insure tenderness. There is nothing more disastrous than fatty, chewy meat! Enhance the meat dish with such interesting garnishes as fresh fruits, roasted and grilled vegetables, condiments such as capers and kumquats, and delectable sauces. Make it a grand presentation!

SIRLOIN WITH BEARNAISE SAUCE

Sirloin roast flavored with garlic and Madeira wine presented with a quick-to-fix blender béarnaise sauce.

> 3 pound sirloin roast
> 2 large cloves garlic, cut into slivers
> 1 large onion, diced
> 1 cup Madeira wine
> 1 teaspoon coarse salt
> 1/2 to 1 tablespoon coarsely ground black pepper
> Béarnaise Sauce (see page 12)

1. Preheat the oven to 425°.

2. With the tip of a sharp knife, cut slits in the roast and insert garlic slivers in the slits. Place in a shallow roasting pan and surround the meat with the diced onion.

3. Rub the roast well with the wine. Season with the salt and pepper.

4. Place the roast in the oven for 25 minutes. Then lower the heat to 325° and continue roasting for 1 hour—or 20 minutes per pound for rare beef, 120° on a meat thermometer. (The roast should be presented rare, as it continues to cook itself once it is removed from the oven.) Baste the roast occasionally.

5. When the meat is done, transfer it to a platter and pour the pan juices over it. Let the roast rest for 10 minutes before carving the meat into thick slices. Present with a dollop of the béarnaise sauce.

6 to 8 portions

CHOPPED SIRLOIN FRANCAISE

A new design for the all-American hamburger—grilled sirloin burgers oozing with an herbed Boursin cheese and chive filling, enhanced by sun-dried tomatoes.

2 pounds chopped sirloin, divided into 6 equal portions
4 ounce package Boursin cheese
2 tablespoons snipped chives
6 sun-dried tomatoes, cut in half (see page 251)
freshly ground pepper to taste
Worcestershire sauce

1. Divide each portion of meat into two equal pieces, and shape each into a neat, flat circle. You should have 12 circles of sirloin.

2. On each of six sirloin patties, spread:

   1 tablespoon Boursin cheese
   1 teaspoon snipped chives
   2 pieces of sun-dried tomato
   freshly ground pepper to taste
   dash of Worcestershire sauce

3. Top each with a plain half of sirloin, pressing around the edges well to seal in the filling. (Up to this point may be done several hours in advance, and kept refrigerated until serving time.)

4. When ready to serve, broil or grill the burgers over hot coals. Rare = 3 minutes per side, medium-to-well = 4 minutes per side. When cooked, transfer the burgers atop slices of sour dough or French bread and serve.

6 portions

FEZ'S EGGPLANT BAKE

A more delicate presentation than moussaka—slices of eggplant smothered in an herbed tomato sauce with ground lamb and pine nuts.

1 tablespoon oil
1 medium onion, diced
1 large clove garlic, crushed
1 pound ground lamb
salt and freshly ground pepper to taste
3 tablespoons chopped fresh parsley
$1/2$ teaspoon dried mint
1 pound 12 ounce can tomatoes with purée
1 large eggplant, sliced lengthwise into $1/2$-inch thick pieces
1 tablespoon lemon juice
$1/4$ cup pine nuts

1. Heat the oil in a large saucepan until hot. Add the onion and garlic, and sauté until the onion is limp.

2. Add the lamb and brown well. Season with salt, pepper, parsley, and mint.

3. Stir in the tomatoes and simmer for 30 minutes.

4. While the sauce is simmering, prepare the eggplant. Sprinkle the eggplant with lemon juice and steam for 10 minutes. Place the eggplant in a colander and let drain well. Arrange the slices in a single layer in a large baking dish.

5. When the sauce is finished, stir in the pine nuts. Spoon the sauce over the eggplant, covering generously. (Up to this point may be prepared as much as 24 hours in advance of serving time, and refrigerated. Return to room temperature before baking.)

6. When ready to serve, bake the eggplant entrée in a 350° oven for 30 minutes and present piping hot with rice pilaf.

6 to 8 portions

BEEF BURGUNDY

A robust beef stew with bacon, assorted chopped vegetables, red wine, and a garnish of sautéed pearl onions and mushrooms. This is definite party fare—well worth the effort! This dish is at its flavor-best when prepared 1 to 2 days in advance.

1/2 pound bacon, diced
5 pounds chuck, cut into 2-inch cubes
1/3 cup flour
1/2 cup butter
1/4 teaspoon pepper
1/4 cup cognac
1 tablespoon tomato paste
2 leeks, coarsely chopped (see page 80—how to clean leeks)
4 carrots, coarsely chopped
2 stalks celery, coarsely chopped
2 cups onions, coarsely chopped
4 cloves garlic, minced
1 tablespoon chopped fresh parsley
2 bay leaves, crumbled
1 teaspoon dried thyme
1 cup sweet sherry
1 1/2 cups Burgundy wine
2 pounds mushrooms
2 teaspoons lemon juice
2 pounds whole pearl onions
4 teaspoons sugar

1. Preheat the oven to 350°.

2. Fry the bacon in a large Dutch saucepan until golden. Remove the cooked bacon from the saucepan and set aside, leaving the bacon fat in the pan.

3. Dredge the beef in the flour, lightly coating each piece.

4. Add 4 tablespoons of butter to the bacon fat. Turn the heat to medium-high, and when the butter is hot, add the meat in batches, browning well on all sides. As the pieces brown, transfer them to a platter. When all the meat is browned, return it to the Dutch oven. Sprinkle with the pepper, douse with the cognac, and ignite. When the flames die, stir in the tomato paste.

5. Add the cooked bacon, chopped vegetables, garlic, parsley, bay leaves, thyme, sherry, and 1 cup of Burgundy.

6. Cover and bake for 2 to 2¹/₂ hours or until the meat is fork tender.

7. Remove the pot from the oven, and remove the meat from the pot. Transfer the cooking liquids and vegetables to a food processor or blender, and purée for a rich, thick sauce. Return the purée and meat to the pot.

8. Prepare the onion and mushroom garnish. Sauté the mushrooms in 2 tablespoons of hot butter in a large skillet over high heat until golden. Sprinkle with the lemon juice and add to the meat. Add the remaining 2 tablespoons butter to the pan. Add the onions and sauté until golden. Add the sugar and ¹/₂ cup Burgundy wine. Cover and simmer for 15 minutes until the onions are tender. Add the onions and pan juices to the casserole when done. Up to this point can be prepared as much as 2 days in advance of serving time and refrigerated, giving the flavors a chance to mellow.

9. To serve, bring the stew to room temperature and reheat the casserole in a 350° oven for at least 30 to 40 minutes until piping hot. Serve at once with buttered noodles.

10 to 12 portions

HERBED RACK OF LAMB

Racks of lamb are painted with an herbed mustard and soy coating. The potpourri of herbs lends an aromatic flavor to the lamb.

> 2 racks of lamb, trimmed of fat
> 2 tablespoons Dijon mustard
> 2 tablespoons soy sauce
> 2 large cloves garlic, crushed
> 1 teaspoon dried rosemary
> 1/2 teaspoon ground ginger
> 1 teaspoon dried thyme
> 1 teaspoon ground marjoram
> freshly ground pepper to taste
> 2 tablespoons olive oil

1. Whisk together the Dijon, soy, garlic, herbs, spices, and oil.

2. Paint the marinade generously over the exposed surfaces of lamb. Place the racks in a roasting pan and let marinate at room temperature for 1 hour.

3. When ready to serve, preheat the oven to 400°.

4. Roast the lamb for 25 minutes for medium-rare. Remove to a platter, carve the rack and present.

4 portions

BUTTERFLIED LEG OF LAMB

Boneless lamb, marinated in a mint-chili sauce, and grilled over hot coals—this always receives rave reviews. It's so simple to make! I like to accompany this meal with a Greek salad and rice pilaf, as lamb is a typically Greek food.

12 ounce bottle chili sauce
5¹/2 ounce bottle mint sauce (Crosse & Blackwell or Raffeto's)
¹/2 cup oil
5 pound boned leg of lamb, butterflied (weight after boned)

1. Combine the chili sauce, mint sauce, and oil in a bowl. Pour the sauce over the lamb and marinate the meat refrigerated for 2 days, turning the meat every 12 hours.

2. When ready to cook, remove the lamb from the sauce, and grill over hot coals 4 inches from the heat source, for 20 to 25 minutes (about 10 to 12 minutes per side for medium-rare), basting often with the reserved marinade.

3. Serve hot off the grill, carving the lamb into thin slices.

8 portions

LAMB WITH RASPBERRY SAUCE

Leg of lamb is roasted with a sauce combining raspberry jam, orange juice, and red wine. The slightly sweet, fruity sauce complements the sometimes "gamey" flavor of the meat.

6 pound leg of lamb
salt and freshly ground pepper to taste
1 large clove garlic, crushed
2 cups dry red wine
1/2 cup seedless red raspberry jam
1/2 cup orange juice

1. Pour 1 cup of red wine over the lamb. Season the leg with salt, pepper, and garlic, rubbing the spices into the meat. Let marinate for at least 2 hours.

2. While the lamb is marinating, prepare the sauce. Stir together the raspberry jam, orange juice, and 1/2 cup of red wine in a small bowl.

3. When ready to roast the meat, preheat the oven to 450°. Remove the lamb from the marinade to a roasting pan, reserving the marinade.

4. Place the lamb in the hot oven for 15 minutes to sear the meat, sealing in the juices. Lower the oven temperature to 350°, pour the marinade over the roast, and continue to bake for 1½ hours, or 15 minutes per pound. After roasting for 20 minutes at 350°, pour the raspberry sauce over the lamb and continue to baste the leg every 15 to 20 minutes. It may be necessary to add an additional 1/2 cup of red wine if you find you do not have sufficient sauce.

5. When the lamb is done, remove to a platter, let sit for 10 minutes before carving. Serve with the pan juices.

8 portions

VEAL CALABRESE

Rolled scallops of veal stuffed with prosciutto and mozzarella and sautéed with red wine and grilled vegetables.

1¹/₂ pounds veal scallops (12 slices)
freshly ground pepper to taste
12 thin slices prosciutto
12 thin slices mozzarella
¹/₄ cup flour
¹/₂ pound mushrooms, thickly sliced
2 onions, sliced
1 green pepper, cut into ¹/₂-inch slices
1 red pepper, cut into ¹/₂-inch slices
4 tablespoons olive oil
4 tablespoons butter
2 tablespoons chopped fresh parsley
1 tablespoon capers
¹/₂ cup red wine

1. Pound the veal scallops with a mallet. Sprinkle with pepper.

2. On each scallop of veal, place a piece of prosciutto. Cover this with a slice of mozzarella cheese and roll the veal up jelly-roll fashion.

3. Dredge the veal rolls in flour and set aside.

4. Drizzle the mushrooms, onions, and peppers with 2 tablespoons of oil. Grill or broil the vegetables until cooked and nicely browned. When the vegetables are done, set aside.

5. Heat the butter and 2 tablespoons of oil in a large skillet until hot. Add the veal rolls and cook 2 minutes on each side until golden brown.

6. Add the parsley, grilled vegetables, capers, and red wine to the skillet, stirring up any browned bits in the pan, and simmer 3 to 4 minutes more. Serve at once.

4 to 6 portions

VEAL FONTINA

Breaded veal cutlets topped with asparagus spears, crabmeat, and Fontina cheese. This preparation also works well with chicken.

1 1/2 pounds veal cutlets (6 cutlets)
salt and freshly ground pepper to taste
1/4 cup flour
1 egg
2 tablespoons water
1 cup fresh bread crumbs
4 tablespoons butter
2 tablespoons oil
1/2 pound crabmeat
12 asparagus spears, peeled and steamed until tender-crisp (see page 232— how to peel asparagus)
1 cup grated Fontina cheese

1. Pound the veal cutlets with a mallet. Season the flour with salt and pepper; dredge the veal in the flour, coating well.

2. Beat the egg with the water in a flat dish. Dip the veal into the egg mixture.

3. Dredge the veal in the bread crumbs, coating well on both sides. Refrigerate the veal for 30 minutes so that the crumbs adhere well.

4. Heat the butter and the oil in a large skillet until very hot. Add the veal, two or three pieces at a time, and sauté until golden, about 1 to 2 minutes per side. Remove the cooked veal to a shallow baking dish. Repeat until all the meat is cooked.

5. Arrange a chunk of crab and 2 asparagus spears on each cutlet. Sprinkle all with the grated Fontina cheese. (This much may be done in advance and refrigerated until serving time.)

6. When ready to serve, place the veal under a hot broiler until the cheese is brown and bubbly.

6 portions

VEAL VERDICCHIO

Veal scallops are sautéed in garlic butter with broccoli, mushrooms, black olives, and artichoke hearts, and finished with Verdicchio wine.

1¹/₂ pounds veal scallops
¹/₄ cup flour
salt and freshly ground pepper to taste
6 tablespoons butter
1 clove garlic, smashed
1 head broccoli, cut into spears, and steamed 5 minutes
1 cup small pitted whole black olives
14 ounce can artichoke hearts, drained and cut in half
6 ounces mushrooms, sliced in half
¹/₂ cup Verdicchio wine
2 tablespoons consommé

1. Pound the veal lightly with a mallet. Season the flour with salt and pepper; dredge the veal in the flour mixture.

2. Heat the butter over medium-high heat in a large skillet. When hot, add the smashed garlic, and swirl it around in the pan. Add the veal, two or three pieces at a time, and cook the scallops 1 minute per side. Remove the browned pieces to a platter and keep warm. Continue until all the veal is cooked.

3. Add the broccoli spears, black olives, artichoke hearts, and mushrooms to the skillet and sauté over medium-high heat for 2 to 3 minutes.

4. Pour the Verdicchio wine and consommé over the vegetables and simmer 3 minutes more. Spoon the vegetables and sauce over the veal scallops and serve immediately.

4 to 6 portions

GRILLED VEAL CHOPS MADEIRA

Veal chops are grilled over hot coals, then covered with a Mushroom-Madeira sauce.

6 loin veal chops, 1-inch thick
olive oil
freshly ground pepper to taste
Mushroom-Madeira Sauce (recipe follows)

1. Rub the chops with olive oil, coating well. Season the veal with pepper.

2. Grill the chops over hot coals 4 inches from heat source, approximately 4 minutes per side for medium-rare. When the chops are cooked, remove them to a platter. Serve with the Mushroom-Maderia sauce spooned over each chop.

6 portions

Mushroom-Madeira Sauce:
4 tablespoons butter
1 clove garlic, crushed
1 pound mushrooms, thinly sliced
2 tablespoons chopped fresh parsley
1/2 cup Madeira wine

1. In a large skillet, heat the butter over high heat until hot.

2. Add the garlic and sliced mushrooms. Season with salt, pepper, and parsley, and sauté quickly, stirring occasionally until the mushrooms are lightly browned.

3. Add the Madeira and cook until the sauce is reduced by 1/3.

4. Pour the sauce over the grilled chops and serve immediately.

VEAL CHOPS MARSALA

Veal chops are breaded and sautéed until crisp, then surrounded by wild mushrooms, scallions, and roasted red pepper. All is splashed with Marsala wine for a distinctively sweet Italian touch.

> *4 veal chops, 3/4-inch thick*
> *pepper to taste*
> *1 egg, beaten*
> *1 cup plain bread crumbs*
> *6 tablespoons butter*
> *6 ounces shiitake mushrooms*
> *1 bunch scallions, coarsely chopped*
> *1 large red pepper, roasted and cut into 1/2-inch wide strips (see page 243)*
> *1/2 cup Marsala wine*

1. Season the chops with pepper. Dip each in the egg and then into the bread crumbs, coating generously. Place in the refrigerator for 1/2 hour so crumbs will adhere.

2. In a large skillet, heat 3 tablespoons butter over medium-high heat. When sizzling, add the mushrooms and scallions and sauté until tender. Remove from the pan and set aside.

3. Add the remaining 3 tablespoons butter to the pan. When hot, add the veal chops and sauté over medium-high heat until browned and crisp, about 3 minutes per side. Cover for 1 minute at the end.

4. Uncover, add the cooked vegetables and roasted pepper. Add the Marsala and let simmer 2 to 3 minutes. Remove to a platter and serve at once.

4 portions

BARBECUED RIBS

Spareribs grilled with a gutsy chili-flavored sauce.

1 cup catsup
2/3 cup water
1 small onion, chopped
1 tablespoon Worcestershire sauce
1/4 cup white vinegar
1/4 cup firmly packed dark brown sugar
2 teaspoons dry mustard
1 teaspoon paprika
1 tablespoon chili powder
1 clove garlic, minced
1/4 teaspoon black pepper
1/8 teaspoon cayenne pepper
salt to taste
1 tablespoon oil
4 pounds meaty spareribs

1. Combine all of the above ingredients, except the spareribs, in a medium-size saucepan and stir well. Cover and simmer over low heat for 30 minutes, stirring occasionally.

2. Remove the cooked barbecue sauce from the heat and let cool. (You may prepare the sauce several days in advance and refrigerate until needed.)

3. Place the ribs in a roasting pan and coat them generously with the rich sauce.

4. Parcook the ribs before grilling—bake in a 350° oven for 30 minutes. This gives the meat a chance to cook through before browning, so you won't have burned ribs! This much may be done a day in advance if you wish.

5. When ready to serve the ribs, grill over hot coals for 20 minutes, basting often with additional marinade.

4 to 6 portions of ribs
2 to 2^1/$_2$ cups barbecue sauce

Note—any leftover sauce may be refrigerated for future use. The sauce will keep 4 to 6 weeks. It also works wonders with chicken and shrimp!

PORK CHOPS WITH POTATOES AND PEPPERS

Sautéed pork chops are surrounded by potatoes, onions, and peppers and finished with red wine vinegar. Pork need not be well done, but can be enjoyed slightly pink, as long as the juices run clear when pricked with a fork.

> $1/2$ cup butter
> 3 medium-size new potatoes, sliced wafer thin
> 1 large red onion, sliced
> 2 large green peppers, sliced into $1/2$-inch thick pieces
> 1 clove garlic, crushed
> 6 loin pork chops, cut $3/4$-inch thick
> salt and freshly ground pepper to taste
> $1/2$ teaspoon dried thyme
> $1/2$ cup red wine vinegar

1. Heat 6 tablespoons of butter in a large skillet until hot. Add the vegetables and cook over high heat for 10 minutes or until the vegetables are cooked and browned.

2. Remove the vegetables from the pan and set aside. Add the remainder of the butter and garlic to the skillet. Lower the heat to medium-high and add the pork chops.

3. Season the meat with salt, pepper, and thyme. Pan fry the chops about 4 minutes per side until cooked and browned.

4. When the chops are done, surround them with the sautéed vegetables, douse with vinegar, and heat through. Transfer the chops and vegetables to a platter and serve at once.

6 portions

ORANGE-FLAVORED PORK ROAST

Loin of pork marinated in orange juice, flavored with the essence of garlic and rosemary, with Madeira wine.

> 1 cup orange juice
> salt and freshly ground pepper to taste
> 1 clove garlic, crushed
> 1/2 teaspoon dried rosemary
> 1 teaspoon finely grated orange peel
> 3 pound boned and rolled pork loin
> 1 to 2 cups Madeira wine
> 1 orange, peeled and cut into thin slices for garnish

1. Combine the orange juice, salt, pepper, garlic, rosemary, and orange peel in a bowl. Set the pork loin in a roasting pan and pour the mixture over the loin. Let the pork marinate for 2 hours.

2. Preheat the oven to 350°.

3. Roast for 2 hours 15 minutes or 45 minutes per pound. After 1/2 hour of cooking, pour 1 cup Madeira over the pork, and baste the meat with the pan juices every 20 to 30 minutes. After 1 hour, make a loose foil tent to cover the meat, and continue roasting, covered, basting until done. It may be necessary to add an additional 1/2 to 1 cup of Madeira to the pan if you find the juices drying up.

4. Remove the roasted loin to a platter and let sit for 10 minutes before carving. Pour the pan juices over all, and serve garnished with orange slices.

6 portions

ROAST PORK WITH ARTICHOKE-MUSTARD SAUCE

Slices of roasted pork loin bathed in an artichoke heart and mustard-flavored sauce. This dish is also delicious when served at room temperature, enabling you to prepare it in advance.

> 3 pound boned and rolled pork loin
> 1 to 1¹/₂ cups dry white wine
> 2 cloves garlic, cut into slivers
> salt and freshly ground pepper to taste
> ¹/₂ teaspoon dried thyme
> Artichoke-Mustard Sauce (see page 13)

1. Preheat the oven to 350°.

2. Place the pork loin in a shallow roasting pan. Rub the roast with ¹/₂ cup white wine. With the tip of a sharp knife, cut slits in the roast and insert the garlic slivers in the slits. Work the seasonings into the meat.

3. Set the loin in the oven. Roast for 2 hours and 15 minutes or 45 minutes per pound. Baste the pork every 20 to 30 minutes with the pan juices. After 1 hour of roasting time, make a loose foil tent and cover the meat for the remainder of the cooking time. It may be necessary to add an additional ¹/₂ to 1 cup of wine at this time, if the pan juices have dried up.

4. When the roast is done, transfer the loin to a platter, and let sit for 10 minutes. Carve into ³/₄-inch thick slices, pour the pan juices over all, and serve with the artichoke-mustard sauce covering the slices. Pass the extra sauce alongside in a gravyboat.

6 portions

FANCY FOWL

Chicken is continuing to be served regularly as a dinner favorite. It is economical, a good source of protein, relatively low in calories, and probably the most adaptable and versatile entrée.

Chicken has 1,000 identities. It teams well with vegetables, makes a great soup, can be served hot or cold, can be roasted with fruits, or prepared with sundry seasonings and sauces, thus changing the flavor, as in different cuisines.

Chicken can be prepared using many different techniques. Boneless breasts can be stuffed, breaded, sautéed, or stir-fried; whole chicken can be roasted; chicken parts can be broiled, baked, sautéed or grilled. Chicken is suitable for all types of gatherings—from a casual picnic of barbecued chicken to a formal dinner party featuring Roast Chicken Boursin.

I frequently use boneless, skinless breasts. They make a nice neat presentation for guests, are easy to serve and to eat, there is no waste, and they're lower in cholesterol. They also cook in a short amount of time, which is an important consideration for busy working people.

The versatility of this main course makes it a splendid choice no matter what the occasion!

CHICKEN GIGI

I will be forever appreciative to Gigi in Paris for inspiring the creation of this glorious dish! Roast chicken is stuffed with Boursin cheese, and seasoned with tarragon. The cheese oozes out of the cavity as the bird cooks, and the flavors blend together forming an incredibly delicious sauce that romances the taste buds!

6 to 7 pound roasting chicken
salt and freshly ground pepper to taste
2 (5 ounce) packages Boursin cheese
2 tablespoons melted butter
1 teaspoon dried tarragon
1/2 cup dry white wine

1. Preheat the oven to 350°.
2. Season the roast with salt and pepper. Stuff the cavity with the Boursin cheese. Place the chicken, breast side up, in a large roasting pan.
3. Baste the roast with the melted butter and sprinkle with tarragon. Pour the wine around the chicken.
4. Set the roast in the oven for 2¾ hours, basting every 30 minutes. As the cheese melts, it will begin to ooze out into the pan juices.
5. When the chicken is done, tip the roaster, allowing the rest of the Boursin stuffing to seep out of the cavity into the pan. Transfer the chicken to a platter.
6. Skim the fat from the pan juices. Mix the sauce well.
7. Carve the roast into serving pieces. Spoon some of the delectable sauce over the chicken and present at once. Pass the remaining sauce alongside.

6 portions

DEVILED CHICKEN

Baked chicken parts with a hot mustard and nutty crumb coating. It makes great picnic fare.

3 pound broiler, cut into eight pieces
1/4 cup Hot Mustard (see page 9)
1/4 cup melted butter
2 cups fresh bread crumbs, made from French bread
1/2 cup finely chopped pecans

1. Preheat the oven to 375°. Grease a shallow baking pan.

2. Mix the mustard and butter together. In a shallow bowl, combine the bread crumbs and pecans.

3. Dip the chicken pieces in the mustard butter, then roll in the crumbs, coating well.

4. Place the pieces in the baking pan, skin-side up. Bake the chicken for 1 hour, until browned and crisp. Serve hot from the oven, or let cool and enjoy at room temperature.

4 portions

APRICOT CHICKEN

Chicken parts are baked with a tangy apricot sauce and garnished with apricot halves. Great with a buttered rice accompaniment to absorb the delectable sauce.

2 whole broilers, cut into serving pieces
1 tablespoon Dijon mustard
1 teaspoon Worcestershire sauce
1 teaspoon soy sauce
1 clove garlic, crushed
freshly ground pepper to taste
1/4 cup brown sugar
2 tablespoons lemon juice
1/2 cup apricot preserves
1 pound canned apricots, drained and cut in half

1. Preheat the oven to 350°.

2. Arrange the chicken pieces in a roasting pan.

3. In a bowl mix the Dijon, Worcestershire, soy, garlic, pepper, brown sugar, lemon juice, and apricot preserves. (The sauce may be prepared up to 4 days in advance and kept refrigerated until needed.)

4. Coat the chicken generously with the apricot mixture.

5. Bake for 1 hour, basting occasionally. Remove from the oven and surround the chicken with apricot halves. Return to the oven and bake 15 minutes more. Transfer to a platter, spoon the pan juices over the chicken, and serve at once.

8 portions

GRILLED CHICKEN WITH PEANUT SAUCE

Chicken breasts are char-grilled, then covered with a spicy Oriental peanut sauce. The peanut sauce also doubles as a favorite dip for snow peas, red peppers, carrots, and cooked shrimp. I oftentimes prepare this dish as an hors d'oeuvre for large parties, serving the chicken cut up into bite-size chunks with the peanut sauce alongside for dipping.

1/4 cup chunky peanut butter
3 tablespoons boiling water
1 tablespoon sugar
1 tablespoon grated gingerroot
1 tablespoon soy sauce
1 teaspoon Oriental sesame oil*
1/8 teaspoon hot oil*
freshly ground pepper to taste
3 boneless, skinless chicken breasts, split in half
2 tablespoons vegetable oil

1. Prepare the sauce. Stir the boiling water into the peanut butter until completely incorporated. Add the sugar, gingerroot, soy, sesame and hot oils, and pepper, and mix well. Set aside. (The sauce may be prepared up to 4 days in advance and kept refrigerated. Return to room temperature before using.)

2. Brush the chicken with the vegetable oil.

3. Grill the chicken over hot coals until cooked and browned, about 4 to 5 minutes per side.

4. Spread a dollop of sauce over each breast and serve.

4 portions

*Available in Oriental markets.

CHICKEN TERIYAKI

The addition of port wine and orange peel to the marinade makes this teriyaki distinctive.

2 pounds boneless, skinless chicken breasts, split in half
1/4 cup oil
1/4 cup port wine
2 large cloves garlic, crushed
2 tablespoons soy sauce
1 teaspoon ground ginger
freshly ground black pepper to taste
2 tablespoons dark brown sugar
1 teaspoon finely grated orange peel

1. Arrange the chicken pieces in a large pan.

2. Stir together the oil, wine, garlic, soy, ginger, pepper, sugar, and orange peel in a small bowl.

3. Pour the marinade over the chicken pieces. Cover and refrigerate for at least 2 hours, and as much as 24 hours.

4. When ready to serve, grill over hot coals 4 to 5 minutes per side, basting with the extra teriyaki sauce. If a grill is unavailable, broil 4 inches from the heat source, 4 to 5 minutes per side, until cooked and browned.

5. Serve hot or cool and refrigerate—it is also tasty served cold as picnic fare.

4 portions

GRILLED ORANGE CHICKEN WITH ORANGE BUTTER

Boneless breasts of chicken are marinated in a rosemary and orange juice sauce before grilling, then served with a dollop of orange butter.

2 pounds boneless, skinless chicken breasts

Marinade:
2 tablespoons olive oil
1/2 cup orange juice
1 clove garlic, crushed
1 teaspoon dried rosemary
1 teaspoon dried grated orange peel (Durkee's)
salt and pepper to taste
Orange Butter (recipe follows)

1. Split the chicken breasts in half and place in a baking pan.

2. Combine the marinade ingredients; pour over the chicken and let sit 1 to 2 hours.

3. Grill over hot coals, 4 to 5 minutes per side, basting with any extra marinade. Serve with a dollop of orange butter atop each portion.

6 portions

Orange Butter:
4 tablespoons butter or margarine, softened
4 tablespoons orange marmalade
generous pinch cayenne pepper

Mix the ingredients together and pack into a crock. Refrigerate until ready to serve. May be prepared 3 to 4 days in advance.

Enough to adorn 6 portions of chicken

CHICKEN WITH GINGER CREAM

Chicken breasts flavored with the essence of fresh ginger, flambéed in brandy, and coated with a cream sauce. This makes for delectable eating!

2 pounds boneless, skinless breasts, split in half
salt and freshly ground pepper to taste
flour for dredging
4 tablespoons butter
2 generous tablespoons grated fresh gingerroot
3 tablespoons thinly sliced scallions
3 tablespoons brandy
1/2 cup heavy cream

1. Season the breasts with salt and pepper and dredge lightly in flour.

2. In a large fry pan, heat the butter over medium-high heat until hot. Add the ginger and let sizzle for 1 minute to allow the essence to be released.

3. Add the chicken and sauté for 5 minutes. Turn the chicken over, and continue to sauté for 5 minutes more.

4. Sprinkle with the scallions. Add the brandy and ignite. When the flames die, add the cream and simmer for 2 minutes, spooning the sauce over the breasts. Serve at once over a bed of white rice.

6 portions

GRILLED CHICKEN HOISIN

Boneless breasts are marinated in an Oriental-inspired barbecue sauce and then grilled over hot coals. I like to accompany this with sesame noodles and an Oriental vegetable salad.

1/4 cup Hoisin sauce*
2 tablespoons lemon juice
1 teaspoon lemon peel
1/4 cup white wine
1 tablespoon soy sauce
freshly ground pepper to taste
1 teaspoon Oriental sesame oil*
4 boneless, skinless breasts, cut in half

1. Prepare the barbecue sauce. Combine the Hoisin sauce, lemon juice, lemon peel, wine, soy, pepper, and sesame oil, and mix well.

2. Pour the barbecue sauce over the chicken and marinate 1 to 2 hours.

3. Grill the chicken over hot coals, approximately 4 to 5 minutes per side. Serve at once.

6 portions

*Available in Oriental markets

CRANBERRY CHICKEN

Sautéed boneless breasts are smothered in a whole berry cranberry sauce accented with Oriental flavorings.

4 boneless, skinless breasts, split in half
flour for dredging
4 tablespoons butter

Cranberry Sauce:
1 cup whole berry cranberry sauce (homemade is preferable)
1 tablespoon soy sauce
1 clove garlic, crushed
1 teaspoon finely grated gingerroot
freshly ground pepper to taste
2 tablespoons red wine

1. Dredge the breasts lightly in the flour.

2. Prepare the sauce. In a saucepan, combine the cranberry sauce, soy, garlic, ginger, pepper, and red wine. Warm over low heat until the cranberry sauce melts and the ingredients can be thoroughly mixed together. Set aside.

3. In a large fry pan, heat the butter over medium-high heat until hot. Add the chicken and sauté for 5 minutes. Turn the chicken over, and continue to sauté for 5 minutes more.

4. Pour the cranberry sauce over the chicken and let simmer 1 to 2 minutes more, spooning the glaze over the breasts. Serve piping hot over a bed of white rice.

6 portions

INDIAN SPICED CHICKEN

An Indian-inspired recipe—the authentic version is baked in a tandoor or clay oven. Chicken parts are first marinated overnight in a highly seasoned yogurt sauce and then baked in a hot oven to effect the same results as from a tandoor oven.

> 5-pound chicken, cut into serving pieces
> 1 teaspoon salt
> 3 tablespoons lemon juice
> 8 ounces plain yogurt
> 1 clove garlic, crushed
> 1 medium onion, chopped
> 1/2 teaspoon coriander seeds, crushed
> 1 teaspoon ground cumin
> 1/4 teaspoon each ground clove, nutmeg, cinnamon, cayenne
>   pepper and black pepper
> 1 teaspoon grated fresh gingerroot
> thin lemon slices, for garnish
> 1/2 medium red onion, sliced into paper thin rings, for garnish

1. Season the chicken with salt and work the lemon juice into the pieces.

2. Stir together the yogurt, garlic, onion, and spices in a small bowl.

3. Place the chicken in a pyrex dish. Rub the sauce into the chicken parts, cover, and marinate in the refrigerator overnight.

4. When ready to serve, preheat the oven to 450°. Transfer the chicken along with the marinade to a shallow baking pan. Roast in the oven for 45 to 50 minutes. Remove to a platter, pour the pan juices over all, and garnish with lemon slices and red onion rings. Serve at once.

6 to 8 portions

CHICKEN MACADAMIA

Chunks of chicken are sautéed in a ginger-flavored butter, and adorned with pineapple and the rich, sweet, buttery taste of macadamia nuts.

> *2 pounds boneless, skinless chicken, cut into 1-inch chunks*
> *flour for dredging*
> *salt and freshly ground pepper to taste*
> *6 tablespoons butter*
> *1 clove garlic, smashed*
> *1 teaspoon finely grated fresh gingerroot*
> *1/8 teaspoon cayenne pepper*
> *8 ounce can pineapple chunks in its own juice (reserve juice)*
> *2/3 cup macadamia nuts*

1. Season flour with salt and pepper; dredge the chicken in flour mixture.

2. Heat the butter in a large skillet until hot. Add the garlic and chicken and sauté over medium-high heat for 5 minutes. Sprinkle with the ginger and cayenne pepper. Turn the chicken over and sauté 3 minutes.

3. Add the pineapple with its juice and nuts to the skillet. Simmer 5 minutes more, basting with the pan juices. Transfer to a platter and serve immediately with buttered rice.

6 portions

CHICKEN CASTILIAN

Chicken topped with a colorful red pepper sauce seasoned with garlic, basil, and toasted almonds.

4 whole boneless breasts, skinned, boned, and cut in half
flour for dredging
salt and freshly ground pepper to taste
1 cup canned Italian plum tomatoes, well drained, and chopped
1 large roasted red pepper, puréed (see page 243)
1/3 cup blanched almonds, toasted and coarsely chopped (see page 273)
1 teaspoon dried basil
1 large clove garlic, crushed
6 tablespoons butter

1. Season the flour with salt and pepper; dredge chicken in flour mixture.

2. Combine the tomatoes, red pepper purée, almonds, basil, and garlic in a bowl, and set aside.

3. In a large skillet, heat the butter until sizzling. Add the chicken and sauté over high heat, 4 to 5 minutes per side, until cooked and browned.

4. Cover the chicken with the red pepper sauce and let simmer 2 to 3 minutes more. Transfer to a platter and serve at once with rice accompaniment.

6 portions

CHICKEN ROSEMARY

Chicken breasts are sautéed in olive oil, aromatically seasoned with garlic and rosemary, and adorned with pine nuts.

4 whole chicken breasts, boned, skinned, and cut in half
flour for dredging
salt and freshly ground pepper to taste
1/4 cup olive oil
1 large clove garlic, crushed
1 teaspoon dried rosemary
1/3 cup pine nuts
1/3 cup chopped fresh parsley

1. Season the flour with salt and pepper; dredge breasts in flour mixture.

2. Heat the olive oil and garlic in a large skillet until hot. Add the chicken.

3. Sprinkle with the rosemary and pine nuts, and sauté the breasts over high heat for 5 minutes.

4. Turn the chicken over, add the parsley, and simmer 5 minutes more until done. Transfer to a platter along with the pan juices and serve immediately.

6 portions

CHICKEN LUCIA

A Northern Italian-inspired dish—sautéed chicken chunks surrounded by artichoke hearts, delicately seasoned with lemon and oregano.

2 pounds boneless, skinless chicken breasts, cut into 1$^{1}/_{2}$-inch chunks
flour for dredging
salt and freshly ground pepper to taste
$^{1}/_{4}$ cup olive oil
2 large cloves garlic, finely chopped
1 teaspoon dried oregano
14 ounce can artichoke hearts, drained and cut in half
3 tablespoons lemon juice
$^{1}/_{4}$ cup chopped fresh parsley

1. Season the flour with salt and pepper; dredge chicken pieces in flour mixture.

2. Heat the oil and garlic in a large skillet. When hot, add the chicken. Sprinkle with the oregano and simmer over medium-high heat for 3 to 4 minutes.

3. Add the artichoke hearts and drizzle with lemon juice. Add the parsley.

4. Simmer 5 minutes more until the chicken is done.

6 portions

CHICKEN CACCIATORE

Sautéed chicken and sweet sausage, adorned with onions, mushrooms, and peppers in a light tomato-red wine sauce.

> 2 pounds boneless, skinless chicken, cut into 2-inch chunks
> salt and freshly ground pepper to taste
> 2 tablespoons butter
> 3 tablespoons olive oil
> 1 large red pepper, cut into 1/2-inch slices
> 1 large green pepper, cut into 1/2-inch slices
> 1 Spanish onion, sliced
> 1/2 pound shiitake mushrooms, thickly sliced
> 1 pound sweet sausage, cut into 1-inch chunks
> 1/2 teaspoon dried basil
> 1/4 cup chopped fresh parsley
> 2 tablespoons tomato paste
> 1 cup red wine

1. Season the chicken with salt and pepper and set aside.

2. Heat 1 tablespoon butter and 1 tablespoon olive oil in a large skillet until hot. Add the vegetables. Season with salt and pepper and sauté over high heat for 5 minutes, stirring occasionally. Remove the vegetables with a slotted spoon and set aside.

3. In the same skillet, add the remaining butter and oil. When sizzling, add the chicken pieces and sausage chunks and brown well.

4. Return the vegetables to the skillet. Season with the basil and parsley, and stir in the tomato paste and wine. Simmer 10 minutes until the chicken is cooked. Transfer to a casserole dish and serve at once over a bed of noodles.

6 to 8 portions

CHICKEN AU POIVRE

Divine and peppery—boneless breasts are coated with lots of freshly cracked black pepper, sautéed in butter, and sauced with Cognac and cream.

3 whole chicken breasts, skinned, boned, and cut in half
1/2 to 1 tablespoon coarsely crushed black peppercorns
4 tablespoons butter
1/2 cup dry white wine
2 tablespoons Cognac
1/2 cup heavy cream

1. Pound the chicken breasts gently to flatten them. Coat the breasts generously with the peppercorns, pressing the seasoning firmly into the flesh.

2. Heat the butter in a large skillet until hot. Add the chicken and sauté over high heat, 4 to 5 minutes per side, until browned. Transfer the chicken to a platter and keep warm.

3. Stir the wine, Cognac, and heavy cream into the pan. Bring the sauce to a boil and reduce for 4 to 5 minutes until slightly thickened. Pour the sauce over the chicken and serve at once.

4 portions

CHICKEN BREASTS BOURSIN

Boneless breasts are stuffed with Boursin cheese and wrapped in bacon before baking. The cheese oozes out during cooking creating a heavenly sauce.

2 whole boneless, skinless breasts, cut in half
freshly ground pepper to taste
5 ounce package Boursin cheese
2 tablespoons snipped chives
4 slices bacon

1. Preheat the oven to 400°.
2. Season the breasts with pepper.
3. Mix the chives into the cheese until evenly distributed.
4. Place a spoonful of the cheese mixture on each breast and roll up. Wrap a slice of bacon around each breast, and place seam side down in a roasting pan.
5. Bake for 40 minutes. Place under the broiler for approximately 5 minutes until the bacon is browned. Serve piping hot with the pan juices spooned over the roll-ups.

4 portions

IDEAS FOR STUFFED CHICKEN BREASTS

Stuff boneless, skinless breasts with such interesting fillings as:
• Pâté.
• Cooked rice mixed with sun-dried tomatoes.
• Montrachet, garlic, and crushed peppercorns.
• Roquefort cheese, grated apple, and chopped walnuts.
• Feta cheese, chopped tomatoes, black olives, and mint.
• Roasted red and green peppers, Parmesan, and garlic, drizzled with olive oil.
• Thick pesto.

GRILLED CURRY CHICKEN

Boneless breasts are char-grilled in a savory honey-mustard curry sauce. You don't have to be a curry fan to enjoy this one! A rice medley of raisins, almonds, coconut, and orange peel makes a good accompaniment.

1/3 cup honey
1/4 cup Dijon mustard
1 to 2 teaspoons curry powder
1/4 cup orange juice
1 clove garlic, crushed
pinch cayenne pepper
4 boneless chicken breasts, skinned and split in half

1. Combine the honey, mustard, curry, orange juice, garlic, and cayenne pepper.

2. Pour the sauce over the breasts, coating well. Let marinate 1 to 2 hours.

3. Cook over a hot grill 4 inches from heat source, about 4 to 5 minutes per side, basting with any extra marinade.

6 portions

JAMAICAN CHICKEN

This is my rendition of typical Jamaican street food—it's a peppery marinated and grilled chicken, tempered with allspice.

2 tablespoons soy sauce
4 scallions
1 medium onion, cut into chunks
2 teaspoons allspice
1/4 teaspoon cayenne pepper (or more to taste if you like it fiery)
1 teaspoon freshly ground black pepper
1/2 teaspoon cinnamon
2 bay leaves
2 tablespoons oil
4 boneless, skinless chicken breasts, split in half

1. In a food processor, place the soy, scallions, onion, allspice, cayenne, black pepper, cinnamon, bay leaves, and oil, and purée.

2. Rub the paste over the chicken and let marinate in the refrigerator at least 2 hours and as much as overnight.

3. When ready to serve, grill the chicken over hot coals, 4 inches from the heat source, approximately 4 to 5 minutes per side, basting with any extra marinade. Serve hot off the grill. For a special touch, heat your favorite barbecue sauce and serve alongside for dipping.

6 to 8 portions

CHICKEN WITH CAPONATA SALSA

Chicken breasts are fragrantly enhanced by the sweet-sour Italian eggplant specialty, caponata, punctuated with toasted pine nuts, black olives, and capers. This relish makes a hearty hors d'oeuvre presentation when spread on slices of French bread.

2 pound eggplant, peeled and cut into 1-inch cubes
salt
1/2 cup olive oil
pepper to taste
1 large onion, chopped
1 1/2 cups thinly sliced celery
2 red peppers, chopped
28 ounce can Italian plum tomatoes, drained and coarsely chopped
1/4 cup ripe black olives, sliced
2 tablespoons capers
2 tablespoons pine nuts, toasted (see page 273)
1/3 cup balsamic vinegar
2 tablespoons sugar
4 boneless, skinless chicken breasts

1. Salt the eggplant generously and place in a colander to drain for 1/2 hour. Rinse thoroughly and pat dry.

2. Heat 1/4 cup oil in a saucepan and when hot add onion, celery, and red pepper. Cook over medium heat for 15 minutes.

3. Remove the cooked vegetables from the pan and set aside. Add the remaining oil to the pan and when hot, add the eggplant. Sauté 10 minutes until golden brown. Return the celery-onion mixture to the pan along with the rest of the ingredients, except the chicken.

4. Bring to a boil, reduce to a simmer, and cook uncovered 25 to 30 minutes, stirring occasionally. Cool and refrigerate. (The caponata may be made up to 3 days in advance so flavors have a chance to mellow.)

5. When ready to serve, return the caponata to room temperature. Either grill or poach the chicken breasts, seasoning them first with salt and pepper. Present the breasts with the caponata salsa.

6 to 8 portions

CHICKEN CHESAPEAKE

Boneless breasts are stuffed with crabmeat and Swiss cheese, then broiled with a mustard butter, and garnished with broccoli.

> 4 whole large breasts, boned, skinned, and split in half
> salt and freshly ground pepper to taste
> 3/4 pound crabmeat
> 1/4 pound Swiss cheese, thinly sliced
> 1 tablespoon Dijon mustard
> 1/4 cup melted butter
> 1 head broccoli, separated into stalks

1. With a wooden mallet, pound the breasts lightly. Season with salt and pepper.

2. Divide the crabmeat and cheese evenly into 8 portions. Place equal amounts of crabmeat and Swiss cheese on each piece of chicken. Roll breasts jelly-roll fashion and place seam side down in a shallow roasting pan.

3. Combine the Dijon and melted butter and pour over the chicken.

4. Place the chicken under a hot broiler, 4 inches from heat source, for 5 minutes. Baste with the mustard butter; turn the rolls over and broil 5 minutes more. While the chicken is cooking, steam the broccoli. Transfer the chicken to a serving dish and surround with the broccoli. Pour the pan juices over all, and serve.

6 to 8 portions

CHICKEN TARRAGON

Boneless breasts sautéed with mushrooms and laced with a creamy tarragon-mustard sauce. A great company dish, as it can be prepared in advance and then placed in the oven when the guests arrive.

4 whole chicken breasts, skinned, boned, and cut in half
flour for dredging
salt and freshly ground pepper to taste
6 tablespoons butter
1 pound mushrooms, thickly sliced
1 clove garlic, smashed
1 teaspoon dried tarragon
1/2 cup Dijon mustard
1/2 cup dry white wine

1. Preheat the oven to 350°.

2. Season the flour with salt and pepper; dredge chicken in flour mixture.

3. Heat 3 tablespoons butter in a large skillet until hot. Add the mushrooms and sauté over high heat until golden. Remove from pan and set aside.

4. Add the remaining 3 tablespoons butter and garlic, and when hot add the chicken breasts. Sprinkle with the tarragon and brown over high heat 3 minutes per side. Remove the chicken to a casserole dish. Cover with the sautéed mushrooms.

5. Stir the mustard and wine together and pour the sauce over the chicken and mushrooms. (Up to this point may be prepared 6 to 8 hours in advance and refrigerated. Return to room temperature before baking.)

6. Cover and bake for 15 to 20 minutes. To serve, transfer the breasts to a platter and spoon the mushrooms and sauce over all. Present immediately.

6 to 8 portions

CHICKEN WITH TOMATO PESTO

Boneless breasts are sautéed in a fragrant sun-dried tomato and basil pesto sauce.

> *4 boneless, skinless breasts, cut in half*
> *flour for dredging*
> *salt and freshly ground pepper to taste*
> *3 tablespoons olive oil*
> *Tomato Pesto (recipe follows)*

1. Season the flour with salt and pepper; dredge chicken in flour mixture.

2. Heat the olive oil in a large skillet over high heat. When hot, add the chicken and sauté until golden brown, about 3 to 4 minutes per side.

3. Add the tomato pesto, lower the heat and simmer for 5 to 10 minutes more. Serve piping hot with the sauce spooned over each breast.

6 portions

> ### Tomato Pesto:
> *2 large cloves garlic*
> *1/2 cup blanched almonds*
> *2 cups loosely packed fresh basil*
> *1/2 cup olive oil*
> *1 cup canned, puréed Italian plum tomatoes*
> *5 sun-dried tomatoes, chopped (see page 251)*

1. Place the garlic, almonds, basil, oil, and plum tomatoes in the bowl of a food processor and purée.

2. Remove the tomato purée to a bowl and mix in the sun-dried tomatoes. Refrigerate until needed. (The sauce may be prepared 1 week in advance.)

Enough sauce to dress 4 breasts generously.

CHICKEN PAPRIKA

A variation on a classic Hungarian favorite—chicken browned in butter and blanketed in a rich paprika-cream sauce. This is best when teamed up with buttered noodles.

3 pound chicken, cut into eighths
salt and freshly ground pepper to taste
4 tablespoons butter
1 clove garlic, smashed
1 tablespoon lemon juice
1/4 cup white wine
1 tablespoon paprika (use sweet Hungarian)
1 cup heavy cream
2 tablespoons snipped chives

1. Season the chicken pieces with salt and pepper.

2. In a large Dutch oven, heat the butter and the smashed garlic until hot. Add the chicken and fry on both sides until browned.

3. Add the lemon juice and wine. Cover, lower the heat, and simmer 15 minutes.

4. Mix the paprika and cream together and stir into the chicken. Cover and cook 5 minutes. Uncover, add the chives and simmer 5 minutes more, basting occasionally. Present on a bed of buttered noodles.

4 portions

TUSCAN CHICKEN

Boneless breasts are sautéed in an egg batter, then surrounded by roasted peppers, capers, and a dusting of Romano cheese. Although a little time consuming to prepare, most of the work can be done in advance, allowing you to be a gracious hostess. This is wonderful served with an antipasto.

> *4 red peppers, roasted (see page 243)*
> *4 whole chicken breasts, boned, skinned, and cut in half*
> *flour for dredging*
> *salt and freshly ground pepper to taste*
> *4 eggs, beaten with 1 1/2 tablespoons water*
> *4 tablespoons butter*
> *4 tablespoons olive oil*
> *2 to 3 tablespoons capers*
> *3 tablespoons Romano cheese*

1. Slice the roasted peppers into 1/2-inch thick strips and set aside in a bowl. The peppers release their juices and it is important to save the syrup for the finishing of the dish.

2. Pound the chicken breasts with a mallet to flatten.

3. Season the flour with salt and pepper; dredge chicken in flour mixture.

4. Place the egg mixture in a small bowl.

5. Dip the chicken in the egg wash, coating each piece well. Set on a large platter.

6. Heat 2 tablespoons butter and 2 tablespoons oil in a large skillet. Add half of the chicken pieces along with any extra egg and sauté over medium-high heat for 3 to 4 minutes per side until golden. Remove the cooked chicken and fried egg bits to a large greased baking dish, arranging them in a single layer.

7. Add the remaining butter and oil to the saucepan and cook the rest of the chicken and egg mixture. Transfer the pieces to the baking dish.

8. Add the roasted peppers, pepper juice, and capers to the skillet and sauté for 1 minute. Spoon the pepper mixture and any browned bits of egg over the chicken. The juice from the peppers will deglaze the pan.

9. Sprinkle all generously with Romano cheese. (You may choose to refrigerate at this point until needed. When ready to serve, return to room temperature before broiling.) Run the dish under a hot broiler, 4 inches from the heat source, for 3 to 4 minutes to brown slightly. Serve immediately.

6 portions

CHICKEN WITH RED WINE

A new rendition of a classic favorite—boneless chicken marinated in a flavorful red wine sauce, sautéed, and presented with a bacon, pearl onion, and mushroom garnish.

> *4 boneless, skinless chicken breasts, split in half*
> *1 1/4 cups dry red wine*
> *2 tablespoons lemon juice*
> *1 clove garlic, crushed*
> *1 tablespoon Worcestershire sauce*
> *1/4 teaspoon dried thyme*
> *freshly ground pepper*
> *1/4 pound bacon, diced*
> *1/2 pound pearl onions*
> *1/2 pound whole mushrooms*
> *1/2 cup flour*
> *4 tablespoons butter*
> *1/4 cup chopped fresh parsley*

1. Place the chicken in a deep pan.

2. In a small bowl, whisk together the red wine, lemon juice, garlic, Worcestershire, thyme, and pepper.

3. Pour the marinade over the chicken and let sit for 2 hours.

4. While the chicken is marinating, fry the bacon in a large skillet until crisp. Remove the bacon from the pan and set aside.

5. Sauté the onions and mushrooms in the bacon fat until golden. Remove the sautéed vegetables from the pan and set aside, discarding any excess bacon fat.

6. When ready to serve, remove the chicken from the marinade, reserving the sauce. Dredge the chicken in the flour, coating generously.

7. Heat the butter in the fry pan until hot, and add the chicken. Sauté over medium-high heat 4 to 5 minutes per side until cooked and browned. Sprinkle with parsley.

8. Add the cooked bacon and sautéed mushrooms and onions to the chicken.

9. Pour the reserved marinade over all and simmer 5 minutes more. Serve at once.

6 to 8 portions

ROCK CORNISH HENS A L'ORANGE

Hens are roasted in a hot oven until brown and crisp, then covered with a divine orange sauce.

> *2 large oranges*
> *4 plump Rock Cornish hens*
> *salt and freshly ground pepper to taste*
> *Orange Sauce (recipe follows)*

1. Preheat the oven to 450°.

2. Quarter one orange, leaving the peel on. Peel the second orange and cut into 1/4-inch thick slices. Set the slices aside for garnish.

3. Season the hens with salt and pepper. Insert an orange quarter inside the cavity of each hen. (This keeps the chicken moist.) Place the hens breast side up in a shallow roasting pan. Bake for 1 hour, basting occasionally with the pan drippings. If you see the hens getting too brown, turn them over—breast side down to crisp the underside.

4. Remove the hens from the oven and cover with the orange sauce. (This much may be done several hours in advance, if desired.)

5. Lower the oven temperature to 350° and return the hens to bake 15 to 20 minutes more.

6. To serve, slice each hen in half down the mid-line, remove the quartered orange, and discard it. Garnish with an orange slice, and serve any extra orange sauce alongside.

6 to 8 portions

Orange Sauce:
3 tablespoons sugar
1/4 cup red wine vinegar
10 1/2 ounce can beef consommé
3 tablespoons port wine
2 tablespoons cornstarch mixed with 1/4 cup water
grated peel of 1 orange
2 tablespoons Grand Marnier
1 tablespoon butter

1. Boil the sugar and the vinegar in a saucepan over high heat for several minutes until the mixture turns into a rich brown syrup. Remove from the heat and add the consommé.

2. Return the syrup to the heat, stir to dissolve the mixture, and simmer for 1 minute.

3. Add the port, cornstarch mixture, and orange peel. Simmer 4 to 5 minutes until the sauce is clear and slightly thickened.

4. Whisk in the Grand Marnier and butter, remove from the heat, and serve immediately, or may be stored in the refrigerator. When ready to serve, warm over low heat until hot.

Enough sauce for 4 cornish hens

ROAST DUCKLING WITH APRICOT SAUCE OR PINEAPPLE-ALMOND SAUCE

This is probably the easiest way to prepare a succulent, crisp roast duckling. It requires no attention and is done in advance.

> *2 ducklings, each 5 pounds*
> *salt and freshly ground pepper to taste*
> *Apricot Sauce (recipe follows)*
> *Pineapple-Almond Sauce (recipe follows)*

1. Preheat the oven to 250°.

2. Season the ducks with salt and pepper and place them in a deep roasting pan, breast side up.

3. Roast for 8 hours. Do not baste, season, or turn the ducks. By cooking the ducks in this manner, all the fat cooks down, and the ducks remain moist.

4. When the birds are cooked, drain off the fat. Cool and cut the ducks into quarters. Refrigerate for as much as 24 hours—until ready to serve.

5. When ready to serve, return the birds to room temperature. Preheat the oven to 450°. Place the quartered ducks in a shallow baking pan, and bake for 15 minutes. Remove from the oven and cover each piece generously with your choice of sauce. Return to the oven to heat for 5 to 10 minutes more. Transfer the pieces to a platter and serve with extra sauce alongside. This final cooking at a high temperature crisps the skin.

6 to 8 portions

Apricot Sauce:
17 ounce can apricot halves in heavy syrup
2 tablespoons lemon juice
1 tablespoon butter
3 tablespoons apricot brandy mixed with 1 tablespoon cornstarch

1. Drain the apricots and reserve 1/2 cup of the syrup.

2. Place the apricot halves, reserved syrup, and lemon juice in a food processor and purée until smooth.

3. Pour the apricot mixture into a saucepan. Add the butter, and apricot brandy mixture. Warm over low heat for 5 to 10 minutes until sauce thickens.

1½ cups sauce, enough to sauce 2 ducklings

Pineapple Almond Sauce:
1 pound 14 ounce can unsweetened crushed pineapple with juice
2 tablespoons honey
1 tablespoon lemon juice
3 tablespoons butter
¼ cup Amaretto mixed with 2 tablespoons cornstarch
¼ cup sliced almonds, toasted (see page 273)

1. Place the pineapple and juice, honey, and lemon juice in the bowl of a food processor and purée.

2. Transfer the pineapple purée to a saucepan. Add the butter and Amaretto mixture and simmer 5 to 10 minutes until the sauce thickens.

3. Pour the sauce over the ducks and sprinkle with sliced almonds.

2½ cups sauce. This makes enough sauce for 3 ducks. Extra sauce will keep refrigerated in a closed container for 4 weeks. (Try the sauce warm over vanilla ice cream!)

ROAST TURKEY BREAST WITH PEACH CHUTNEY

This chutney is a sophisticated subtlety of tastes—slightly sweet, slightly tart, and slightly spicy. It turns ordinary turkey into an exciting blast of flavor.

Peach Chutney:
3 large peaches, peeled and chopped
1 medium onion, chopped
1 cup currants
$1/2$ cup chopped pecans
1 teaspoon salt
3 large cloves garlic, crushed
$1/4$ cup chopped crystallized ginger
$11/2$ cups lightly packed dark brown sugar
$1/2$ cup balsamic vinegar
$1/4$ teaspoon cayenne pepper
1 teaspoon chili powder
$1/4$ teaspoon ground cloves
$1/2$ teaspoon cinnamon

1. Put all of the ingredients in a large saucepan. Bring to a boil, lower heat, and simmer gently for 2 hours until thickened; stir occasionally.

2. Pack in sterile jars, and store in your pantry until needed. Refrigerate after opening.

3 pints

Roast Turkey Breast:
5 to 6 pound turkey breast
$1/4$ cup melted butter
$1/4$ cup dry white wine
salt, pepper, and paprika to taste

1. Preheat the oven to 350°.

2. Place breast in a large roasting pan. Drizzle with melted butter and wine; sprinkle seasonings over bird.

3. Roast 20 minutes per pound or until the internal temperature reaches 165°. Baste occasionally with the pan juices.

4. To serve, slice the breast and garnish with dollops of chutney.

6 portions

SUCCULENT ROAST TURKEY

This cooking method of roasting the turkey, breast side down, truly results in a moist, delicious bird—one that will make Thanksgiving memorable. Corn pudding, a toasted pecan and prune salad, and cranberry mousse round out this special holiday meal.

1 turkey, 12 to 16 pounds
salt and freshly ground pepper to taste
2 teaspoons finely grated orange peel
favorite stuffing (See Apple, Pear, and Sausage Stuffing, page 260)
paprika to taste
1¹/₂ cups dry red wine
³/₄ cup orange juice

1. Preheat the oven to 350°.

2. Season the interior of the turkey with salt, pepper, and ¹/₂ teaspoon orange rind. Fill the turkey with your favorite stuffing. Truss up the cavity with string. (Stuff the turkey just before roasting—not in advance of cooking—to insure no bacteria forming.)

3. Place the turkey, breast side down, in a roasting pan.

4. Pour the red wine and orange juice over the bird.

5. Rub the remainder of the orange peel over the outside of the bird. Sprinkle with salt, pepper, and paprika.

6. Place the turkey in the oven and roast for 1¹/₄ hours, basting once. Turn the turkey over, breast side up. Continue roasting for the remainder of the time, basting every 20 to 30 minutes with the pan juices. This helps keep the bird moist. After 2 hours, the turkey should be a beautiful golden brown. Cover it loosely with a foil tent until done, and ready to serve.

7. Roast for 3¹/₄ to 4¹/₄ hours in total, or until the drumstick moves easily in the socket. Transfer the bird to a platter, and let rest 10 minutes. Remove the stuffing to a bowl. Carve the bird and serve with the pan juices.

10 to 14 portions

FRUITS OF THE SEA

American eating habits are continuing to focus more on light eating. Fish seems to fit the bill perfectly, as it is lower in calories and fats than beef and chicken, and rich in protein.

You might pay a high price for fish, but there is literally no waste. There are several tips you should consider when purchasing and storing seafood. Always buy fresh fish. It's delicate texture breaks down when frozen.

The great variety of fish available—ranging from shellfish to fresh and salt water fish—gives the cook a large choice, thus expanding fish cookery in the home.

Fish can be prepared imaginatively and relatively simply in a variety of ways. Try seasoning the seafood with herbed butters and broil or grill it; poach, steam, sauté, stir-fry, deep-fry, or bake it. All methods lend themselves to presentations with delectable sauces.

Be spontaneous and try the catch of the day!

SCALLOPS WITH PUMPERNICKEL CRUMBS

Scallops are sautéed in butter, and tossed with an onion-pumpernickel crumb coating—similar to baked stuffed, but much lighter and more delicate.

2 pounds bay scallops
salt and pepper to taste
6 tablespoons butter
1/2 cup finely chopped sweet onion—Spanish or Vidalia
1/2 cup fresh pumpernickel bread crumbs
1/4 cup chopped fresh parsley

1. Season the scallops with salt and pepper and set aside.

2. In a large skillet melt 4 tablespoons butter over high heat. Add the onion and sauté until golden. Add the bread crumbs and sauté 1 minute more. Remove from pan and toss with the parsley. Set aside.

3. Heat the remaining 2 tablespoons butter in the pan. When sizzling, add the scallops and sauté over high heat until lightly browned, about 3 to 4 minutes. Sprinkle with the crumb mixture, toss together, and serve.

6 portions

BARBECUED SCALLOPS HOISIN

Scallops and red pepper are skewered and brushed with a Hoisin-inspired barbecue sauce before being char-grilled for an Oriental flavor sensation.

1¹/₄ pounds bay or sea scallops
2 medium red peppers, cut into 1¹/₂-inch squares
3 tablespoons Hoisin sauce (available in Oriental markets)
1 tablespoon soy sauce
2 tablespoons dry sherry
1 tablespoon sugar

1. Alternately thread the red pepper and scallops on wooden skewers, beginning and ending with peppers.

2. Mix together the Hoisin, soy, sherry, and sugar. Brush the shellfish and peppers with the sauce, coating well.

3. Grill the kebobs over hot coals 4 inches from the heat source, 3 to 4 minutes per side. Remove to a platter and serve.

6 to 8 appetizer portions; 3 main-course portions

SCALLOPS WITH RED PEPPER COULIS

Grilled scallops are adorned with a colorful and rich red pepper purée.

2¹/₂ pounds bay scallops
1 to 2 tablespoons oil
salt and freshly ground pepper to taste
Coulis (recipe follows)

1. Skewer the scallops and brush them lightly with oil. Season the fish with salt and pepper.

2. Grill over hot coals 3 to 4 minutes per side. (Broil when weather does not permit grilling.)

3. Place spoonfuls of the coulis on each plate and top with a serving of scallops. Present at once.

6 generous portions

Coulis:

3 large or 4 medium-size red peppers, roasted and puréed (see page 243)
6 tablespoons butter
salt and freshly ground pepper to taste
generous pinch cayenne pepper

1. Place the puréed peppers and butter in a saucepan. Season with salt, pepper, and cayenne pepper. (The coulis may be prepared several hours in advance up to this point and refrigerated until needed.)

2. Heat and simmer for 2 minutes. Serve piping hot.

Enough coulis to sauce 2¹/₂ pounds scallops

SCALLOPS PESARO

Sautéed scallops are finished with a delicate pesto sauce, and garnished with pine nuts.

> *3 pounds bay scallops*
> *salt and freshly ground pepper to taste*
> *6 tablespoons butter*
> *Pesto Sauce (recipe follows)*
> *3 tablespoons pine nuts*

1. Pat scallops dry with a towel. Sprinkle with salt and pepper.

2. Heat the butter in a large skillet over high heat until sizzling. Add the scallops and sauté for 5 minutes, stirring occasionally until they lose their translucency.

3. Spoon the pesto sauce over the scallops, tossing gently. Add the pine nuts. Continue to cook until the scallops are evenly coated with the sauce—approximately 2 to 3 minutes more. Transfer to a platter and serve immediately.

8 portions

Pesto Sauce:
> *1 clove garlic, crushed*
> *1 cup firmly packed fresh basil leaves*
> *3 tablespoons pine nuts*
> *1 tablespoon olive oil*
> *2 tablespoons white wine*

Place all of the ingredients in the bowl of a food processor. Process until the mixture is puréed. Remove the pesto to a container and refrigerate until needed. This keeps up to 2 weeks.

Enough to sauce 3 pounds of scallops

GRILLED SHRIMP MARNIER

Raw shrimp are marinated in Grand Marnier, wrapped in prosciutto, and then grilled over hot coals. The orange essence of the liqueur heightens the flavor of the cured ham.

2 pounds large-size raw shrimp, peeled
1/2 cup Grand Marnier
1/2 pound prosciutto, sliced
freshly ground pepper to taste
4 tablespoons butter, melted

1. Place the shrimp in a glass bowl. Pour the Grand Marnier over the shellfish, set aside, and marinate at room temperature for 2 to 3 hours.

2. When ready to serve, wrap each shrimp in half a slice of prosciutto. Skewer the shrimp, season with pepper, drizzle with the melted butter and any leftover marinade.

3. Place over hot coals and grill 2 to 3 minutes per side, spooning with the Grand Marnier. Transfer to a platter and serve at once.

8 to 10 appetizer portions; 4 to 5 entrée portions

CURRIED SHRIMP

Curry is a popular Indian seasoning. Contrary to what most people think, curry powder is not a single spice, but rather a unique mixture of many ground herbs and spices. Different brands of curry powder vary greatly from mild to quite fiery. I prefer the Madras brand. This is an Indian-inspired dish—shrimp, green pepper, and onion are sautéed together, bathed in a piquant curry-mustard sauce, and garnished with peanuts.

2 tablespoons Dijon mustard
1 teaspoon curry powder
1 teaspoon finely grated gingerroot
1¹/₂ tablespoons lemon juice
4 tablespoons oil
1 medium-size onion, cut into ¹/₂-inch chunks
1 medium-size green pepper, cut into ¹/₂-inch chunks
1¹/₂ pounds medium-size raw shrimp, peeled
salt and freshly ground pepper to taste
2 tablespoons coarsely chopped unsalted peanuts

1. Prepare the sauce. In a small bowl, combine the Dijon, curry, gingerroot, and lemon juice. Set aside.

2. Heat the oil in a large skillet over high heat. When hot, add the onion and green pepper, and sauté until the vegetables are tender-crisp.

3. Add the shrimp, season with salt and pepper, and continue to stir-fry until the shrimps turn pink 2 to 3 minutes.

4. Blanket with the sauce, lower the heat to medium-high, and simmer for 1 to 2 minutes.

5. Turn the sauté onto a platter, garnish with the chopped nuts, and serve. Present with steamed white rice.

4 portions

SHRIMP SCAMPI

Jumbo shrimp are broiled in a dashing herb butter. A bed of freshly cooked linguine makes a nice base for these tasty prawns.

1 to 2 large cloves garlic, crushed
6 tablespoons melted butter
2 pounds jumbo raw shrimp, peeled
salt and freshly ground pepper to taste
generous pinch cayenne pepper
1/4 cup chopped fresh parsley
3 tablespoons snipped chives

1. Place the garlic in the melted butter and let sit for 30 minutes.

2. While the garlic is flavoring the butter, arrange the shrimp in a large shallow baking dish.

3. Sprinkle the shrimp with the herbs and seasonings. Pour the garlic butter over the prawns. Place under a hot broiler, 4 inches from the heat source, for 2 to 3 minutes per side. Serve immediately.

8 appetizer portions; 4 main-course portions

SHRIMP AND MUSHROOM BAKE

Shrimp, wild mushrooms, and grated cheese team together with a buttery crumb topping.

> 2 pounds large-size raw shrimp, peeled
> 1 pound assorted mushrooms—cultivated, shiitake, and cremini
> 6 tablespoons butter
> freshly ground pepper to taste
> 1^1/$_2$ cups grated Swiss cheese
> 1/4 cup lightly toasted French bread crumbs

1. Preheat the oven to 400°.

2. In a large fry pan, heat 3 tablespoons butter. When hot, add mushrooms and sauté until lightly browned and liquid has evaporated.

3. Pile the shrimp and mushrooms into a large greased baking dish. Season with pepper. Sprinkle with the grated cheese and bread crumbs.

4. Melt the remaining 3 tablespoons butter and drizzle over the shrimp mixture. (Up to this point may be prepared in advance and refrigerated. Return to room temperature before baking.)

5. Bake for 20 minutes until shrimp are cooked and cheese is brown and bubbly. Serve immediately.

6 portions

MIXED SEAFOOD GRILLE

A colorful riot of vegetables sautéed with assorted shellfish in a piquant orange-ginger sauce.

3 tablespoons chili sauce
2 tablespoons orange juice
1 tablespoon finely grated gingerroot
2 tablespoons oil
1 large clove garlic, smashed
1/2 pound snow peas
1 red pepper, cut into thin julienne slices
1 medium onion, sliced
1/4 pound shiitake mushrooms, sliced
3/4 pound bay scallops
3/4 pound medium-size raw shrimp, peeled
3/4 pound squid, cleaned and cut into 1/2-inch wide rings
salt and freshly ground pepper to taste

1. Combine the chili sauce, orange juice, and gingerroot in a bowl and set aside.

2. Heat the oil over medium-high heat in a large skillet or wok. Add the garlic and vegetables and stir-fry for 3 minutes.

3. Add the seafood. Season with salt and pepper. Pour the ginger sauce over the sauté, and stir-fry 5 to 8 minutes more until the shrimps turn firm and pink, the scallops and squid white, and are no longer translucent. Transfer to a serving dish, spooning the sauce over all. Present with a rice accompaniment.

6 to 8 portions

LOBSTER FRA DIAVOLO

Sautéed lobster meat and vegetables are piquantly spiced, laced with a cream sauce, and presented on a bed of linguine for heavenly eating.

4 tablespoons butter
1 large onion, chopped
3 stalks celery, diced
1 medium green pepper, diced
1 medium red pepper, diced
3 cups cooked lobster meat, cubed
salt and freshly ground pepper to taste
1/2 teaspoon dry mustard
1/8 teaspoon cayenne pepper
1/3 cup dry white wine
1 cup heavy cream

1. Heat the butter in a large skillet over medium-high heat and sauté the onion, celery, and peppers until tender.

2. Add the lobster. Season with salt, pepper, mustard, and cayenne pepper and mix well.

3. Add the wine and simmer for 3 minutes. Pour the cream into the pan, and simmer 2 to 3 minutes more. Present the lobster sauce spooned over freshly cooked pasta.

6 portions

GRILLED BLUEFISH WITH CITRUS BUTTER

Marinating the bluefish in lime juice helps to remove the strong fish flavor. The citrus butter and kiwi garnish add a refreshing taste and dashing touch.

2 pounds bluefish filets
2 limes
salt and freshly ground pepper to taste
1 to 2 tablespoons olive oil
2 kiwis, peeled and sliced, for garnish
Citrus Butter (recipe follows)

1. Place the filets in a Pyrex dish.

2. Squeeze the limes over the bluefish. Set aside to marinate at room temperature for 30 minutes. Lift the fish from the lime juice, and season the filets with salt and pepper.

3. Brush the filets with the oil, coating generously.

4. Place the fillets on a hot grill for 5 to 7 minutes per side until cooked and browned. Transfer to a platter. Garnish each portion with a dollop of citrus butter and kiwi slices. Serve immediately.

5 to 6 portions

Citrus Butter:
6 tablespoons butter, at room temperature
1 teaspoon finely grated lemon peel
1 teaspoon finely grated orange peel
1 teaspoon finely grated lime peel
2 tablespoons chopped fresh parsley

1. Mix the butter, citrus peels, and parsley, stirring until evenly combined.

2. Pack into a crock and refrigerate until needed. This will keep for several days.

Enough butter to sauce 2 pounds of fish

ORANGE MARINATED BLUEFISH

Bluefish filets are marinated in a savory sauce of orange juice, white wine, and tarragon.

2¹/₂ pounds bluefish filets
2 tablespoons olive oil
2 tablespoons orange juice
2 tablespoons dry white wine
1 tablespoon lemon juice
salt and freshly ground pepper to taste
1 teaspoon dried tarragon
2 teaspoons finely grated orange peel

1. Place the bluefish filets in a Pyrex dish.

2. Make a marinade by whisking together the oil, orange juice, wine, lemon juice, and seasonings in a bowl. Spoon the orange sauce over both sides of the bluefish and marinate for at least 30 minutes at room temperature.

3. When ready to serve, place the bluefish in a shallow baking pan, and baste with the marinade. Place under a hot broiler 4 inches from heat source for 10 minutes. Do not turn the fish. It stays moist and juicy cooking on one side only. Transfer to a platter along with the pan juices and serve at once.

6 generous portions

PAN-FRIED MACKEREL

Pan-fried mackerel filets are enhanced by the flavors of garlic and rosemary.

3 pounds mackerel filets
salt and freshly ground pepper to taste
flour for dredging
6 tablespoons butter
2 cloves garlic, crushed
1 teaspoon dried rosemary
2 tablespoons lemon juice

1. Season the filets with salt and pepper and dredge lightly in flour.

2. Melt the butter in a large skillet over medium-high heat. Add the garlic, and when the butter sizzles, place the mackerel in the pan, skin side down.

3. Sprinkle with the rosemary and lemon juice. Fry for 5 to 6 minutes until browned and crusty.

4. Turn the filets over and fry on the second side 4 minutes until brown, basting with the pan juices. Transfer the filets to a serving platter, spooning the pan juices over all, and present.

8 portions

SAUTEED TROUT PISTACHIO

Pan-fried brook trout are enhanced by pistachio nuts and Amaretto.

4 whole brook trout
flour for dredging
6 tablespoons butter
1/4 cup shelled and skinned pistachio nuts
2 tablespoons chopped fresh parsley
1/4 cup Amaretto

1. Dredge the trout in flour.

2. Heat the butter in a large non-stick skillet over medium-high heat, until sizzling. Add the trout, nuts, and parsley to the skillet. Sauté 4 to 5 minutes until browned, spooning the butter over the fish. Turn the trout over, and fry 3 to 5 minutes more until cooked and browned.

3. Working quickly, douse the trout with the Amaretto, swirl it around in the pan, and serve immediately. The Amaretto gets syrupy very quickly, so you have to work fast.

4 portions

SWORDFISH AMANDINE

Swordfish is an extremely adaptable fish—well suited to many flavorful and colorful presentations. In this recipe, swordfish steaks take on a fresh orange and almond taste.

3 pounds swordfish steaks, cut 1-inch thick
salt and freshly ground pepper to taste
flour for dredging
1/2 cup butter
2 cloves garlic, smashed
1 cup sliced almonds
peel of 1 orange, cut into thin julienne strips
1/2 cup orange juice

1. Sprinkle the swordfish steaks with salt and pepper and dredge in flour.

2. In a large skillet, heat the butter with the garlic until the butter foams. Add the swordfish and cook over medium-high heat for 5 minutes. Turn the steaks over. Add the almonds and orange peel, and sauté for 5 minutes, basting the fish with the pan juices.

3. Splash the orange juice over all and simmer 2 to 3 minutes more. Transfer the steaks to a platter, garnish with the almond butter sauce, and serve at once.

8 portions

SWORDFISH WITH CAPERS AND PINE NUTS

Swordfish steaks are sautéed in garlic butter and adorned with capers and pine nuts. Capers are actually the flowering bud of a shrub. They're used as a condiment to jazz up food.

> *2 pounds swordfish steaks, cut 1-inch thick*
> *salt and freshly ground pepper to taste*
> *flour for dredging*
> *4 tablespoons butter*
> *1 large clove garlic, crushed*
> *1 tablespoon capers*
> *3 tablespoons pine nuts*
> *1 tablespoon lemon juice*
> *1/2 cup white wine*

1. Season the fish with salt and pepper and dredge in flour.

2. In a large skillet, heat the butter and garlic until sizzling. Add the swordfish and sauté over medium-high heat for 5 minutes.

3. Add the capers and pine nuts.

4. Turn the fish over. Add the lemon juice and wine and sauté 5 minutes more, or until the sauce turns into a lovely glaze, spooning the pan juices over the steaks.

5. Remove the fish to a platter and bathe with the pan juices. Serve at once.

5 to 6 portions

GRILLED CAJUN SWORDFISH

Peppery swordfish seared with the fiery flavors of Cajun spices. The mayonnaise coating on the steaks helps to seal in the juices, keeping the fish moist and flavorful. So simple, yet so delicious! This spice mixture also turns salmon filets and chicken breasts into memorable meals.

3 pounds swordfish steaks, cut 1 to 1$^{1}/_{4}$-inches thick
1 teaspoon black pepper
$^{1}/_{2}$ teaspoon white pepper
$^{1}/_{4}$ teaspoon red pepper
1 teaspoon paprika
1 teaspoon garlic powder
2 teaspoons dried thyme
salt to taste
$^{1}/_{2}$ to $^{2}/_{3}$ cup mayonnaise

1. In a small bowl, combine the herbs and spices and mix well. Rub the seasoning mixture onto both sides of the swordfish steaks.

2. Spread a generous coating of the mayonnaise on all surfaces of the steaks.

3. Grill over hot coals 4 inches from heat source, 5 to 7 minutes per side. Transfer to a platter and serve immediately.

8 portions

SWORDFISH SALSA

Grilled swordfish steaks are blanketed in a zesty garlic and thyme tomato salsa. The salsa makes a dashing sauce for other grilled fish—shrimp, scallops, halibut, bluefish—whatever strikes your fancy!

4 ripe plum tomatoes, diced
2/3 cup chopped fresh parsley
1 large clove garlic, crushed
1/3 cup chopped scallions
1 tablespoon fresh thyme leaves or 1 teaspoon dried thyme
1/4 cup red wine vinegar
1/2 cup olive oil
salt and freshly ground pepper to taste
3 pounds swordfish steaks, 1¹/4-inches thick
1 to 2 tablespoons vegetable oil

1. Prepare the salsa. In a small bowl, combine the tomatoes, parsley, garlic, scallions, thyme, vinegar, olive oil, salt, and pepper. Set aside. This may be prepared 6 to 8 hours in advance and refrigerated.

2. Brush the fish lightly on both sides with the vegetable oil and season with salt and pepper.

3. Grill the fish over hot coals 4 inches from heat source, 5 to 7 minutes per side.

4. When cooked, remove the swordfish to a platter, adorn with spoonfuls of salsa, and serve.

8 portions

SWORDFISH SHIITAKE

Swordfish takes on an Oriental flavor when sautéed with shiitake mushrooms and Hoisin sauce in this East meets West creation.

2 pounds swordfish, cut into 1¹/₂-inch chunks
flour for dredging
salt and pepper to taste
6 tablespoons vegetable oil
¹/₄ pound shiitake mushrooms, sliced
1 large clove garlic, crushed
¹/₂ cup chopped scallions
2 tablespoons Hoisin sauce (available in Oriental markets)
¹/₂ cup dry white wine

1. Season the flour with salt and pepper and dredge fish in flour mixture.

2. In a large skillet, heat 2 tablespoons of the oil. When hot, add the mushrooms and sauté until golden. Remove the mushrooms from the pan and set aside.

3. Heat the remainder of the oil in the skillet along with the crushed garlic. When the oil is sizzling, add the fish and sauté over high heat for 2 minutes.

4. Turn the fish over, add the scallions and mushrooms, and sauté 2 minutes more.

5. Mix together the Hoisin sauce and wine and pour over the fish. Simmer 1 to 2 minutes more until done, basting with the sauce. Present with a rice accompaniment.

6 portions

WALNUT STRIPED BASS

Striped bass filets are baked with a topping of grated zucchini, ground walnuts, Parmesan cheese, and cream.

1 medium-size zucchini
salt
2 pounds striped bass filets (you may substitue any white fish—
  sole, flounder, cod, etc.)
freshly ground pepper to taste
1/2 cup heavy cream
1/2 cup Parmesan cheese
1/2 cup ground walnuts
4 tablespoons melted butter

1. Coarsely grate the unpeeled zucchini to measure 1 1/2 cups. Place in layers in a colander, sprinkling each layer with a little salt. Let drain for 30 minutes, then rinse thoroughly and squeeze out any extra liquid.

2. Preheat the oven to 425°.

3. Place the filets in a greased casserole, and season with salt and pepper. Spread the grated zucchini over the filets. Pour the cream over the fish.

4. Combine the Parmesan and ground walnuts in a bowl. Sprinkle the mixture atop the zucchini. Drizzle the melted butter over all. Bake for 20 minutes, and serve at once. (If using white fish, adjust cooking time to 10 to 15 minutes.)

6 portions

INDIAN STRIPED BASS

Filets are marinated in a yogurt-based sauce that is pungently seasoned with garlic, lime juice, and cumin, and then broiled. This also works well with bluefish.

> 2 pounds striped bass filets
> 8 ounces plain yogurt
> 1 large clove garlic, crushed
> 1/4 cup lime juice
> 1/2 teaspoon ground cumin
> 1 teaspoon paprika

1. Place the fish filets in a Pyrex dish.

2. Whisk together the yogurt, garlic, lime juice, cumin, and paprika in a small bowl. Spread the yogurt mixture over the filets, cover, and marinate for 2 to 3 hours at room temperature.

3. When ready to serve, transfer the fish to a shallow baking pan, spooning any of the marinade over the filets. Place under a hot broiler 4 inches away from the heat source, and broil 10 to 12 minutes, on one side only. Transfer to a serving platter, pour the pan juices over the filets, and serve immediately.

4 to 6 portions

HADDOCK PARMESAN

Haddock filets are enhanced by a puffed Parmesan and artichoke heart topping. It's a flavorful, yet simple way to prepare fish.

2¹/2 pounds haddock filets
pepper to taste
1 cup mayonnaise
³/4 cup Parmesan cheese
14 ounce can artichoke hearts, drained and coarsely chopped

1. Preheat the oven to 350°.
2. Season the filets with pepper and place in a baking pan.
3. Combine the mayonnaise, Parmesan, and artichoke hearts, and spread the mixture over the fish, coating it generously. (This much may be prepared in advance and refrigerated until needed. Return to room temperature before baking.)
4. Bake for 30 minutes until browned and puffed. Serve piping hot.

6 portions

HADDOCK MARGHERITA

Haddock filets are coated with an egg-cheese batter and sautéed in lemon butter.

2 pounds haddock filets, skinned and cut into 3-inch wide pieces
salt and freshly ground pepper to taste
flour for dredging
3 eggs, lightly beaten
1/2 cup grated Romano cheese
1/2 cup butter
1 garlic clove, smashed
2 tablespoons lemon juice

1. Preheat the oven to 400°.
2. Season the haddock with salt and pepper, and dredge in flour.
3. In a shallow bowl, make a batter by mixing together the eggs and cheese. Dip the haddock pieces in the batter, coating well.
4. In a large skillet, heat the butter and smashed garlic until hot. Add the haddock, sprinkle with the lemon juice, and sauté over medium-high heat 3 to 4 minutes per side until browned. Transfer the fish to a platter and spoon the pan juices over the pieces. (You may choose to refrigerate at this point for later use. Return to room temperature before crisping.) Crisp in the oven for 10 minutes and serve immediately.

6 portions

SCROD DUGLERE

The taste of fish chowder—scrod filets baked on a bed of sliced onions and potatoes smothered with tomatoes and cream.

> 3 medium-size Idaho potatoes, unpeeled and thinly sliced
> 2 medium-size onions, thinly sliced
> salt and freshly ground pepper to taste
> 4 tablespoons melted butter
> 2 1/2 pounds scrod
> 3/4 cup chopped canned plum tomatoes, drained
> 1/2 cup heavy cream
> paprika

1. Preheat the oven to 350°.

2. Arrange the potato and onion slices in a greased casserole. Season the vegetables with salt and pepper and drizzle with 2 tablespoons butter.

3. Place the scrod filets on top of the vegetables. Season the fish with salt and pepper. Drizzle with the rest of the melted butter.

4. Spread the tomatoes over the scrod and cover with the cream. Dust with a good sprinkling of paprika.

5. Place in the oven for 50 to 60 minutes, basting occasionally. Serve piping hot.

6 portions

PLANKED SCROD WITH OYSTERS

Baked scrod filets are surrounded by a riot of vegetables and oysters, and sauced with a light wine-butter cream.

2 pounds scrod filets, skinned
1/2 pint shucked, raw oysters
3 carrots, cut into matchstick pieces, 1/8 x 2 1/2-inches
1 medium zucchini, cut into matchstick pieces, 1/8 x 2 1/2-inches
3 stalks celery, cut into matchstick pieces, 1/8 x 2 1/2-inches
1/2 pound mushrooms, thinly sliced
1/2 cup coarsely chopped Italian parsley
1 tablespoon lemon juice
1/4 cup melted butter
1/2 cup dry white wine
salt and freshly ground pepper to taste
1/2 cup light cream
4 tablespoons water mixed with 2 tablespoons cornstarch

1. Preheat the oven to 350°.

2. Place the scrod filets in a large buttered casserole. Cover and surround the fish with the oysters, vegetables, and parsley.

3. Stir together the lemon juice, melted butter, wine, salt, and pepper in a bowl. Pour the butter mixture over the fish and vegetables.

4. Cover with a piece of foil. Bake the scrod for 50 to 60 minutes.

5. When the fish is done, drain the pan juices into a saucepan. Cover the fish and keep warm while finishing the sauce.

6. Place the saucepan over high heat and reduce the sauce to half its volume. Stir together the cream and cornstarch mixture. Add to the sauce, bring to a boil, stirring constantly. Continue to heat and stir until the sauce thickens. Pour the cream sauce over the fish and vegetables and serve at once.

6 portions

STEAMED SALMON WITH RED PEPPER MAYONNAISE

Great fare for a hot summer's night—cold, steamed salmon filets presented with a creamy red pepper mayonnaise.

3 pounds salmon filets, cut into serving pieces
salt and freshly ground pepper to taste
1/2 cup dry white wine
water
2 slices of lemon with peel
Red Pepper Mayonnaise (recipe follows)

1. Season the filets with salt and pepper.

2. Fill a steamer basket with the wine, 1 cup or more of water—amount required depends on steamer, and lemon slices.

3. Place the salmon on the rack in the steamer. Cover and steam about 10 minutes until the fish flakes easily. Lift the filets out of the steamer and transfer to a platter. You may choose to serve hot, allow to cool to room temperature, or refrigerate and serve cold. My personal preference is to serve the fish at room temperature—the delicate flavor of the salmon is best appreciated. Present with dollops of the red pepper mayonnaise.

8 portions

Red Pepper Mayonnaise:
2 medium red peppers, roasted (see page 243)
1/2 cup sour cream
1/2 cup mayonnaise
1 tablespoon snipped chives
generous shake cayenne pepper
1/2 teaspoon paprika

1. Purée the roasted peppers until smooth.

2. Combine the puréed peppers, sour cream, mayonnaise, chives, cayenne, and paprika, stirring until well mixed. Refrigerate until needed. (The sauce may be prepared 24 hours in advance.)

GRILLED SALMON WITH GINGER BUTTER

Ginger has a wonderful affinity for salmon—grilled salmon steaks are adorned with a lime-ginger butter that's absolutely divine.

2¹/₂ pounds salmon steaks, ³/₄-inch thick
1 to 2 tablespoons vegetable oil
salt and pepper to taste
Ginger Butter (recipe follows)

1. Brush the steaks with oil and season with salt and pepper.

2. Place over hot coals 4 inches from the heat source and grill 4 minutes per side. Serve with a dollop of ginger-butter crowning each portion.

6 portions

Ginger Butter:
6 tablespoons butter, at room temperature
4 tablespoons ginger preserves
1 teaspoon finely grated lime peel
1 tablespoon snipped chives

1. Cream together the above ingredients until well mixed.

2. Pack the flavored butter into a crock and refrigerate until needed. (The butter may be prepared several days in advance.)

Enough butter to adorn 6 portions

PEKING SALMON

Salmon steaks in an Oriental marinade, grilled over hot coals. This is always a sensational hit! It also works well with tuna steaks.

4 salmon steaks, 3/4-inch thick, about 2 pounds *
1/4 cup Hot Mustard (see page 9)
2 tablespoons soy sauce
2 tablespoons orange juice
2 tablespoons oil

1. Place the steaks in a Pyrex baking dish.

2. Whisk together the mustard, soy, orange juice, and oil in a bowl. Pour the sauce over the salmon steaks and marinate for 2 to 3 hours.

3. When ready to serve, place the salmon over hot coals. Baste with the marinade, and grill 4 minutes per side. Transfer to a platter and serve.

4 to 6 portions

*When the weather makes grilling unreasonable, I purchase 2 pounds of salmon filets instead of steaks. Cover the filets with the sauce, and broil them on one side only for 7 to 8 minutes, 4 inches from the heat source, basting after 5 minutes.

SALMON WITH TARRAGON CREAM

Salmon filets are surrounded by mushrooms and covered with a tarragon cream sauce. Easy and very elegant!

> 2 pounds salmon filets, 3/4-inch thick
> salt and freshly ground pepper to taste
> 1/2 pound sliced mushrooms
> 4 tablespoons butter, melted
> 1 teaspoon lemon juice
> 1 teaspoon dried tarragon
> 1/2 cup heavy cream

1. Place the filets in a large greased shallow baking dish. Season with salt and pepper. Surround the salmon with the sliced mushrooms.

2. Whisk together the melted butter, lemon juice, tarragon, and cream in a bowl. Pour the sauce over the filets and mushrooms.

3. Place under a hot broiler, 4 inches from the heat source, and broil for 7 to 8 minutes. Do not turn! Serve at once, spooning the pan juices over each portion.

6 portions

TUNA SHANDONG

Tuna steaks are marinated in a fiery Oriental oyster-flavored sauce and then grilled.

> 2 tablespoons oyster sauce*
> 1 tablespoon soy sauce
> 1 tablespoon mirin*
> 1 teaspoon Oriental sesame oil*
> $1/8$ teaspoon hot oil*
> 1 clove garlic, crushed
> 1 teaspoon grated gingerroot
> 2 pounds tuna steaks, 1-inch thick

1. Combine the oyster sauce, soy, mirin, sesame oil, hot oil, garlic, and ginger. Pour the marinade over the tuna and let sit for 1 to 2 hours.

2. When ready to serve, grill the steaks over hot coals 4 inches from heat source approximately 3 minutes per side for medium—pink on the inside, so the fish stays moist.

6 portions

*Available in Oriental markets

GRILLED TUNA WITH TOMATO-CAPER BUTTER

Tuna is a real meaty fish; we find it at its juiciest and flavor best when presented medium—pink in the interior. In this recipe, fresh tuna steaks are grilled and then capped with a balsamic vinegar flavored tomato-caper butter. The sauce is also tantalizing on grilled swordfish.

> *8 tablespoons butter, softened*
> *2 tablespoons capers*
> *2 tablespoons balsamic vinegar*
> *1 tablespoon tomato paste (I buy it in the tube and that way I'm*
> *   able to use small amounts at a time.)*
> *freshly ground pepper*
> *2 1/2 pounds tuna steaks, cut 1-inch thick*

1. Prepare the caper butter. In a small bowl, whisk together 6 tablespoons of the butter with the capers, balsamic vinegar, tomato paste, and pepper to taste. Set aside.

2. Melt the remaining 2 tablespoons of butter and brush over the steaks. Season with pepper.

3. Grill the steaks over hot coals, 4 inches from the heat source, approximately 3 minutes per side for medium rare. Remove to a platter and place dollops of the caper butter over the fish. Serve at once.

6 portions

SOLE WITH BALSAMIC VINEGAR

Tasty, refreshing and easy to prepare—sole filets are pan-fried in olive oil and butter, and doused with balsamic vinegar for a sweet, tangy flavor enhancer. Sure to set your taste buds dancing!

 $1^1/2$ pounds filet of sole
 salt and pepper to taste
 flour for dredging
 3 tablespoons butter
 2 tablespoons olive oil
 $^1/3$ cup balsamic vinegar
 1 to 2 teaspoons capers

1. Season the filets with salt and pepper. Dredge in flour.

2. In a large non-stick fry pan, heat the butter and oil over medium high heat. When hot, add the fish and sauté 3 to 4 minutes per side until golden.

3. Douse the filets with the vinegar, sprinkle with the capers, and sauté 1 minute more, basting constantly. Let the vinegar cook down and become syrupy and the fish glazed before removing to a platter to serve.

4 portions

SOLE TOULOUSE

Filet of sole stuffed with scallop mousse, sauced with a ginger cream, and garnished with shiitake mushrooms.

1/2 pound scallops
2 tablespoons sour cream
salt and freshly ground pepper to taste
1 3/4 pounds sole (6 filets)
4 ounces shiitake mushrooms, sliced
1/4 cup melted butter
3 tablespoons heavy cream
2 tablespoons lime juice
1 tablespoon grated gingerroot

1. Preheat the oven to 350°.

2. Place the scallops and sour cream in the bowl of a food processor. Season with salt and pepper and purée.

3. Spread an equal amount of the purée over each filet. Roll up the sole and place seam side down in a greased casserole. Surround the fish with the sliced mushrooms.

4. Stir together the butter, heavy cream, lime juice, and gingerroot in a bowl. Pour the cream sauce over the fish.

5. Bake for 30 to 35 minutes, basting occasionally. Serve immediately.

6 portions

CRAB-STUFFED SOLE

Rolled filets of sole are stuffed with an herbed spinach and crabmeat filling and adorned with sliced almonds.

2 pounds sole (6 filets)
salt and freshly ground pepper to taste
10 ounce package frozen chopped spinach, thawed and squeezed of excess liquid
5 ounce package Boursin cheese
1 1/2 cups crabmeat, flaked
1/4 cup chopped fresh parsley
1/3 cup sliced almonds
5 tablespoons melted butter

1. Preheat the oven to 350°. Grease a large casserole dish.
2. Season the filets with salt and pepper.
3. Combine the spinach, Boursin, and crabmeat in a bowl.
4. Divide the spinach mixture evenly among the filets and spread the filling over each piece. Roll up each filet and place seam side down in the prepared baking dish.
5. Garnish the fish with the parsley and almonds, and drizzle with the melted butter.
6. Bake the sole for 30 to 40 minutes, basting occasionally with the pan juices. Serve immediately with the buttery sauce spooned over each roll-up.

5 to 6 portions

FRESH FROM THE GARDEN

Vegetables—the current trend is toward fresh, away from frozen, canned, and processed. Always select crisp, firm vegetables. I hand-pick mine at a produce market, choosing the very best possible—small, young vegetables, ones free from bruises and blemishes. Young vegetables are more delicate in taste and texture than thick, fat ones. By buying them fresh, you are insured of getting more nutrients, more healthful goodness, and better flavor! Take advantage of seasonal offerings, for example, parsnips in winter, asparagus in springtime, and native corn and tomatoes in summer. The simplest way to prepare vegetables is probably my favorite. Just steam them until tender-crisp, season with a good sprinkling of salt and pepper, and flavor with an herbed butter. Most vegetables can also be eaten raw. Raw or cooked, vegetables are an important part of our diet, providing the body with vitamins and fiber. No longer do people have to shy away from eating cooked vegetables, as their presentation enhances their appeal. With the colorful array of garden vegetables, one can indulge in a different vegetable every day of the week. For a real treat, try growing your own next summer. Vegetables fresh from the garden are the best pickings!

SHELLEY'S APPLESAUCE

A thick pulp of cooked apples and apricot preserves flavored with vanilla and cinnamon. It makes an awesome accompaniment to roasted pork, and it's scrumptious served warm over vanilla ice cream!

> 12 medium-size apples (preferably MacIntosh)
> 3/4 cup apricot preserves
> 1 tablespoon vanilla extract
> 1 tablespoon lemon juice
> 1/2 cup dark brown sugar, firmly packed
> 2 tablespoons butter
> 1 teaspoon cinnamon

1. Peel and core the apples, and cut them into 1/4-inch thick slices.

2. Cook the apples in a large covered pot, on low heat for 20 to 30 minutes until the apples are cooked down to a pulpy consistency. Make sure that you stir the apples occasionally while cooking.

3. After the apples are soft, lower the heat more and stir in the apricot preserves, vanilla, lemon juice, sugar, butter, and cinnamon.

4. Remove the applesauce from the heat and cool completely before refrigerating in an air tight container.

5. When ready to serve, present the applesauce hot, warm, or cold—whatever your personal preference.

Approximately 2 quarts—will keep refrigerated 3 weeks

ASPARAGUS WITH MUSTARD BUTTER

Steamed asparagus are covered with a Dijon-flavored butter. I always peel asparagus, as the stalk can be quite tough, especially on mature asparagus. If you purchase the pencil thin asparagus, it is not necessary to peel them, as they are generally quite tender.

2 pounds asparagus
salt and freshly ground pepper to taste
4 tablespoons butter, melted
1/4 cup Dijon mustard

1. Cut off the tough portion at the stem end of the asparagus. Peel the stalks almost up to the tip.

2. Poach the asparagus in a large pot of boiling water for 5 minutes until tender. Drain well and arrange the spears in a serving dish. Season with salt and pepper.

3. Mix together the melted butter and Dijon. Pour the mustard butter over the asparagus and serve at once.

6 portions

PICKLED BEETS

Shredded raw beets and cucumbers marinated in a red wine vinaigrette. These are reminiscent of a recipe my grandmother used to make.

1 pound raw beets, peeled and coarsely grated
1 large pickling cucumber, peeled and coarsely grated
1/3 cup very thinly sliced red onion

Vinaigrette:
1/4 cup red wine vinegar
salt and freshly ground pepper to taste
1/2 teaspoon dried dill
1 tablespoon sugar
1/3 cup oil

1. Heap the grated beets, cucumber, and onion in a bowl.

2. Prepare the vinaigrette. In a separate bowl, mix together the vinegar, salt, pepper, dill, and sugar. Slowly drizzle in the oil, stirring constantly until all the oil has been incorporated.

3. Pour the vinaigrette over the vegetables, toss, and let marinate 1 to 2 hours in the refrigerator. Serve chilled.

4 portions

CURRIED BROCCOLI

Serve steamed broccoli with flair—finish it with a piquant curry mayonnaise. This can also be served cold and toted to picnics for dining al fresco.

1 large head broccoli (about 2 pounds)
1/4 cup mayonnaise
3 tablespoons butter, melted
2 teaspoons lemon juice
1/2 teaspoon curry powder
1/2 teaspoon Worcestershire sauce
salt and freshly ground pepper to taste
2 tablespoons chopped cashews

1. Cut off the heavy bottom portion of the stem. Peel the stalk. Separate the broccoli into reasonable-size serving pieces. Steam the broccoli for 8 minutes.

2. While the broccoli is cooking, make the sauce. Combine the mayonnaise, butter, lemon juice, curry powder, Worcestershire sauce, salt, and pepper in a bowl and blend well.

3. Drain the cooked broccoli and arrange the stalks in a casserole dish. Pour the curry sauce over the stalks, garnish with the cashews and serve at once.

6 portions

BUTTERNUT SQUASH PUREE

Creamy butternut squash with a hint of nutmeg.

2 pound butternut squash
4 tablespoons butter, melted
salt and freshly ground pepper to taste
1/4 teaspoon nutmeg
1/3 cup sour cream

1. Peel the squash, remove the seeds, and cut into 1-inch chunks.

2. Steam the squash for 15 to 20 minutes until tender. Remove the cooked squash to a colander and let drain for 5 minutes.

3. Transfer the drained squash to a food processor and purée until very smooth.

4. Spoon the purée into a casserole dish. Add the butter, seasonings, and sour cream and stir well. Serve at once. (If made in advance, it may be warmed in a 350° oven or in a microwave.)

6 portions

DILLY CARROTS, PARSNIPS, AND ZUCCHINI

A splashy sauté of vegetable rounds seasoned with dill. Unlike other recipes, these vegetables should be cooked until soft, allowing the carrots and parsnips to release their natural sugars.

> 1/2 pound carrots, peeled
> 1/4 pound parsnips, peeled
> 1/2 pound zucchini
> 4 tablespoons butter
> salt and freshly ground pepper to taste
> 1 teaspoon dried dill

1. Slice all the vegetables into 1/8-inch thick rounds.

2. Steam the carrots and parsnips 4 to 5 minutes and drain well. (Up to this point may be prepared several hours in advance.)

3. Heat the butter in a large skillet. Add the zucchini and sauté over medium heat until the slices are soft. Add the carrots and parsnips.

4. Season the vegetables with salt, pepper, and dill and cook, stirring often, until the vegetables are tender. Transfer the vegetable mélange to a casserole dish and serve.

4 to 6 portions

DEVILED CAULIFLOWER

Steamed cauliflower is dressed with a mustard mayonnaise and crumb topping.

> 1 large head cauliflower
> salt and freshly ground pepper to taste
> 1/2 cup mayonnaise
> generous pinch cayenne pepper
> 1 tablespoon Dijon mustard
> 1/2 cup fresh bread crumbs, toasted
> 4 tablespoons melted butter

1. Preheat the oven to 350°.

2. Break the cauliflower into flowerettes, and steam for 8 minutes. Drain well and place in a baking dish. Season with salt and pepper.

3. Combine the mayonnaise, cayenne, and mustard and pour over the steamed flowerettes, mixing well. Sprinkle with the bread crumbs, and drizzle with the melted butter. (Up to this point may be prepared several hours in advance and refrigerated. Bring to room temperature before heating.)

4. Set the casserole in the oven and bake for 10 to 15 minutes until golden. Serve piping hot.

4 to 6 portions

CORN PUDDING

Freshly grated corn is baked in a sumptuous egg custard. This is always received with accolades. It adds an extra special touch to the Thanksgiving meal, and has become a tradition with our family.

4 cups (12 ears) freshly grated corn (If fresh corn is unavailable,
   substitute corn niblets.)
1/2 cup flour
2 cups whole milk
8 eggs, beaten
1 cup butter, melted
1 1/2 cups sugar
1 teaspoon salt
2 teaspoons vanilla extract

1. Preheat the oven to 350°. Grease a 10 x 15-inch baking dish.

2. Blend the corn and flour together, and set aside.

3. Whisk together the milk and eggs in a large mixing bowl. Beat in the butter, sugar, salt, and vanilla. Stir in the corn mixture.

4. Pour the custard into the prepared pan.

5. Bake for 45 to 60 minutes until the pudding is set and golden. Cut into squares and serve at once.

8 to 10 portions

ROAST GARLIC

When roasted, garlic takes on a mellow, nutty flavor that is marvelous. It's a great partner for grilled or roasted meats and fabulous spread on crusty French bread.

6 heads of garlic
3 tablespoons olive oil
salt and freshly ground pepper to taste

1. Remove the white outer skins from the heads of the garlic, leaving the heads in tact.

2. Arrange the heads in a baking dish and drizzle with the olive oil, coating them lightly. Season with salt and pepper.

3. Roast in a 375° oven for 1 hour and 10 to 15 minutes until golden, basting occasionally.

6 portions

WAYS TO TREAT GARLIC

- Smash—place garlic clove on cutting board. Cover with the side of a knife, and pound the blade.
- Crush—place garlic clove in a press and squeeze, releasing the pulp.
- Mince—dice the clove of garlic finely with a knife.
- Work to a paste—purée the clove in a food processor, or dice and smash it with a knife until a smooth consistency.

GREEN BEANS GREMOLATA

Poached green beans are sauced in a zesty lemon-garlic butter. The sauce may be prepared a day ahead and refrigerated, making serving hassle-free.

1 pound green beans
4 tablespoons butter, melted
1/4 cup finely chopped fresh parsley
1 teaspoon grated lemon peel
2 large cloves garlic, crushed
salt and freshly ground pepper to taste

1. Poach the green beans for 5 minutes until they are tender-crisp.

2. While the beans are cooking, prepare the sauce. Combine the melted butter, parsley, lemon peel, garlic, and seasoning.

3. Pour the sauce over the cooked beans, toss, and serve.

6 portions

MUSHROOM SAUTE

A variation on a popular theme—similar in taste to baked stuffed mushrooms. A mélange of sautéed mushrooms coated with garlic crumbs.

1 pound assorted fresh mushrooms—white, brown, shiitake,
   and oyster—sliced
6 tablespoons butter
1 clove garlic, crushed
salt and freshly ground pepper to taste
3 tablespoons chopped fresh parsley
1/4 cup fresh bread crumbs, toasted

1. In a large skillet, heat the butter and garlic. When the butter is sizzling, add the mushrooms. Season with salt and pepper, and sauté over high heat until the mushrooms are golden.

2. Sprinkle with the parsley and bread crumbs, toss, and serve.

4 portions

SAUTEED PEAS AND SNOW PEAS

A delicate blend of fresh peas and snow peas seasoned with mint for zesty flavor.

3 tablespoons butter
1 cup shelled peas
1/2 pound snow peas, stems removed
salt and freshly ground pepper to taste
1 teaspoon dried mint

1. Heat the butter in a medium-size skillet. When it sizzles, add the peas and snow peas.

2. Season with the salt, pepper, and mint. Stir-fry over high heat 2 to 3 minutes. Serve at once.

4 to 6 portions

ROASTED PEPPERS

Roasted peppers boast a wonderful richness and delicious flavor! They make a fanciful addition to salads, omelettes, quiches, and sandwiches; puréed they add a distinctive touch to sauces. I always keep some on hand for spontaneous creating.

red and/or green peppers
olive oil

1. Place the peppers on a baking sheet and set under a hot broiler.
2. Broil the peppers until the skin is charred all over, turning the peppers as each side blackens. (It is also possible to cook over an open flame.)
3. Place the roasted peppers in a plastic bag and fold down the top to seal. Let the peppers steam in the bag for 10 minutes.
4. Remove the peppers from the bag. Rinse under cold water. The skins should slip off easily.
5. Core and seed the peeled peppers. Place the pieces in a container, cover with oil, and refrigerate until ready to use. The peppers will keep up to 1 week.

CARAWAY BAKED POTATOES

Caraway has a wonderful affinity for potatoes. A dollop of sour cream blended with Parmesan cheese and caraway seeds adorn these baked potatoes.

6 medium-size Idaho potatoes
3 tablespoons butter, melted
1/2 cup sour cream
1/4 cup Parmesan cheese
1 teaspoon caraway seeds
1 clove garlic, crushed
salt and freshly ground pepper to taste

1. Preheat the oven to 400°.

2. Scrub the potato skins well and pat dry. Prick the end of each potato. Put the potatoes in the oven and bake for 1 hour, or until fork tender.

3. While the potatoes are baking, prepare the topping. Combine the butter, sour cream, Parmesan cheese, caraway seeds, and garlic, and blend well.

4. When the potatoes are done, remove them from the oven. Cut each potato open by making a cross-cut on the top of each and arrange on a platter.

5. Season the potatoes with the salt and pepper. Spoon a dollop of the sour cream sauce on each potato and present at once.

6 portions

HERB-BAKED RED-SKINNED POTATOES

Baked potatoes are accented with a sprinkling of rosemary, parsley, and chives.

6 medium-size red-skinned potatoes
3 tablespoons olive oil
salt and freshly ground pepper to taste
1 teaspoon dried rosemary
3 tablespoons chopped fresh parsley
3 tablespoons snipped chives

1. Preheat the oven to 400°.

2. Cut the potatoes into quarters, leaving the skin on. Place the potatoes in a roasting pan. Drizzle them with oil, rolling the potatoes in the pan to completely coat them. Sprinkle with the seasonings.

3. Bake for 45 to 60 minutes until fork tender. Baste the potatoes with the herbed oil every 15 minutes.

4. Remove the potatoes to a serving dish, and drizzle with the pan drippings.

6 portions

POTATOES CELESTE

A rich and creamy potato cake of thinly sliced potatoes laced with Brie. It's outrageous!

3 large Idaho potatoes, sliced 1/4-inch thick (with the skin)
salt and pepper to taste
2/3 pound Brie, white rind removed and thinly sliced
2 tablespoons melted butter

1. Preheat the oven to 400°. Grease a 10-inch deep-dish pie pan.

2. Place a layer of potatoes in the pan and season with salt and pepper. Cover with a scant layer of sliced Brie. Continue layering in this fashion until all the ingredients are used, ending with a layer of cheese. Drizzle the melted butter over the top.

3. Cover and bake for 50 minutes. Uncover and bake 25 minutes more or until browned and bubbly. Slice into wedges to serve.

6 to 8 portions

POTATO PANCAKES

Crispy pancakes of grated potatoes and onion are pan-fried until brown. These make a terrific hors d'oeuvre when made silver dollar size and served with a sour cream and caviar dipping sauce. They may be prepared in advanced and reheated in the oven for tasty nibbling.

3 large Idaho potatoes, well-scrubbed
1 medium onion, grated
3 eggs, beaten
2 tablespoons flour
1/4 cup fresh bread crumbs
1 teaspoon salt
freshly ground pepper to taste
1/4 cup vegetable oil
1/4 cup butter

1. Coarsely grate the potatoes, skin and all. Let the grated potatoes drain in a colander for at least 10 minutes. Pat dry with a paper towel.

2. Combine the potatoes, onion, eggs, flour, bread crumbs, and seasonings in a mixing bowl.

3. In a large fry pan, heat 2 tablespoons of the butter and 2 table-spoons of the oil until hot. Drop the potato batter by large spoonfuls into the pan. Fry over medium to high heat until brown and crisp on both sides. Repeat, adding more oil and butter to the pan with the second batch. Keep the first batch warm in a low oven while cooking the second batch. Serve at once—either plain or if you prefer with a dollop of sour cream or applesauce.

12 to 15 pancakes

SWEET POTATOES WITH PECAN BUTTER

Baked sweets are capped with a praline topping for mouth-watering eating! This makes a dashing accompaniment to roast turkey at holiday time.

6 sweet potatoes
1/2 cup butter
3 tablespoons dark brown sugar
1/4 cup finely chopped pecans
1/4 teaspoon ground ginger

1. Preheat the oven to 350°. Scrub the sweet potatoes, and prick them with a fork.

2. Bake the potatoes for 1 hour or until tender.

3. While the potatoes are baking, prepare the topping. Cream the butter and sugar. Add the pecans and ginger and mix well. (Actually, the pecan butter may be prepared several days in advance and refrigerated until needed.)

4. When the potatoes are done, split each one open, top each half with a dollop of the pecan butter, and serve.

6 portions

SWEET POTATO FRIES WITH MAPLE CREAM

A new and dazzling version of the all-American French fry—wafers of sweet potato baked until crispy, then served with a maple-sour cream dipping sauce. An outrageous accompaniment to the burger, and a divine nibble for parties or friendly get-togethers.

2 large sweet potatoes, peeled and cut into wafer thin rounds—use a mandoline or food processor
4 tablespoons vegetable oil
salt and pepper to taste

Maple Cream:
1 cup sour cream
1/4 cup maple syrup
1/4 teaspoon ground ginger

1. Preheat the oven to 450°. Grease two baking sheets.

2. Put the sweet potato slices in a bowl. Pour the oil over all to coat.

3. Spread the fries out on the baking sheets. Season with salt and pepper.

4. Bake in the middle of the oven for 20 to 25 minutes.

5. While the fries are cooking, prepare the sauce. In a bowl, combine the sour cream, maple syrup, and ginger, mixing until smooth. (The sauce may be prepared as much as 24 hours in advance and refrigerated until needed.)

6. Serve the fries hot from the oven with the dipping sauce alongside.

3 to 4 side portions

BAKED SPINACH AND CHEESE

A crustless quiche of spinach, with Swiss and cottage cheeses. This is always a favorite, and is so versitile it can be used in a number of different settings—as a vegetable, for luncheon, as an entrée, or even as a first course. When teamed up with a tomato salad and crusty peasant bread, it makes a light, yet filling repast.

> 1 pound cottage cheese
> 3 eggs, beaten
> 1/4 cup butter, melted
> 1/4 pound Swiss cheese, grated
> 10 ounce package frozen chopped spinach, thawed and squeezed of its
> excess water
> 3 tablespoons flour

1. Preheat the oven to 350°. Butter a 1½ quart casserole.

2. Combine the cottage cheese, eggs, butter, and Swiss cheese in a large mixing bowl.

3. Add the spinach and flour and blend thoroughly.

4. Transfer the quiche mixture to the prepared casserole. (The pudding may be prepared 6 to 8 hours in advance up to this point and refrigerated. Return to room temperature before baking.)

5. Bake for 60 minutes until the custard sets. Let cool for 10 minutes before cutting into portions and serving.

6 to 8 side-dish portions; 4 to 6 luncheon portions

SUN-DRIED TOMATOES

Once you sample sun-dried tomatoes, you'll be hooked for life. The deep, rich flavor of the Italian plum tomato is incomparable. These are costly to buy, yet very easy and inexpensive to make. I put them in the oven in the evening, and they're ready by the next morning. I always have a supply on hand, as they make wonderful additions to salads, sauces, and pastas.

6 pounds ripe Italian plum tomatoes
coarse salt

1. Preheat the oven to 200°. Line baking sheets with wire racks.

2. Wash the tomatoes well. Slice them in half lengthwise. Arrange them on the racks, cup side up. Sprinkle lightly with coarse salt.

3. Dry (bake) in the oven until the tomatoes are shriveled, deep red, leathery, and dry (but not hard), 10 to 13 hours.* Remove the tomatoes as they are ready, and cool for 1 hour.

4. Store the dried tomatoes in an airtight jar or container—or pack them in a sterile jar and cover them completely with olive oil for a softer, richer taste—and store in the refrigerator for up to 2 months.

2 to 3 pints

*The tomatoes dry at varying rates, depending on how large and juicy each one is. Therefore, check them at 10 hours, and every 30 minutes thereafter, removing those that are done. On occasion, some have taken as long as 14 to 15 hours to dry, so don't be discouraged—it's worth the wait.

TOMATOES PROVENCAL

Baked tomato halves are encrusted with a zesty herbal crumb topping. Use the reddest, vine-ripened or home-grown tomatoes for peak flavor.

3 large ripe tomatoes
1/2 cup fresh bread crumbs
1/4 cup chopped fresh parsley
3 tablespoons chopped fresh basil or 1 tablespoon dried basil
1 to 2 cloves garlic, minced
1/8 teaspoon dried thyme
salt and freshly ground pepper to taste
3 tablespoons chopped scallions
1/4 cup olive oil

1. Preheat the oven to 350°.

2. Cut the tomatoes in half through the middle of each piece of fruit.

3. Mix together the bread crumbs, parsley, basil, garlic, thyme, salt, pepper, scallions, and oil. Place a large spoonful of the topping mix on each tomato half, dividing it evenly.

4. Arrange the tomatoes in a shallow baking pan and place in the oven for 15 to 20 minutes until golden. Serve at once.

6 portions

VEGETABLE TEMPURA

Assorted vegetables deep-fried in a light, crispy Japanese-inspired batter. This makes a wonderful accompaniment to grilled chicken or fish. I've also prepared several batches and served them as hors d'oeuvres.

> 1 large carrot, peeled, cut into 1/4 x 3-inch matchstick pieces
> 1 to 2 stalks celery, peeled, cut into 1/4 x 3-inch matchstick pieces
> 1/2 small sweet potato, peeled, cut into 1/4 x 3-inch matchstick pieces
> 3 scallions, cut into 3-inch lengths
> 1/2 green pepper, sliced into 1/2-inch thick strips
> 1/2 red pepper, sliced into 1/2-inch thick strips
> 1/8 pound string beans
> 1 cup cold water
> 1 egg
> 1 cup flour
> 1 teaspoon baking powder
> 1 teaspoon salt
> 4 cups vegetable oil

1. Make the batter. Gently stir the water into the egg.

2. Sift together the flour, baking powder, and salt, and add it quickly to the egg mixture. Stir just to mix, as the batter should be slightly lumpy.

3. Heat the oil until hot over high heat in a wok or deep fry pan.

4. Dip the vegetables into the batter and drop them, piece by piece, into the hot oil. Do not put too many in at one time.* Cook the vegetables about 3 to 5 minutes until they are crisp and lightly browned. Remove the cooked vegetables with a slotted utensil to a paper lined tray to drain. (Up to this point may be prepared several hours in advance, and refrigerated until serving time. When ready to serve, place the tempura on a baking sheet and set in a 400° oven for 8 to 10 minutes.) Serve at once.

6 portions

*It will be necessary to cook the vegetables in batches—overcrowding them in the pan will cause them to stick together.

ZUCCHINI MANDOLINE

A good mandoline is an expensive slicing machine made in France. The mandoline comes with several blades for slicing vegetables, cheeses, etc. in different shapes. Recently a moderately priced plastic version has been marketed, and is quite good; I recommend it. You must use a mandoline in order to slice the zucchini properly for this recipe. The mandoline slices the zucchini into long thin julienne strands resembling linguine. When the vegetable is prepared this way it takes on a different taste. Even people who are not zucchini fans will become devoted squash eaters!

> 3 medium-size zucchini
> 4 tablespoons butter
> salt and freshly ground pepper to taste
> 1 tablespoon fresh dill or 1 teaspoon dried dill

1. Slice the zucchini lengthwise on the finest julienne blade of the mandoline up to the seeds. Dispose of core.

2. In a large skillet, heat the butter until foaming. Add the shredded zucchini and sprinkle with the seasonings.

3. Sauté over high heat, stirring frequently, only until tender, about 2 to 3 minutes. The flesh of the fruit loses its bright white color when soft.

4. Transfer the vegetable to a casserole dish and serve at once.

4 to 6 portions

ZUCCHINI PUFFS

Grated zucchini, cheese, onions, and eggs are baked in muffin cups forming quiche-like puffs. This doubles as a tasty hors d'oeurve.

2 cups unpeeled coarsely grated zucchini
1 cup coarsely grated Swiss cheese
3 tablespoons finely chopped onion
1/2 cup fresh bread crumbs
1 tablespoon chopped fresh parsley
salt and freshly ground pepper to taste
2 eggs, beaten
1 tablespoon oil

1. Preheat the oven to 375°. Grease a 12-cup muffin pan.

2. Combine all of the ingredients in a large mixing bowl and stir until well blended.

3. Carefully spoon the batter into the prepared muffin tins, filling each cup 3/4 full.

4. Bake for 25 minutes or until the muffins are golden brown and puffed. Remove the muffins to a platter and serve at once.

12 large muffins; 8 to 12 portions

RICE PILAF

A Middle Eastern rice dish featuring sautéed onions, noodles, and pine nuts simmered in chicken broth. Even though of ethnic origin, I find this dish marries well with many foods, particularly lamb, chicken, and fish. When I have leftover roast chicken, I cut it into bite-size chunks and mix it into the cooked rice for a complete meal.

6 tablespoons butter
1 medium onion, diced
2 cups raw thin noodles (vermicelli)
1/3 cup pine nuts
2 1/2 cups chicken broth
1 cup raw long-grain rice

1. Heat the butter in a 3-quart casserole or saucepan. Add the onion and sauté over medium heat until it is a light golden color.

2. Add the noodles and pine nuts and continue to sauté, stirring often, until the pasta is somewhat softened.

3. Add the chicken broth, and when it comes to a boil, stir in the rice.

4. Cover the casserole, reduce the heat to low, and simmer undisturbed for 20 minutes or until all the liquid has been absorbed. Uncover the pan, fluff the pilaf with a fork and serve at once. (This may also be prepared in advance of serving, and refrigerated. Return to room temperature before reheating in a low oven or microwave.)

6 portions

RICE PARMESAN

Rice baked with a creamy Parmesan sauce—somewhat similar to the rich Italian rice dish, risotto.

1 cup raw long-grain rice
2 cups chicken broth
1/4 cup heavy cream
1/3 cup plus 1 tablespoon Parmesan cheese
2 tablespoons butter, melted
freshly ground pepper to taste

1. Bring the chicken broth to a boil in a large saucepan. Stir in the rice and cover the pot. Lower the heat to a simmer, and cook the rice undisturbed for 20 minutes, or until all the liquid is absorbed. Remove the pan from the heat and let stand for 5 minutes.

2. Uncover the pan, and fluff the rice with a fork.

3. Combine the cream, 1/3 cup Parmesan, melted butter, and freshly ground pepper. Add to the cooked rice and stir gently.

4. Transfer the rice to a buttered 1 1/2 quart baking dish. Sprinkle the top with 1 tablespoon Parmesan and run under the broiler to brown. Serve at once.

6 portions

PECAN RICE WITH FIGS

Rice is teamed with the sweet taste of dried figs and the nuttiness of pecan meats for a dynamite flavor sensation.

1/4 cup butter
1 medium-size onion, chopped
6 dried figs, destemmed and coarsely chopped
1/2 cup coarsely chopped pecans
2 cups chicken broth
1 cup raw long-grain rice

1. Heat the butter in a 3-quart casserole. When the butter is hot, add the onion and sauté over medium heat until soft. Add the figs and pecans and continue to sauté until the onions are lightly golden.

2. Pour in the chicken broth, and when it comes to a boil, stir in the rice.

3. Cover the casserole, reduce the heat to low, and simmer undisturbed for 20 minutes or until all the liquid has been absorbed. Fluff the rice with a fork and serve piping hot. (You may choose to refrigerate the rice at this point for later use. Return to room temperature before reheating in a low oven or microwave.)

6 portions

AUTHENTIC CHINESE FRIED RICE

A medley of rice, scrambled eggs, roasted pork, and Chinese vegetables with Oriental seasonings. This dish was originally conceived to use up leftovers!

1 teaspoon salt
1 tablespoon dry sherry
4 teaspoons soy sauce
3 tablespoons oil
2 eggs, scrambled in 2 tablespoons oil and broken into chunks
²/3 cup roasted pork, cut into ¹/2-inch chunks
8 to 10 canned water chestnuts, chopped
1 cup bean sprouts
8 large mushrooms, sliced
¹/2 cup fresh shelled peas
5 scallions, chopped
3 cups cooked long-grain rice, cooled

1. Combine the salt, sherry, and soy and set aside.

2. In a wok or large fry pan, heat the oil. When the oil is hot, add the eggs, pork, water chestnuts, bean sprouts, mushrooms, peas, and scallions and stir-fry for 1 minute.

3. Add the rice to the wok and stir-fry 1 minute more, tossing gently.

4. Add the soy mixture, and continue to stir-fry until the sauce is evenly distributed and the rice is heated. Serve at once. (This dish reheats well in a low oven.)

6 to 8 portions

APPLE, PEAR, AND SAUSAGE STUFFING

I find stuffing a bird to be messy, especially at serving time. I prefer to make my stuffing separately and cook it alongside the turkey. This stuffing is quite savory and aromatic—seasoned with thyme and sage, it combines toasted French bread, vegetables, sausages, almonds, and the sweet scent of apples and pears.

1 large French baguette (15 to 18 inches long)
olive oil
1/2 teaspoon dried thyme
1/4 cup olive oil
2 cups chopped onion
2 cups chopped celery
1/2 pound sliced mushrooms
2 apples, peeled, cored, and chopped
2 pears, peeled, cored, and chopped
3/4 cup slivered almonds
3/4 cup chopped fresh parsley
1 tablespoon fresh thyme
1 teaspoon ground sage
pepper to taste
1 pound sweet sausage, cooked and crumbled (I use chicken
    sausage to reduce the fat intake.)
2 cups chicken broth

1. Preheat the oven to 350°.

2. Slice the bread in half lengthwise. Spread with olive oil and sprinkle with dried thyme. Bake for 10 minutes or until brown and crunchy. When cooled, cut into 3/4-inch cubes and place in a large bowl.

3. Heat 1/4 cup olive oil in a large sauté pan. When hot, add the onion, celery, mushrooms, apples, pears, almonds, parsley, thyme, sage, and pepper. Sauté over medium-high heat for 10 minutes until vegetables are soft. Remove from heat and add to the bread cubes.

4. Add the cooked sausage and chicken broth, stirring until well mixed. Turn the mixture into a large casserole. Drizzle the top with 1/4 to 1/2 cup of pan drippings from the turkey. Bake in a 375° oven for 45 minutes. Enjoy piping hot.

10 to 12 portions

GLORIOUS GREENERY

Salads have as many variations as the people preparing them. Color, taste, and texture are the composite factors to consider when assembling a salad. A salad should combine the freshest of ingredients, using only crisp, firm vegetables. The best ones are those that are carefully and simply put together—a compatible marriage of ingredients with distinctive flavors enhanced by the dressing. Salads should be served well chilled and dressed sparingly just before presenting. There are salads for all occasions. Be adventurous and try them all, accompanied by slices of assorted freshly baked breads.

VEGETABLE SALADS

Americans are passionate salad eaters. Because of the popularity of this dish, chefs and cooks have created countless variations on the basic theme, making them colorful, tasty, and imaginative. Some form of salad should be an intrisinic part of the day's food.

SPRINGTIME ASPARAGUS SALAD

Steamed asparagus marinated in a zesty onion and Parmesan flavored vinaigrette, garnished with pine nuts, and served cold.

2 pounds asparagus, peeled (see page 232—how to peel asparagus)
1/2 cup olive oil
1/4 cup white wine vinegar
1/2 teaspoon Dijon mustard
1 large clove garlic, crushed
salt and freshly ground pepper to taste
1 teaspoon Worcestershire sauce
dash Tabasco sauce
1/2 cup chopped onion
1/2 cup chopped fresh parsley
1/2 cup Parmesan cheese
3 tablespoons pine nuts, toasted (see page 273)

1. Steam the asparagus spears for 5 minutes. Drain well and place in a serving dish.

2. In a bowl, whisk together the oil, vinegar, Dijon, garlic, salt, pepper, Worcestershire, Tabasco, onion, parsley, and Parmesan. Stir in the pine nuts.

3. Pour the vinaigrette over the asparagus. Cover and let marinate in the refrigerator 6 to 8 hours or overnight. Serve chilled with the marinade spooned over the spears.

6 portions

BROCCOLI CALEDONE

Broccoli spears dressed in a Dijon vinaigrette, enhanced by black olives, pimiento, and capers.

1 large bunch broccoli
1/2 cup olive oil
2 tablespoons white wine vinegar
1 teaspoon Dijon mustard
salt and freshly ground pepper to taste
1/2 tablespoon chopped fresh parsley
1 tablespoon capers
1 head Boston lettuce
1 cup sliced ripe black olives
2 ounces pimiento, thinly sliced

1. Cut off the tough end portion of the stalk. Separate the stalk into reasonable-size serving pieces, and peel the spears. Steam for 5 to 7 minutes until tender-crisp. Drain well and transfer to a bowl.

2. Combine the oil, vinegar, Dijon, salt, pepper, parsley, and capers in a bowl and blend well. Pour the vinaigrette over the broccoli and refrigerate until serving time—up to 8 hours.

3. Wash the Boston lettuce, pat dry, and place the leaves on a serving platter.

4. Arrange the broccoli on the bed of lettuce. Adorn the spears with the black olives and pimiento; pour the vinaigrette over the salad and serve.

6 portions

BEETS WITH HORSERADISH SAUCE

Shredded beets dressed in a piquant horseradish cream sauce garnished with chives.

4 medium-size beets

Horseradish Sauce:
1/2 cup sour cream
1 tablespoon red horseradish
1 tablespoon lemon juice
1 teaspoon sugar
1/4 teaspoon dried dill
1/4 teaspoon salt

1 head Boston lettuce
2 tablespoons snipped chives

1. Scrub the beets well and cut off the roots and stems. Plunge them into a pot of boiling water and cook until fork tender, about 40 minutes. When cooked, drain well and cool. Peel the beets and coarsely grate them.

2. Stir together the sour cream, horseradish, lemon juice, sugar, dill, and salt.

3. On each of six salad plates, place 2 to 3 leaves of Boston lettuce. Put a scoopful of grated beets atop the lettuce, and cover each salad with a dollop of dressing. Garnish with a sprinkling of chives and serve.

6 portions

COLESLAW

A shredded red and green cabbage slaw in a piquant creamy dressing.

1 medium head of cabbage, coarsely shredded
1 cup coarsely shredded red cabbage
2 carrots, coarsely grated

Piquant Dressing:
1 cup mayonnaise
1 tablespoon milk
1 tablespoon white horseradish
1 tablespoon sugar
2 tablespoons white vinegar
3/4 teaspoon salt
freshly ground pepper to taste

1. Put the cabbages and carrots together in a large bowl.

2. In a small bowl, mix together the mayonnaise and milk. Stir in the horseradish, sugar, vinegar, salt, and pepper.

3. Pour the dressing over the slaw, tossing to coat the vegetables evenly. Cover and chill at least 3 to 4 hours or as much as overnight to marinate. Toss before serving.

6 to 8 portions

SALAD A LA CAESAR

My rendition of the classic Caesar salad—leaves of romaine garnished with pumpernickel croutons in a zesty garlic and Parmesan dressing. With the concern for avoiding raw eggs, I've eliminated the egg in the dressing and have added mayonnaise (I use the cholesterol free kind) as a thickening agent. Friends swear this is "The Best Caesar they've ever had" . . . the proof is in the eating!

1 large head romaine
1 to 2 slices pumpernickel bread

Zesty Dressing:
1 clove garlic, smashed
1 teaspoon Dijon mustard
1/2 teaspoon Worcestershire sauce
1/4 teaspoon salt
lots of freshly ground pepper to taste
2 tablespoons mayonnaise
2 tablespoons lemon juice
1/4 cup olive oil
3 tablespoons Parmesan cheese

1. Wash the romaine well, as it is usually quite sandy. Pat dry with a paper towel, and cut the leaves into fork-size pieces. Place in a large salad bowl.

2. Make the pumpernickel croutons. Toast the bread directly on the middle rack in a 400° oven for 5 minutes per side. Slice into 3/4-inch squares.

3. In a small bowl, beat together the garlic, Dijon, Worcestershire, salt, pepper, mayonnaise, and lemon juice.

4. Whisk in the oil, and continue to beat until the dressing gets thick.

5. Stir in the Parmesan cheese, and pour the dressing over the romaine. Add the croutons. Toss well and serve on chilled plates.

6 portions

CREAMY MUSHROOM SALAD

Boston lettuce and sliced mushrooms generously coated with a creamy, garlic dressing.

2 heads of Boston lettuce
1 pound mushrooms, sliced

Creamy-Garlic Dressing:
1/2 cup olive oil
2 tablespoons red wine vinegar
1 clove garlic, crushed
1 teaspoon Dijon mustard
1/4 cup heavy cream
1/4 teaspoon salt
freshly ground pepper to taste

1. Wash the Boston lettuce well, and pat dry. Break the leaves into a salad bowl.

2. Add the sliced mushrooms to the greens.

3. Whisk together the oil, vinegar, garlic, mustard, cream, salt, and pepper until thick and creamy. Pour the dressing over the salad, toss gently, and serve at once.

6 portions

BUTTERMILK DRESSED GREENS

A creamy ranch-style dressing enhanced by buttermilk, Parmesan cheese, and garlic covers mixed greens with a sliced apple garnish. Try the dressing as a dip for favorite crudités—it dazzles!

Buttermilk Dressing:

$1^1/2$ cups mayonnaise
$1/2$ cup buttermilk
$1/2$ cup Parmesan cheese
1 clove garlic, crushed
2 tablespoons red wine vinegar
$1/4$ to $1/2$ teaspoon Worcestershire sauce
salt and freshly ground black pepper to taste

12 cups mixed salad greens—Boston, red leaf, and romaine
1 tart apple, thinly sliced (Granny Smiths work well)

1. In a bowl, whisk together vigorously the mayonnaise and buttermilk. Add the Parmesan, garlic, vinegar, Worcestershire, salt, and pepper and mix well.

2. Transfer to a covered container and store in the refrigerator until needed. (The dressing will keep up to 2 weeks in the refrigerator—if it lasts that long!)

3. When ready to serve, arrange the salad greens on 8 individual salad plates. Garnish each serving with several apple slices. Spoon dollops of the dressing atop each salad and serve.

Approximately 2 cups of dressing—enough for 8 portions with extra dressing

HERB SALAD

Fabulous, refreshing, and aromatic—a potpourri of fresh herbs with a balsamic vinegar dressing. It makes a marvelous accompaniment to roasted lamb or beef.

> *4 cups coarsely chopped Italian parsley*
> *6 tablespoons snipped chives*
> *2 tablespoons fresh thyme*
> *2 tablespoons fresh rosemary*
> *2 tablespoons balsamic vinegar*
> *1/4 cup olive oil*
> *salt and freshly ground pepper to taste*

1. Combine the herbs in a bowl.

2. In a separate bowl, whisk together the vinegar, oil, salt, and pepper. Pour the dressing over the herbs and toss gently to mix.

3. Present at once or let marinate 1 to 2 hours before serving.

4 to 6 side portions

SHREDDED ROMAINE SALAD

A salad of romaine lettuce, covered with a garlic and Parmesan dressing, and adorned with toasted pine nuts. Similar to a Caesar salad, but more delicate. My family's absolute favorite!

> 1 large head romaine lettuce, cut into 1/4-inch wide pieces
> 1/4 cup pine nuts, lightly toasted

Parmesan Dressing:
1 large clove garlic, smashed
1 teaspoon Hot Mustard (see page 9)
salt and freshly ground pepper to taste
2 tablespoons white vinegar
1/3 cup vegetable oil
2 tablespoons Parmesan cheese

1. Place the shredded romaine and pine nuts in a large salad bowl.

2. In a separate small bowl, combine the garlic, mustard, salt, pepper, and vinegar. Whisk in the oil until completely incorporated. Stir in the Parmesan cheese.

3. Cover the romaine with the dressing and toss to mix. Serve at once.

6 portions

HOW TO TOAST NUTS

Spread nuts out on a cookie sheet and bake in a 350° oven for 5 to 10 minutes until golden. Different sizes and types of nuts toast at varying times; the smaller the nut, the faster it browns, so you have to keep a watchful eye on the oven.

PEPPER TRIO

A spectacular vision—a blast of color—a mélange of julienned red, yellow, and green bell peppers tossed in a teriyaki dressing and sprinkled with cashew nuts.

2 large red peppers, sliced in thin julienne strips
2 large yellow peppers, sliced in thin julienne strips
2 large green peppers, sliced in thin julienne strips
1/2 cup unsalted cashew nuts

Teriyaki Vinaigrette:
3 tablespoons soy sauce
1 teaspoon grated gingerroot
1 clove garlic, crushed
1 tablespoon honey
black pepper to taste
2 tablespoons red wine vinegar
1/4 cup vegetable oil

1. Combine the pepper slices and cashews in a serving bowl.

2. In a separate small bowl, whisk together the dressing ingredients.

3. Pour the vinaigrette over the pepper mélange and toss well. Serve at once or let marinate 1 to 2 hours.

6 to 8 portions

ENDIVE AND HEARTS OF PALM

Bibb lettuce and sliced endive are garnished with hearts of palm in a creamy tarragon dressing.

1 head Bibb or Boston lettuce
4 endive, cut into thin julienne strips
14 ounce can hearts of palm, drained and cut into 1/2-inch thick slices

Tarragon Dressing:
1 teaspoon Dijon mustard
2 tablespoons sour cream
1/3 cup olive oil
1 tablespoon lemon juice
1 tablespoon red wine vinegar
1/2 teaspoon dried tarragon
1 tablespoon chopped fresh parsley
salt and freshly ground pepper to taste

1. Wash the lettuce and pat dry. Heap the greenery into a large salad bowl.

2. Adorn the salad with the endive and hearts of palm.

3. Whisk together the Dijon, sour cream, oil, lemon juice, vinegar, herbs, and spices. Drizzle the dressing over the salad, toss, and serve.

6 portions

TOASTED PECAN AND PRUNE SALAD

Red leaf lettuce is embellished with prunes, scallions, and toasted pecans in a sweet and sour poppy seed dressing. Poppy seeds are the tiny black seeds of the poppy flower, known for their crunchy, nutty flavor.

1 large head red leaf lettuce, washed and torn into bite-size pieces
12 large pitted prunes
1/4 cup sliced scallions
1/4 cup pecans, toasted (see page 273)

Poppy Seed Dressing:
1 tablespoon balsamic vinegar
1 tablespoon red wine vinegar
1 tablespoon honey
salt and pepper to taste
1 teaspoon dry mustard
1 tablespoon poppy seeds
1/2 cup vegetable oil

1. Heap the lettuce into a large bowl.
2. Adorn the lettuce with the prunes, scallions, and pecans.
3. In a separate small bowl, whisk together the dressing ingredients until well combined. Pour the dressing over the salad, toss, and serve.

6 portions

PANZANELLA

A rustic, crunchy bread salad with savory Mediterranean influences—roasted peppers, sun-dried tomatoes, black olives, capers, and pine nuts in a thyme-scented dressing, coupled with lots of toasted chunky French bread cubes.

12-inch long piece of French bread
2 medium-size red peppers, roasted (see page 243)
2/3 cup coarsely chopped sun-dried tomatoes (see page 251)
3/4 cup coarsely chopped ripe black olives
2 tablespoons capers
1/4 cup pine nuts, toasted (see page 273)

Vinaigrette:
1 clove garlic, smashed
salt and lots of freshly ground pepper to taste
1 teaspoon dried thyme
1 tablespoon red wine vinegar
1 tablespoon balsamic vinegar
1/3 cup olive oil

1. Make the croutons. Cut the bread into 1-inch thick slices. Toast until golden and crunchy. Cut into 1-inch cubes and set aside.

2. In a large bowl, combine the chopped vegetables and pine nuts.

3. In a separate small bowl, whisk together the dressing ingredients.

4. Pour the vinaigrette over the vegetables and toss well. Cover and marinate 1 to 4 hours.

5. When ready to serve, add the croutons and toss thoroughly. Present at once.

6 portions

SUCCOTASH SALAD

A new twist to the traditional bean-corn medley—roasted red pepper and scallions join forces and all are coated with a dill-sour cream sauce. This makes great picnic fare.

4 cups corn niblets (fresh or frozen), cooked until tender crisp
2 cups lima beans, steamed until barely tender
1/2 pound stringbeans, cut into 1-inch pieces, steamed until
*   tender crisp*
1 large roasted red pepper, coarsely chopped (see page 243)
1/4 cup thinly sliced scallions
1/2 cup sour cream
1/4 cup mayonnaise
1 teaspoon dried dill
salt and lots of freshly ground black pepper to taste
pinch of cayenne pepper

1. In a large bowl, combine the corn, limas, stringbeans, red pepper, and scallions.

2. In a separate small bowl, stir together the sour cream, mayonnaise, and seasonings.

3. Pour the sauce over the vegetable medley and mix thoroughly until dressing is evenly distributed. Serve at once or refrigerate until needed. Return to room temperature before presenting.

6 to 8 portions

TOMATO AND AVOCADO SALAD

South-of-the-Border flavors and ingredients are highlighted in this composition—tomatoes, avocado, and red onion are laced with a cilantro dressing and topped with cornbread croutons.

3 x 5-inch piece of cornbread
1/2 tablespoon vegetable oil
1 ripe avocado, peeled
2 medium tomatoes, cut into wedges
1 small red onion, thinly sliced
1 large or 2 small heads Boston lettuce, coarsely shredded into 1/2-inch wide strips

Vinaigrette:
1/4 cup loosely packed fresh cilantro leaves
1 clove garlic, crushed
1 teaspoon dry mustard
salt and lots of freshly ground pepper to taste
2 tablespoons lemon juice
1/3 cup olive oil

1. Preheat the oven to 400°.

2. Prepare the croutons. Cut the cornbread into 1/2-inch wide slices. Cut each slice into 1/2-inch cubes. Brush the tops of the cubes lightly with the vegetable oil. Bake 20 to 23 minutes until golden brown. Let cool. (These may be prepared as much as a day in advance and kept in an airtight container.)

3. Cut the avocado in half. Remove the pit. Cut each piece in half lengthwise, and then into bite-size chunks.

4. In a large bowl, combine the lettuce, avocado, tomato, red onion, and croutons.

5. Prepare the vinaigrette. Finely chop the cilantro. In a small bowl, mix the cilantro, garlic, mustard, salt, pepper, and lemon juice. Slowly pour in the olive oil, stirring briskly until well incorporated.

6. Pour the dressing over the salad. Toss well and serve.

4 portions

CLAREMONT DINER SALAD

A pickled cabbage slaw featuring cucumbers, carrots, peppers, and onion.

1 small head cabbage, coarsely shredded
3 medium-size cucumbers, peeled, seeded, and coarsely grated
3 to 4 carrots, coarsely grated
1 green pepper, diced
1 medium red onion, thinly sliced

Sweet-Sour Vinaigrette:
1/4 cup vegetable oil
1/2 cup cider vinegar
1/4 cup sugar
1 1/2 teaspoons salt
1/4 teaspoon pepper

1. Combine the cabbage, cucumbers, carrots, green pepper, and onion in a large mixing bowl.

2. Whisk together the oil, vinegar, sugar, salt, and pepper in a small bowl, and pour over the slaw.

3. Cover the salad and refrigerate for at least 24 hours so that the vegetables can marinate in the dressing. Turn the salad over several times while marinating; toss just before serving.

8 portions

CUCUMBER SALAD

Dill has a marvelous affinity for cucumbers. Thin slices of cucumber are covered with a dill-yogurt sauce.

4 large pickling cucumbers
salt
8 ounces plain yogurt
2 scallions, cut into 1/4-inch slices
1 tablespoon fresh dill or 1/2 teaspoon dried dill
freshly ground pepper to taste

1. Peel the cucumbers and slice them thinly.

2. Place a layer of cucumbers in a colander and salt them lightly. Continue adding layers of cucumbers and salting each until all are used. Let the colander stand in the sink for 5 to 10 minutes. Rinse the cucumbers well under cold water. Let them drain for 30 minutes, and then place them in a glass serving bowl.

3. Combine the yogurt, scallions, dill, and pepper.

4. Pour the yogurt dressing over the cucumbers and toss gently. Refrigerate until serving time. This should be made 3 to 4 hours in advance for flavors to properly blend.

4 portions

CUCUMBER SALAD WITH TOMATO VINAIGRETTE

Thin slices of cucumber are donned with a tomato-vinaigrette spiked with the illustrious flavor of cilantro.

2 cucumbers, thinly sliced
2 scallions, thinly sliced

Tomato Vinaigrette:
1 medium ripe tomato, peeled and finely chopped
1/2 teaspoon salt
lots of freshly ground black pepper
3 tablespoons coarsely chopped fresh cilantro
pinch cayenne pepper
2 tablespoons white wine vinegar
1/3 cup olive oil

1. Pile the cucumbers and scallions in a serving bowl.
2. In a separate small bowl, whisk together the dressing ingredients until well mixed.
3. Pour the vinaigrette over the salad, toss, and serve.

4 portions

SOY-DRESSED CUCUMBERS

Thinly sliced cucumbers in an Oriental-inspired marinade.

2 medium-size cucumbers
2 tablespoons soy sauce
2 teaspoons rice vinegar (available in Oriental markets)
1 teaspoon vegetable oil
1 teaspoon sugar
1 tablespoon sesame seeds, toasted in a 350° oven until golden, about
   5 minutes

1. Peel and thinly slice the cucumbers; place them in a bowl.

2. Whisk together the soy, vinegar, oil, and sugar in a small bowl.

3. Pour the Oriental sauce over the cucumbers and mix well. Cover and refrigerate for 1 to 2 hours. Garnish with the sesame seeds before serving.

4 portions

CUCUMBERS AND STRAWBERRIES

A very colorful, refreshing, and unusual combination—the sweet, yet slightly tart fruit enhanced by a light sweet and sour dressing.

1 European cucumber, thinly sliced
1 pint strawberries, thinly sliced
salt and freshly ground pepper to taste
3 tablespoons white wine vinegar
1 tablespoon sugar

1. Delicately arrange the cucumber and strawberry slices in a glass serving bowl.

2. Mix together the salt, pepper, vinegar, and sugar, and pour over the fruits.

3. Cover the salad and chill in the refrigerator for 1 to 2 hours before serving.

6 portions

SPINACH AND MUSHROOM SALAD

Spinach and sliced mushrooms in a zesty vinaigrette, finished with shredded Gruyère and chopped prosciutto.

1 pound fresh spinach
1 pound mushrooms, sliced
³/4 cup finely grated Gruyère cheese
3 slices prosciutto, cut ¹/8-inch thick, coarsely chopped

Vinaigrette:
³/4 cup olive oil
3 tablespoons lemon juice
1 clove garlic, smashed
¹/2 teaspoon sugar
¹/2 teaspoon dry mustard
salt to taste
¹/4 teaspoon black pepper

1. Wash the spinach and pat dry. Remove any stems and discard. Heap the cleaned spinach in a large salad bowl.

2. Add the mushrooms.

3. Garnish the salad with the cheese and prosciutto.

4. Whisk together the olive oil, lemon juice, garlic, sugar, mustard, salt, and pepper.

5. Pour the vinaigrette over the salad and toss well. Serve at once.

6 to 8 portions

SPINACH AND MANDARIN ORANGES

Fresh greenery is dotted with vivid orange segments and toasted almonds before being coated with a honey-mustard dressing.

12 ounces fresh spinach, washed, thick stems removed
1/2 cup thinly sliced scallions
2 (11 ounce) cans mandarin oranges, drained
1/2 cup slivered almonds, toasted (see page 273)

Honey-Mustard Vinaigrette:
1 teaspoon dry mustard
salt to taste
1/8 teaspoon black pepper
1 tablespoon honey
2 tablespoons cider vinegar
1/2 cup vegetable oil

1. Heap the spinach leaves in a large bowl.
2. Adorn the greenery with the scallions, fruit, and nuts.
3. In a small bowl, whisk together the dressing ingredients.
4. Pour the vinaigrette over the salad, toss well, and serve.

6 portions

SALAD GOURMANDISE

Delicate and refreshing—showcasing Boston lettuce, pear slices, and Gourmandise cheese finished with a creamy ginger sauce. The pungency of the ginger complements the savory, sweet taste of the fruit and cheese.

1 head Boston or Bibb lettuce
1 to 2 pears (Bosc or Bartlett), thinly sliced into wedges
4 ounces Gourmandise cheese, cut into julienne strips

Ginger Dressing:
3 tablespoons vegetable oil
1 tablespoon white vinegar
pinch salt
dash of white pepper
1 tablespoon finely chopped candied ginger
2 tablespoons sour cream

1. Wash the lettuce and pat dry. Arrange the lettuce on a platter.
2. Decorate the bed of lettuce with the pear and cheese slices.
3. In a bowl, combine the oil, vinegar, salt, pepper, ginger, and sour cream, blending well.
4. Dress the salad with the ginger vinaigrette and serve.

4 to 6 portions

GAZPACHO SALAD

A take-off on the traditional soup—a layered salad of chopped vegetables, bread crumbs, and tomatoes, with a mouth-watering marinade. It makes a very colorful presentation.

1 large red pepper, diced
1 large green pepper, diced
1 large yellow pepper, diced
2 large pickling cucumbers, peeled and diced
3 stalks celery, diced
1/2 cup thinly sliced scallions
1 cup ripe black olives, coarsely chopped

Herbal Vinaigrette:
1 to 2 cloves garlic, crushed
1 teaspoon Dijon mustard
3 tablespoons balsamic vinegar
3/4 teaspoon salt
1/4 teaspoon black pepper
1 teaspoon dried basil
2 tablespoons chopped fresh parsley
1/2 cup extra virgin olive oil

3 cups chopped and drained plum tomatoes
1/2 cup chopped sun-dried tomatoes
2 cups fresh bread crumbs, made from French bread, toasted
1 head Boston lettuce

1. Mix together the red, green, and yellow peppers, cucumbers, celery, scallions, and black olives in a large bowl.

2. Combine the garlic, mustard, vinegar, salt, pepper, basil, and parsley in a separate bowl. Whisk the mixture briskly while slowly drizzling in the oil until the dressing thickens.

3. In a separate bowl, combine the plum and sun-dried tomatoes.

4. Assemble the salad in a large glass bowl. Place 1/4 of the bread crumbs on the bottom of the bowl. Cover the crumbs with 1/3 of the chopped vegetable mixture. Spread 1/3 of the chopped tomatoes over the vegetables. Pour 1/4 of the dressing over all. Repeat these layers two more times. Cover with a layer of crumbs, and pour the remaining dressing over all.

5. Cover and refrigerate at least 6 to 8 hours, and up to 24 hours.

6. When ready to serve, line each plate with several leaves of lettuce. Scoop out wedges of salad and mound on the greenery.

8 portions

MIXED GREEN SALAD

A colorful array of greenery tossed with a savory balsamic vinaigrette. Whenever nectarines are available, especially during the summer season, I slice up 2 of the succulent fruits and add them to the salad. They lend a delightfully refreshing touch. This recipe won 1st prize in a salad contest run by a Boston area newspaper.

12 to 14 cups assorted salad greens—Boston, red leaf, romaine,
    watercress, arugula, radicchio, and endive
2 nectarines, sliced in wedges
1/3 cup toasted walnut meats (see page 273)

Balsamic Vinaigrette:
2/3 cup olive oil
2 tablespoons balsamic vinegar
1/4 cup orange juice
1 tablespoon Dijon mustard
1 clove garlic, smashed
1/4 teaspoon salt
freshly ground black pepper to taste

1. Choose at least three of the varied salad greens—I usually select Boston and red leaf as my base and add two other types for their color and flavor.

2. Wash the greens, pat dry, and pile them into a large salad bowl. Adorn the greenery with the fruit and toasted walnuts.

3. Beat together the oil, vinegar, orange juice, mustard, garlic, salt, and pepper in a bowl.

4. Pour the dressing over the greenery and toss well to coat evenly. Present at once.

6 portions

WATERCRESS, TOMATOES, AND ROQUEFORT

Roquefort has a curious affinity for tomatoes. Bunches of watercress, chopped tomatoes, and Roquefort are sprinkled with walnuts in a shallot vinaigrette. A must for blue cheese lovers!

> 2 large or 3 medium-size bunches watercress
> 3 medium-size ripe tomatoes, coarsely chopped
> 2 ounces Roquefort cheese, coarsely crumbled
> $1/2$ cup walnuts, toasted (see page 273)

Shallot Vinaigrette:
2 tablespoons dry sherry wine
$1/2$ cup olive oil
salt and freshly ground pepper to taste
1 tablespoon minced shallots

1. Wash the watercress well, pat dry, trim the stems, and separate into bite-size sprigs. Place the greenery in a salad bowl.

2. Heap the tomatoes, Roquefort, and walnuts onto the watercress.

3. In a small bowl, whisk together the sherry, oil, salt, pepper.

4. Pour the dressing over the salad, and toss well. Present on salad plates and serve at once.

6 portions

CREAMY PEA SALAD

Steamed fresh peas served cold in a delicate yogurt-tarragon dressing, garnished with sliced scallions. It makes a great accompaniment to poached salmon for the traditional July 4th celebration!

1 pound fresh peas (unshelled weight)

Yogurt Dressing:
4 tablespoons olive oil
1 tablespoon lemon juice
1/4 teaspoon salt
white pepper to taste
2 tablespoons chopped fresh parsley
1/2 teaspoon dried tarragon
1/4 cup plain yogurt

Boston or Bibb lettuce
1 scallion, thinly sliced

1. Shell the peas and steam for 3 to 4 minutes until tender. Drain well and set aside to cool.

2. Whisk together the oil, lemon juice, salt, pepper, parsley, tarragon, and yogurt in a large bowl. Add the peas and mix gently. Place in the refrigerator to chill.

3. When ready to serve, arrange the lettuce leaves on a platter.

4. Heap the pea salad onto the lettuce and garnish with the sliced scallion. Serve at once.

4 to 6 portions

ZUCCHINI AND CARROTS DIJON

A colorful slaw of grated zucchini and carrots in a savory Dijon vinaigrette. This totes well to picnics and barbecues.

4 medium-size carrots, peeled and coarsely grated
3 medium-size zucchini, coarsely grated
Basic Dijon Vinaigrette (see page 10)

1. Mix the grated carrots and zucchini in a serving bowl.

2. Prepare the Basic Dijon Vinaigrette and pour the dressing over the slaw, tossing well. Cover and marinate at least 3 to 4 hours in the refrigerator. When ready to serve, toss again and present.

6 portions

HERBED NEW POTATOES AND ROASTED PEPPERS

The rich flavor of roasted red and green peppers team up with new potatoes in a savory, herbal vinaigrette.

Herbal Vinaigrette:
1/2 cup olive oil
2 tablespoons white wine vinegar
1 teaspoon mustard seeds
1 tablespoon snipped chives
1 tablespoon chopped fresh parsley
1/2 teaspoon dried basil
1/4 teaspoon dried thyme
1/2 teaspoon salt
1/4 teaspoon pepper

5 medium-size new potatoes, unpeeled and cut into 1/2-inch chunks
2 large red peppers, roasted and sliced into 1/2-inch wide strips (see page 243)
2 large green peppers, roasted and sliced into 1/2-inch wide strips (see page 243)

1. Prepare the dressing by whisking together the oil, vinegar, herbs, and spices in a bowl. Set aside.

2. Boil or steam the potatoes for 5 to 10 minutes or until fork tender. Drain the potatoes well. Place them in a serving dish along with the roasted peppers.

3. While the potatoes are still hot, bathe the vegetables with the vinaigrette—they will absorb more of the savory flavor of the herbs. Cover the salad and marinate in the refrigerator for at least 1 to 2 hours and as much as 24 hours.

4. When ready to serve, return to room temperature and toss gently.

6 portions

ROQUEFORT POTATO SALAD

New potatoes and Roquefort pair up for a dynamite combination—the pungency of the cheese enhancing the bland flavor of the potato.

1¹/₂ pounds new potatoes, cubed (unpeeled)

Roquefort Dressing:
1 large clove garlic, crushed
³/₄ teaspoon salt
freshly ground pepper to taste
2 tablespoons chopped fresh parsley
2 tablespoons red wine vinegar
1/3 cup olive oil
3 ounces Roquefort cheese, crumbled

1. Steam the potatoes until fork tender.

2. While the potatoes are cooking, prepare the dressing. In a small bowl, mix together the garlic, salt, pepper, parsley, vinegar, oil, and Roquefort until thick and creamy.

3. While the potatoes are still hot, pour the dressing over them and toss gently. Serve warm or at room temperature, whatever your preference.

6 portions

SWEET POTATO SALAD

Savory and delicious—julienned sweet potato fries adorn romaine, all dressed in a light sweet-sour vinaigrette. The orange potato fingers against the green lettuce make a splashy presentation.

1 head romaine, washed and cut into bite-size pieces
1 large sweet potato
1 tablespoon vegetable oil

Vinaigrette:
1 shallot, finely diced
1 teaspoon Dijon mustard
1 tablespoon honey
salt and pepper to taste
2 tablespoons red wine vinegar
1/3 cup olive oil

1. Heap the romaine in a large bowl.

2. Prepare the fries. Preheat the oven to 400°. Grease a cookie sheet. Peel the sweet potato and cut into thin julienne pieces. Place on the prepared baking sheet, brush with the vegetable oil, and season with salt and pepper. Bake for 20 to 25 minutes.

3. While the fries are baking, make the dressing. In a small bowl, mix the shallot, mustard, honey, salt, pepper, and vinegar. Whisk in the oil. (Up to this point may be prepared several hours in advance.)

4. Adorn the romaine with the sweet potato fries. Drizzle the vinaigrette over all, toss well, and serve.

6 portions

GREENBEANS, WALNUTS, AND SUN-DRIED TOMATOES

Fruits, nuts, and vegetables all in one! A vibrant salad of chopped walnuts, steamed greenbeans, and sun-dried tomatoes in a Dijon-garlic vinaigrette. The sun-dried tomatoes impart a rich flavor to this composition.

> *1 pound greenbeans, steamed for 5 minutes*
> *1 cup coarsely chopped walnuts, lightly toasted (see page 273)*
> *2/3 cup sun-dried tomatoes, cut in julienne pieces (see page 251)*

> ### Dijon Vinaigrette:
> *1/3 cup olive oil*
> *2 tablespoons red wine vinegar*
> *1 teaspoon Dijon mustard*
> *salt and freshly ground pepper to taste*
> *1 clove garlic, minced*
> *1 tablespoon chopped fresh parsley*

1. Place the greenbeans, walnuts, and tomatoes in a glass serving bowl.

2. Whisk together the oil, vinegar, mustard, salt, pepper, garlic, and parsley in a small bowl.

3. Pour the dressing over the vegetables and toss.

4. Chill and let marinate for at least 4 hours and up to 24 hours. Toss again before serving.

6 portions

ORIENTAL VEGETABLE SALAD

A fabulous colorful mixed vegetable salad dressed with a light sweet and sour ginger-soy dressing. It's sure to bring raves at any dinner.

2 heads red leaf lettuce, washed and torn into bite-size pieces
4 scallions, chopped
8 ounce can waterchestnuts, drained and sliced
1 large or 2 small red peppers, cut into 1-inch chunks
16 ounce can baby corn, drained

Sweet and Sour Dressing:
3 tablespoons soy sauce
1^1/$_2$ tablespoons sugar
2 tablespoons rice vinegar (available in Oriental markets)
^{1}/$_2$ tablespoon grated fresh gingerroot
^{1}/$_2$ cup vegetable oil

1. In a large salad bowl, heap the lettuce. Add the scallions, waterchestnuts, red pepper, and baby corn.

2. In a separate small bowl, whisk together the soy, sugar, vinegar, gingerroot, and oil until the ingredients are well mixed. Pour the dressing over the salad and serve.

8 portions

TABBOULI

A cracked wheat salad of Middle-Eastern origin with chopped tomatoes, scallions, parsley, and mint, enhanced by a hint of aromatic spices.

> 1 cup bulgur (cracked wheat)
> boiling water
> 3 medium-size tomatoes, diced
> 1 cup chopped scallions
>
> ### Parsley-Mint Vinaigrette:
> 1/2 cup olive oil
> 1/2 cup lemon juice
> salt to taste
> 1/2 teaspoon pepper
> 1 tablespoon dried mint
> 1/4 teaspoon each allspice, cinnamon, and nutmeg
> 2 cups finely chopped fresh parsley

1. Place the cracked wheat in a 2 quart mixing bowl and add enough boiling water to come 2 inches above the bulgur. Allow this to stand 1 hour, or until the bulgur is light and fluffy. Toss with a fork, and squeeze out any excess water.

2. Combine the bulgur, tomatoes, and scallions in a large serving bowl.

3. Briskly whisk together the oil, lemon juice, salt, pepper, mint, spices, and parsley. Pour the dressing over the cracked wheat salad and stir well.

4. Cover the salad and chill for at least 3 to 4 hours or overnight. This is actually better the next day, as the flavors have had a chance to mellow. Bring the salad to room temperature before serving.

6 to 8 portions

MEDITERRANEAN BULGUR

An exotic cracked wheat salad enhanced with the essence of fresh basil, spiked with sun-dried tomatoes and pine nuts, and sweetened slightly with raisins.

1 cup cracked wheat
boiling water
1/4 cup raisins
1/2 cup pine nuts, toasted (see page 273)
1 cup chopped sun-dried tomatoes (see page 251)
2 cups coarsely chopped, loosely packed fresh basil
salt and pepper to taste
1/4 cup lemon juice
1/4 cup olive oil
1/3 cup Parmesan cheese

1. Place the cracked wheat in a 2 quart mixing bowl and add enough boiling water to come 2 inches above the bulgur. Allow to stand 1 hour, or until bulgur is light and fluffy. Toss with a fork, and squeeze out any excess water.

2. Combine the bulgur, raisins, nuts, sun-dried tomatoes, and basil in a large bowl.

3. In a small bowl, whisk together the salt, pepper, lemon juice, oil, and Parmesan. Pour the vinaigrette over the cracked wheat salad and toss well.

4. Cover and chill at least 2 to 3 hours so flavors have a chance to mellow. Return to room temperature to serve.

6 to 8 portions

HEARTY SALADS

Hearty salads combine meats, chicken, fish, cheeses, or pasta with greens and selective fruits and vegetables creating a one-dish meal. Salads of this type are especially popular during warm summer months, but are really year-round pleasers! They offer a substantial meal of light cuisine.

THE B.L.T. SALAD

A layered salad of bacon, lettuce, tomato, hard-boiled egg, and cheddar cheese, finished with a curry mayonnaise.

1 head iceberg lettuce, shredded
1 cup chopped celery
4 hard-boiled eggs, chopped
2 medium tomatoes, chopped

Curry Mayonnaise:
1¼ cups mayonnaise
1 tablespoon curry powder
salt and freshly ground pepper to taste
2 teaspoons lemon juice

1 cup grated cheddar cheese
½ pound bacon, cooked and crumbled

1. In a large, deep glass bowl, make a base layer with the shredded lettuce.

2. Sprinkle the celery over the lettuce.

3. Top with the chopped egg, and cover with the chopped tomatoes.

4. Blend the mayonnaise with the curry powder, salt, pepper, and lemon juice. Spread the mixture evenly over the top of the vegetables.

5. Garnish the salad with the grated cheddar cheese and the crumbled bacon. Cover and refrigerate the salad for 24 hours. Do not toss at serving time; use large serving spoons to divide the salad into wedges.

8 to 10 portions

ANTIPASTO ROMANO

A salad fit for a king—roasted peppers, Italian meat, fish, cheese, and melon with assorted vegetables in a tangy, herbed marinade.

1 head red leaf lettuce
2 sweet Italian sausages, broiled and sliced into $1/4$-inch rounds
$1^1/2$ cups cantaloupe or honeydew melon, cut into 1-inch chunks, wrapped with prosciutto
2 ounce can anchovies, rolled with capers, drained
$3^3/4$ ounce can sardines, drained
$6^1/2$ ounce can tuna, drained
4 ounces provolone cheese, sliced into $1/4$-inch thick julienne pieces
$1^1/2$ cups canned cannelli beans, rinsed and drained
1 large red pepper, roasted, and cut into 1-inch wide strips (see page 243)
1 large green pepper, roasted, and cut into 1-inch wide strips (see page 243)
1 pint cherry tomatoes
2 large carrots, cut into rounds and steamed 5 minutes
12 Tuscan peppers
12 colossal ripe black olives
1 small red onion, thinly sliced into rings

Herbal Vinaigrette:
$1/4$ cup red wine vinegar
2 tablespoons dry red wine
1 to 2 cloves garlic, crushed
1 teaspoon dry mustard
1 teaspoon dried basil
1 teaspoon dried oregano
2 tablespoons chopped fresh parsley
$1/2$ teaspoon salt
$1/8$ teaspoon black pepper
$1/4$ cup Romano cheese
$2/3$ cup olive oil

1. Line a large platter with a layer of lettuce.

2. Attractively arrange the meat, fish, cheese, beans, and vegetables in mounds atop the bed of lettuce. Reserve the black olives and red onion for garnish. When setting up the antipasto, consider the colors

of the food. Try to balance the color scheme of the dish—put red peppers on one side, tomatoes on the other, beans and tuna opposite each other, etc.

3. Decorate the salad with the black olives and red onion.

4. Briskly whisk together the vinegar, red wine, garlic, herbs, spices and Romano cheese in a bowl. Continue to whisk, adding the oil in a slow, steady stream until the dressing is thick and creamy. Bathe the antipasto with the vinaigrette and serve at once.

8 generous portions

CHICKEN DIVINE

Cold poached chicken and artichoke hearts covered with Hollandaise sauce and garnished with almonds. Heavenly on a hot summer's night!

3 large whole chicken breasts
1 lemon, cut into quarters
salt and pepper to taste
3 sprigs parsley
14 ounce can artichoke hearts, drained and cut in half
Hollandaise Sauce (see page 11)
1/4 cup sliced almonds, toasted (see page 273)

1. Place the chicken in a saucepan with enough water to cover. Add the quartered lemon, and season with salt, pepper, and parsley. Bring to a boil, reduce heat, and poach until the flesh turns white. Remove the chicken from the broth and cool. Remove the skin and bones, and cut the meat into thin slices.

2. To serve, arrange the chicken slices in a single layer on a serving platter. Cover with the artichoke hearts and the Hollandaise sauce.

3. Garnish with the toasted almonds and present at once, or refrigerate for later use. If prepared ahead, return to room temperature before serving.

6 portions

CHICKEN WITH PESTO MAYONNAISE

A simple, yet tasty chicken salad—chicken, cherry tomatoes, and scallions, finished with a pesto mayonnaise.

2 pounds boneless chicken, poached and cut into 1/2-inch chunks
1/2 pint cherry tomatoes, sliced in half
3 scallions, thinly sliced
1/4 cup pine nuts, toasted (see page 273)
salt and pepper to taste
1 cup mayonnaise
3/4 cup pesto (see page 128)

1. In a large mixing bowl, combine the chicken, tomatoes, scallions, and pine nuts. Season with salt and pepper.

2. In a separate small bowl, mix together the mayonnaise and pesto until well blended.

3. Spoon the pesto sauce over the chicken and toss gently. Serve at once, or refrigerate until needed. Return to room temperature before presenting.

4 to 6 portions

GRILLED ORANGE CHICKEN SALAD

Grilling the chicken adds a marvelous barbecued flavor and dimension to the orange-marinated breasts. The salad is then punctuated with toasted almonds, mandarin oranges, and scallions. I often serve this at buffet parties, and no matter how much I prepare, it's never enough. For a real flavor sensation and a change of pace, try making this salad with swordfish—it's out of this world!

1/3 cup orange juice
1 tablespoon soy sauce
1/4 cup olive oil
1 teaspoon dried grated orange peel (Durkee's)
1 teaspoon dried rosemary
1 teaspoon mustard seeds
freshly ground pepper to taste
4 large boneless, skinless chicken breasts, split in half
2 (11 ounce) cans mandarin oranges, drained
1/2 cup chopped scallions
3/4 cup whole blanched almonds, toasted (see page 273)
1/2 cup mayonnaise

1. In a bowl, combine the orange juice, soy, oil, and seasonings. Mix well.

2. Pour the orange sauce over the breasts and marinate at least 1 hour and as much as overnight.

3. Grill the chicken over hot coals, 4 inches from the heat, about 4 to 5 minutes per side, basting with any extra marinade.

4. As the chicken is cooked, remove it to a pan and keep it covered until cooled. The chicken will exude its natural juices—this is the secret ingredient to the sauce. When the chicken has cooled, remove it from the pan, reserving the juices.

5. Cut the chicken into 3/4-inch chunks. Combine the chicken, orange segments, scallions, and almonds in a bowl.

6. Mix the mayonnaise with the reserved juices until smooth. Add the sauce to the salad and gently fold in until evenly distributed. Heap onto a bed of salad greens to present.

6 to 8 portions

ORIENTAL CHICKEN SALAD

Julienne of chicken and cucumber sauced in a ginger-soy marinade, garnished with chopped peanuts. A light, yet filling main-course salad, especially geared for those dog days of summer.

> 4 cups cooked chicken, cut into julienne strips
> 1¹/2 cups beansprouts
> 2 scallions, diced
> 1 medium cucumber, peeled, seeded, and coarsely grated

> ### Ginger-Soy Vinaigrette:
> 3 tablespoons soy sauce
> 2 teaspoons grated gingerroot
> 2 tablespoons rice vinegar (available in Oriental markets)
> ¹/2 cup oil

> 1 small head romaine lettuce, shredded
> 3 tablespoons chopped unsalted peanuts

1. Place the chicken, beansprouts, scallions, and cucumber in a glass bowl and mix.

2. In a separate bowl, whisk together the soy, gingerroot, vinegar, and oil. Pour the dressing over the chicken mixture, tossing well. Let marinate 1 to 2 hours.

3. When ready to serve, arrange the shredded romaine on a platter. Mound the chicken mixture onto the bed of lettuce.

4. Sprinkle with the chopped peanuts and serve.

5 to 6 main-course portions

WARM LIVER SALAD

Sautéed chicken livers in a warm vinaigrette, delicately flavored with shallots and chives. This is truly a very elegant dish, and an especially good meal opener.

1 head Boston lettuce
1 clove garlic, crushed
1 tablespoon finely chopped shallots
2 tablespoons snipped chives
2 tablespoons chopped fresh parsley
4 tablespoons butter
1/2 pound chicken livers, cut in half, sinews removed
salt and freshly ground pepper to taste
1/4 cup olive oil
1/4 cup red wine vinegar

1. Place 3 to 4 leaves of Boston lettuce on each of six salad plates.

2. Combine the garlic, shallots, chives, and parsley in a small bowl.

3. Heat the butter in a large skillet until hot. Add the livers, season with salt and pepper, and sauté about 3 to 4 minutes per side over high heat, or until the livers lose their redness and turn brown. Transfer them to a bowl with a slotted spoon, and cover to keep warm.

4. Quickly add the olive oil to the skillet, and when sizzling, add the bowl of herbs, shaking the skillet.

5. Add the vinegar and cook over high heat for 1 minute.

6. Pour the warm vinaigrette over the livers; spoon the livers and sauce atop the lettuce-lined plates and serve immediately.

6 portions

CARAWAY EGG SALAD

A creamy, zesty egg spread flavored with the nutty caraway seed and Parmesan cheese. It is especially delicious when teamed with black bread and served as an appetizer spread.

8 extra-large hard-boiled eggs, shelled
4 ounces cream cheese, at room temperature
1/4 cup sour cream
1/4 cup grated onion
2 tablespoons Parmesan cheese
1 teaspoon caraway seeds
pinch cayenne pepper
salt and freshly ground pepper to taste

1. Coarsely grate the eggs into a mixing bowl.

2. In a separate bowl, blend the cream cheese with the sour cream until the mixture is smooth.

3. Add the softened cream cheese to the eggs, along with the onion, Parmesan, caraway, and cayenne.

4. Season the egg mixture with salt and pepper and stir until well blended. Refrigerate overnight for flavors to mellow. Serve at room temperature.

6 portions

HERRING SALAD

A creamy salad of marinated herring and chopped vegetables, seasoned with dill.

16 ounce jar herring pieces in wine, well drained
1 cup sour cream
1/2 red onion, thinly sliced
1 tomato, diced
1/2 cucumber, peeled and diced
1/2 green pepper, diced
1/2 teaspoon dried dill
freshly ground pepper to taste
romaine lettuce

1. Combine the herring, sour cream, vegetables, and seasonings and blend well. Cover and refrigerate for at least 4 hours, and as much as overnight.

2. When ready to serve, line salad plates with the romaine.

3. Toss the herring mixture. Scoop spoonfuls onto the lettuce and serve with slices of black bread.

4 portions

FEZ'S GREEK SALAD

Typically Greek in composition, showcasing tomato, feta cheese, red onion, and black olives, all covered with a mint-flavored vinaigrette. There is no need to add salt to the dressing, since the olives and feta provide the characteristically salty taste.

1 large head iceberg lettuce
2 medium-size tomatoes, cut into chunks
1/2 cucumber, peeled and sliced
1/2 medium-size red onion, sliced
6 to 8 radishes, sliced
1/2 large green pepper, sliced
12 Kalamata black olives
6 ounces feta cheese

Vinaigrette:
1/2 cup olive oil
2 tablespoons lemon juice
3 tablespoons chopped fresh parsley
1 teaspoon dried mint
1/4 teaspoon freshly ground black pepper

1 medium-size round of pita bread, toasted and broken into bite-size
    pieces

1. Heap the lettuce into a large salad bowl. Add the vegetables to the bowl and garnish with the black olives. Crumble the feta over the top.

2. Whisk together the olive oil, lemon juice, and seasonings in a small bowl. Pour the dressing over the salad. Adorn the salad with the toasted pita bread. Toss gently but thoroughly, and serve.

6 to 8 portions

TARRAGON CRABMEAT SALAD

A light, yet hearty composition—this dish features crabmeat, hard-boiled egg, and chopped vegetables piquantly seasoned with a tarragon-mustard vinaigrette.

4 cups shredded romaine lettuce
1 cup chopped tomato
1 ripe avocado, peeled, pit removed, and diced
1 cup diced celery
1 cup coarsely grated carrots
1 cup coarsely grated radish
1 cup diced cucumber
1 cup diced green pepper
1 cup chopped ripe black olives
3 hard-boiled eggs, chopped
3/4 pound crabmeat, shredded

Tarragon-Mustard Vinaigrette:
1 tablespoon Dijon mustard
salt and freshly ground pepper to taste
1 tablespoon capers
2 tablespoons tarragon vinegar
1 teaspoon dried tarragon
1/2 cup olive oil

1. On a serving platter, make a base layer with the shredded lettuce.

2. Arrange the chopped vegetables, eggs, and crabmeat in separate mounds atop the lettuce. (Place the crabmeat in the center and surround it with the other accompaniments.)

3. In a small bowl, whisk together the Dijon, salt, pepper, capers, vinegar, and tarragon. Add the oil in a slow stream, beating until incorporated.

4. Pour the dressing over the salad and serve.

4 to 6 main-course portions

SCALLOPS NICOISE

The unique sweet and delicate nature of scallops makes this a dazzling dish. Poached scallops are topped with a chopped plum and sun-dried tomato sauce; a garnish of pine nuts, black olives, and capers is highlighted by orange essence. It's outrageous!

1¹/₂ pounds scallops, poached 2 minutes
salt and freshly ground pepper to taste
2 cups chopped plum tomatoes
6 sun-dried tomatoes, coarsely chopped
¹/₄ cup pine nuts, toasted (see page 273)
¹/₂ cup ripe black olives, sliced
1¹/₂ tablespoons capers
1 tablespoon finely grated orange peel
¹/₄ cup chopped fresh parsley
1 clove garlic, crushed
1 tablespoon balsamic vinegar
2 tablespoons olive oil

1. Place the poached scallops in a large bowl. Season with salt and pepper.

2. Add the chopped tomatoes, sun-dried tomatoes, pine nuts, black olives, and capers.

3. In a separate small bowl, combine the orange peel, parsley, garlic, vinegar, and oil. Pour the vinaigrette over the scallop mixture and toss to blend. Serve at once or refrigerate for later use. Return to room temperature to present.

4 portions

GRILLED SHRIMP AND RED GRAPES

The grilled flavor of the shrimp, along with the complementary tastes and textures of bacon and red grapes, gives a refreshing lift to this extraordinary salad.

1¹/₂ pounds large-size raw shrimp, peeled
2 tablespoons vegetable oil
salt and freshly ground pepper to taste
4 slices bacon, cooked and cut into ¹/₂-inch pieces
1¹/₂ cups seedless red grapes
1 cup whole pecans, toasted (see page 273)
¹/₂ cup mayonnaise

1. Skewer the shrimp and brush them with oil. Season with the salt and pepper. Cook over a hot grill, 2 to 3 minutes per side, just until pink.

2. Combine the shrimp, bacon, grapes, and pecans in a large serving bowl.

3. Add the mayonnaise and toss gently. Serve at once or refrigerate until needed. Return to room temperature before serving.

6 portions

BLUSHING SHRIMP AND PASTA SALAD

A spicy grilled shrimp and pasta medley accented by roasted red peppers, peaches, and pecans. I like adding summer fruits to salads as a refreshing and surprise ingredient. Easy to prepare and a real palate dazzler.

> 1¹/₂ pounds large-size raw shrimp, peeled
> 1 teaspoon dried thyme
> 1 tablespoon Worcestershire sauce
> ¹/₄ teaspoon cayenne pepper
> ¹/₄ teaspoon black pepper
> 1 large clove garlic, crushed
> ¹/₂ cup olive oil
> 1 pound fusilli
> 2 medium-size red peppers, roasted and cut into ¹/₂-inch wide strips
>   (see page 243)
> 2 large peaches or nectarines, sliced into wedges
> ¹/₂ cup pecans, toasted (see page 273)

1. Place the shrimp in a bowl.

2. In a separate bowl, whisk together the thyme, Worcestershire, cayenne, black pepper, garlic, and olive oil. Pour the marinade over the shrimp and let sit for 30 minutes.

3. While the shrimp are marinating, cook the pasta according to package direction. Drain well and place in a large bowl.

4. Remove the shrimp from the marinade, reserving the sauce, and thread the shellfish on skewers. Either grill or broil the shrimp, 4 inches from the heat source, for 2 to 3 minutes per side. Remove from the skewers and add to the pasta.

5. Add the peaches and pecans to the salad and dress with the reserved marinade. Toss thoroughly. Present at once or refrigerate until needed. Return to room temperature to serve.

6 to 8 portions

TORTELLINI SALAD

A trio of cheese-filled pastas accented by Mediterranean ingredients—artichoke hearts, black olives, and sun-dried tomatoes in an oregano-scented balsamic vinaigrette. This is a standard buffet party dish in our house.

10 ounce package fresh cheese-filled egg tortellini
10 ounce package fresh cheese-filled spinach tortellini
10 ounce package fresh cheese-filled hot pepper tortellini
2 (14 ounce) cans artichoke hearts, drained and quartered
1 large can (drained weight 6 ounces) pitted, small, ripe black olives, drained
1 cup coarsely chopped sun-dried tomatoes (see page 251)
1/3 cup pine nuts, toasted (see page 273)

Vinaigrette:
1 tablespoon Dijon mustard
1 1/2 teaspoons dried oregano
lots of freshly ground black pepper (I use 1/8 to 1/4 teaspoon.)
3 tablespoons balsamic vinegar
3/4 cup olive oil

1. Cook the tortellini according to package directions. Drain well.

2. In a large bowl, combine the cooked pasta, artichoke hearts, black olives, sun-dried tomatoes, and pine nuts.

3. In a small bowl, whisk together the dressing ingredients. Pour the vinaigrette over the warm pasta and toss well. Serve at room temperature. (This may be prepared up to 24 hours in advance and refrigerated until needed. Return to room temperature to present.)

10 to 12 portions

ITALIAN PASTA SALAD

A flavorful, hearty repast featuring pasta, sweet Italian sausage, roasted peppers, and provolone cheese bathed in a zesty vinaigrette.

1/2 pound elbow macaroni

1/2 pound sweet Italian sausage, broiled, and sliced into 1/4-inch thick rounds

2 large green peppers, roasted and sliced into 1/2-inch wide strips (see page 243)

1/3 pound provolone cheese, coarsely grated

1 small red onion, diced

Dressing:

3/4 cup olive oil

3 tablespoons red wine vinegar

1 clove garlic, crushed

3 tablespoons chopped fresh parsley

salt and freshly ground pepper to taste

1. In a large pot of boiling salted water, cook the elbows according to the package directions. Place in a colander to drain.

2. Combine the sausages, roasted peppers, provolone, red onion, and cooked pasta in a large serving bowl.

3. In a small bowl, whisk together the oil, vinegar, garlic, parsley, salt, and pepper.

4. Pour the dressing over the pasta mixture and toss gently. Serve at room temperature. This will keep for 3 to 4 days in the refrigerator.

6 to 8 main-course portions

PASTA, CAESAR, AND SHRIMP SALAD

Acomplete meal in one, incorporating some special favorites—pasta, Caesar salad, and shrimp. Cool food for hot weather.

3 slices (3/4-inch thick) sour dough or French bread
1 to 2 tablespoons olive oil
freshly ground black pepper
1 pound fusilli, cooked
1 large head romaine, shredded into 1/4-inch wide strips
11/2 pounds medium-size shrimp, cooked
2 ounce tin anchovies, rinsed, drained, and coarsely chopped

Dressing:
1 teaspoon dry mustard
1 large or 2 small cloves garlic, smashed
1/4 teaspoon salt
1/8 teaspoon black pepper
1/3 cup lemon juice
1 cup olive oil
6 ounces freshly shredded Parmesan cheese

1. Preheat the oven to 350°.

2. Prepare the croutons. Brush the bread slices with 1 to 2 tablespoons olive oil. Sprinkle generously with black pepper. Place on a baking sheet and bake for 20 minutes until golden. Remove, cut into 3/4-inch cubes, and let cool.

3. In a large bowl, heap the pasta, romaine, shrimp, and anchovies.

4. In a small bowl, whisk together the dressing ingredients until well combined.

5. Pour the vinaigrette over the salad and mix thoroughly. Add the croutons and toss to blend. Serve at once.

8 portions

TUNA SALAD

Canned tuna never tasted so good! Tuna sauced in a Dijon-balsamic vinaigrette, piquantly spiked with capers. When the hot weather strikes, I double the amount of dressing and combine it with a pound of cooked pasta for light summer dining.

2 (13 ounce) cans tuna, packed in water, drained
3 scallions, cut into 1/4-inch thick slices

Dressing:
2 teaspoons Dijon mustard
1 teaspoon dried oregano
freshly ground black pepper to taste
3 tablespoons balsamic vinegar
2/3 cup olive oil
2 tablespoons capers

1. In a bowl, break up the tuna with a fork. Mix in the scallions.

2. In a separate bowl, whisk together the dressing ingredients. Pour over the tuna mixture and mix well. Let marinate 2 to 3 hours for the tuna to absorb the flavors of the vinaigrette. Present at room temperature on a bed of lettuce or with slices of sour dough bread to make sandwiches. (This will keep 2 to 3 days under refrigeration, if it lasts that long!)

4 to 6 portions

MEDITERRANEAN RICE SALAD

A cold rice salad featuring a medley of vegetables—artichoke hearts, black olives, and roasted red peppers with pine nuts, all highlighted by a goat cheese dressing.

> 2 cups raw long-grain white rice
> 14 ounce can artichoke hearts, drained and cut in half
> 1 large or 2 small red peppers, roasted and chopped (see page 243)
> 1/4 cup toasted pine nuts (see page 273)
> 3/4 cup sliced ripe black olives
> 1/2 cup olive oil
> 1 large clove garlic, crushed
> 3 tablespoons chopped fresh parsley
> freshly ground pepper to taste
> 3 ounces goat cheese, crumbled

1. Cook the rice according to the package directions.

2. Add the artichoke hearts, roasted pepper, pine nuts, and black olives to the cooked rice.

3. In a separate bowl, combine the olive oil, garlic, parsley, pepper, and goat cheese. Mix well and pour over the rice medley. Stir until evenly distributed and present. (May be refrigerated for later use—return to room temperature to serve.)

8 to 10 portions

SALMON, TOMATOES, AND SCALLIONS

A colorful mélange of cold, poached salmon chunks, chopped tomatoes, and scallions.

1 head romaine, shredded
1 bunch watercress, washed, and stems trimmed
1 pound salmon, poached and broken into chunks
4 medium-size tomatoes, coarsely chopped
1 bunch scallions, chopped (approximately 1/2 cup)

Raspberry Vinaigrette:
3/4 cup olive oil
1/4 cup raspberry wine vinegar
salt and freshly ground pepper to taste

1. Toss the romaine and watercress together and arrange the greens on a platter.

2. Combine the salmon, tomatoes, and scallions in a bowl; mix gently so as not to break up the chunks of fish. Heap the salmon mixture onto the bed of greens.

3. Combine the oil, vinegar, salt, and pepper and whisk together vigorously. Pour the vinaigrette over the salad and serve.

3 to 4 portions

SALAD NICOISE

The classic French cold potato, tuna, green bean, tomato, olive, egg, and artichoke salad with an herbal vinaigrette. A lot of preparation, but well-worth the effort, as this salad always receives raves.

2 heads Boston lettuce
13 ounce can tuna, drained and flaked
5 medium-size new potatoes, steamed with the peel, and cut into $1/4$-inch
　　thick slices
$1^1/2$ pounds green beans, steamed 5 minutes
1 pint cherry tomatoes
14 ounce can artichoke hearts, drained and cut in half
2 cups sliced celery
2 green peppers, sliced into rings
2 ounce can anchovy fillets, rinsed and drained
6 hard-boiled eggs, sliced in half
$1/2$ cup imported black olives
$1/4$ cup sliced scallions
2 tablespoons capers
1 medium-size red onion, thinly sliced and separated into rings

Herbal Vinaigrette:
4 teaspoons Dijon mustard
$1/4$ cup red wine vinegar
salt to taste (I use about $1/2$ teaspoon.)
$1/4$ teaspoon black pepper
2 cloves garlic, crushed
1 teaspoon dried thyme
2 teaspoons dried basil
$2/3$ cup chopped fresh parsley
$1^1/2$ cups olive oil

1. Make a bed of lettuce on a large circular platter.

2. Arrange the tuna, potatoes, beans, tomatoes, artichoke hearts, celery, peppers, anchovies, eggs, and olives in separate mounds atop the greenery.

3. Garnish the salad with the scallions, capers, and red onion rings.

4. Whisk together the dressing ingredients until thick and creamy.

5. Pour the vinaigrette over the salad and present.

8 to 10 side portions; 6 to 8 main-course portions

ORIENTAL STEAK SALAD

We are not meat eaters, but my family craves this salad from time to time. Cooked julienned beef presented in a soy and sesame vinaigrette. This is a great way to use leftover meat.

3 cups broiled, grilled, or roasted beef (done rare to medium-rare),
    julienned
1 large red pepper, cut into 1/2-inch chunks
2/3 cup sliced waterchestnuts
2 scallions, finely chopped

Sesame-Soy Vinaigrette:
1/2 cup vegetable oil
2 tablespoons white wine vinegar
1 teaspoon Dijon mustard
1 clove garlic, smashed
1 tablespoon soy sauce
freshly ground pepper to taste
1 teaspoon Oriental sesame oil (available in Oriental markets)
2 tablespoons sesame seeds, toasted in a 350° oven until golden, about
    5 minutes

shredded lettuce

1. Combine the beef, red pepper, waterchestnuts, and scallions in a mixing bowl.

2. Whisk together the oil, vinegar, Dijon, garlic, soy, pepper, sesame oil, and sesame seeds until blended.

3. Pour the vinaigrette over the salad and toss well. (The salad may be made several hours in advance to this stage and refrigerated. Return to room temperature to serve.)

4. Arrange the salad atop a bed of shredded lettuce, pouring the dressing over all, and serve.

4 portions

THE FINISHING TOUCH

What better way to crown a glorious meal than with something sweet! Desserts are as varied as tastes. Choices may include something light and refreshing in the form of fruit, a luscious mousse, a heavenly cake, a bowl of ice cream garnished with a crispy wafer, or a decadent chocolate torte. Whatever you decide to serve, make it complement the rest of the meal. Do not serve a fruit dessert if you have presented melon wedges as an appetizer; cheesecake is an overindulgence if the meal began with cheese and crackers. Make the dessert dazzle. Present it with a special garnish such as grated chocolate, chopped nuts, or even a fresh flower. A person will always look forward to something sweet if it is appealing, regardless of how much he has eaten! Desserts should be fanciful; they are the stuff dreams are made of.

A special reminder—use extra-large eggs when baking!

MOUSSES, FRUITS, AND ICED MAGIC

CRANBERRY MOUSSE

A refreshingly light and tart cranberry custard.

1 envelope unflavored gelatin
2 tablespoons cold water
1/4 cup boiling water
2 cups fresh cranberries
1/4 cup water
1/4 cup cranberry liqueur
1 cup sugar
1 1/2 cups heavy cream

1. In a small bowl, soften the gelatin in the cold water and let sit for 10 minutes. Stir in the boiling water and mix until the gelatin dissolves. Set aside to cool to room temperature.

2. Combine the cranberries, 1/4 cup water, and cranberry liqueur in a medium saucepan. Bring the mixture to a boil, cover, reduce heat, and simmer for 5 minutes.

3. Press the cooked berries and the juice through a sieve, discarding the skins. Add the sugar and the dissolved gelatin to the berry purée and mix well. Set aside to cool.

4. Whip the cream until soft peaks form. Fold gently into the cooled cranberry mixture and turn the mousse into 6 to 8 individual custard cups. Chill for 4 hours until set and ready to serve.

6 to 8 portions

LEMON MOUSSE

A refreshing and delicate lemony dessert, presented in hollowed-out lemons.

1 envelope unflavored gelatin
2 tablespoons cold water
1/4 cup lemon juice
6 eggs, separated
3/4 cup sugar
1/8 teaspoon salt
1 teaspoon finely grated lemon peel
1 cup heavy cream
8 hollowed-out large lemons

1. Sprinkle the unflavored gelatin over the cold water and let sit for 10 minutes. Heat the gelatin mixture with the lemon juice and bring to a boil, stirring until the gelatin is dissolved. Cool to room temperature.

2. Beat the egg yolks and the sugar until they are thick and pale yellow in color. Add the salt, lemon peel, and the cooled gelatin to the egg mixture and stir until well blended.

3. Beat the egg whites with an electric mixer to stiff peaks.

4. In a separate bowl, whip the heavy cream until soft peaks form.

5. Gently fold the egg whites and whipped cream into the lemon mixture.

6. Slice the point off of the bottom of the lemons so that they stand flat.

7. Spoon the mousse into the hollowed-out lemons and chill for at least 4 hours or even overnight until firm. (Sit the lemons in a muffin pan so they stand upright.)

8 portions

FRUITS MIDORI

A potpourri of vivid summer fruits macerated in melon-flavored liqueur. Absolutely heavenly! Use ripe fruit to ensure peak flavor.

1 pint strawberries, hulled
1 pineapple, trimmed, cored, quartered, and cut into ¹/₂-inch thick slices
3 kiwis, peeled and cut into ¹/₄-inch thick slices
1 cantaloupe, cut into 1-inch chunks
1 honeydew melon, cut into 1-inch chunks
¹/₂ to ³/₄ cup Midori liqueur

1. Heap the fruits into a large bowl.
2. Drizzle the Midori generously over the fruit and let marinate at least 1 to 2 hours (and as much as 6 hours) in the refrigerator. Serve chilled.

6 to 8 portions

MACEDOINE OF STRAWBERRIES

Whole strawberries splashed with an orange-sherry sauce. A large bowl of berries at a buffet table makes an impressive presentation.

1 quart strawberries
1/2 cup cream sherry
1/2 cup orange juice
2 to 4 tablespoons sugar (amount depends on the sweetness of the berries)

1. Wash and hull the berries and heap them into a large glass bowl.

2. Combine the cream sherry, orange juice, and sugar and mix well. Pour the orange sauce over the berries and marinate at least 3 to 4 hours or overnight in the refrigerator, stirring occasionally. To serve, toss gently and present.

6 portions

HEAVENLY STRAWBERRIES ADORNED

Strawberries enveloped in a brown sugar and ginger sour cream. This is equally as good with red and green seedless grapes.

1 pint strawberries
¹/2 cup sour cream
¹/4 cup light brown sugar
¹/2 teaspoon ground ginger

1. Wash and hull the berries, and pile them into a glass bowl.

2. Combine the sour cream, brown sugar, and ginger and blend well. Blanket the strawberries with the sauce. Serve at once or refrigerate until needed.

3 to 4 portions

MIXED BERRIES FRAMBOISE

A splashy mélange of summer berries covered in a raspberry cream.

6 cups of berries—blueberries, raspberries, and blackberries
1 cup all-purpose whipping cream
2 tablespoons confectioners' sugar
2 tablespoons lemon juice
1 teaspoon finely grated lemon peel
2 tablespoons raspberry preserves

1. Wash and dry the berries and heap them into a glass bowl.

2. In the bowl of an electric mixer, whip the cream until thick. Add the sugar, lemon juice, lemon peel, and raspberry preserves and continue to beat until stiff peaks form. Smother the berries in the raspberry cream and present.

6 to 8 portions

CRANBERRY ICE

Delicately refreshing! A good sorbet to accompany the Thanksgiving feast.

> 2 cups cranberries
> 1 cup water
> 1 cup sugar
> 1/2 cup cranberry liqueur
> 2 tablespoons lemon juice

1. Combine the cranberries and water in a medium-size saucepan. Bring the mixture to a boil, then lower the heat and simmer for 10 minutes. Drain well.

2. Purée the berries in a food mill or press them through a sieve and cool.

3. Add the sugar, cranberry liqueur, and lemon juice to the puréed berries. Pour the mixture into a container and freeze.

4. The ice will get quite hard. When you are ready to serve, remove the ice from the freezer for 20 to 30 minutes before scooping into individual bowls.

6 portions

LEMON ICE

A light and sparkling, smooth and creamy lemon sorbet dotted with candied ginger.

    2 cups lemonade
    1 cup light corn syrup
    1 teaspoon grated lemon peel
    1 tablespoon minced candied ginger

1. Combine all of the ingredients and mix well.

2. Process the mixture in an ice cream maker according to manufacturer's directions.

3. Serve at once or store in the freezer for later use.

6 portions

APRICOT FREEZE

A creamy, cool, and uplifting apricot sorbet distinguished by Amaretto liqueur and adorned with a sprinkling of toasted almonds.

> *2 cups apricot nectar*
> *1 cup light corn syrup*
> *1 teaspoon lemon juice*
> *¼ cup Amaretto*
> *2 tablespoons slivered almonds, toasted (see page 273)*

1. Combine the apricot nectar, corn syrup, lemon juice, and Amaretto and mix well.

2. Process in an ice cream maker according to manufacturer's directions.

3. When smooth and creamy, serve immediately, sprinkling each portion with toasted almonds. Any leftover sorbet may be stored in the freezer for later use.

4 to 6 portions

ORANGE FREEZE

A smooth, velvety, and definitely refreshing orange ice, made with freshly squeezed orange juice. Its creamy texture makes you think you're eating rich ice cream.

2 cups freshly squeezed orange juice with pulp
finely grated peel of a large orange
1 cup light corn syrup
1 teaspoon vanilla

1. Mix all of the ingredients together. Process in an ice cream maker according to manufacturer's directions. Serve at once.

2. Any extra ice may be frozen for later use.

4 portions

NOTATIONS

STRAWBERRY ICE CREAM

Old-fashioned goodness—homemade ice cream featuring a strawberries and cream theme. This version is not excessively rich, but is smooth and creamy and bursting with flavor.

1 pint half and half
1/2 cup sugar
1 teaspoon vanilla
pinch salt
10 ounce package frozen strawberries with syrup, puréed

1. Combine all of the ingredients and mix well.

2. Pour the mixture into an ice cream maker and process according to manufacturer's directions.

3. Enjoy the freshly churned ice cream; any leftover may be frozen for later use.

4 portions

DELECTABLE ICE CREAM MIX-INS

Ice cream has been an American classic since Colonial times. Now with the advent of ice cream machines, homemade varieties of this frozen delight—and its contemporary counterpart, frozen yogurt—have reached new heights. Especially popular, soft-serve frozen yogurt has swept America by storm. When you're in the mood for something simple, yet unusual for dessert, try a bowl of ice cream or frozen yogurt with a creative touch!

Try one at a time, or be daring and try several mix-ins together!

1. Favorite preserves rippled into vanilla ice cream; ginger preserves are especially refreshing.

2. Crushed oatmeal, oreo, vanilla creme sandwich, or any favorite cookie.

3. Berries and cut up fruits—blueberries, raspberries, strawberries, bananas, peaches, apricots, pineapple, or cherries.

4. Chocolate chips, butterscotch chips, or peanut butter chips.

5. Peanut butter rippled into vanilla or chocolate ice cream.

6. Granola and toasted coconut.

7. Raisins and chopped nuts—macadamias, pecans, pistachios, almonds, or unsalted peanuts.

8. M & M's, Reese's Pieces, or favorite chopped candy bars—Heath Bars, Peppermint Patties, Nestle's Crunch, Snickers, or white chocolate.

9. Chocolate covered peanuts and raisins.

10. Mini-marshmallows.

11. Applesauce with cinnamon and sugar mixed into vanilla ice cream.

12. Real maple syrup swirled into coffee ice cream.

13. Fudge, caramel, or butterscotch sauce.

14. Liqueurs drizzled into vanilla, chocolate, or coffee ice cream—Crème de Menthe, Crème de Cacao, Kahlua, Grand Marnier.

15. Crumbled brownie chunks.

16. Chocolate mousse.

17. Chopped candied orange peel mixed into vanilla or chocolate ice cream.

PASTRIES PLUS

ALMOND RUSKS

This is also known as German Mandelbrot, which is hard, dry, and crunchy!

3/4 cup vegetable oil
1 cup sugar
3 eggs
3 cups all-purpose flour
2 teaspoons baking powder
1/8 teaspoon salt
1 teaspoon vanilla extract
1 teaspoon almond extract
1 cup coarsely chopped blanched almonds
1 cup sweetened, shredded coconut
cinnamon-sugar mixture for topping

1. Preheat the oven to 375°. Grease two large cookie sheets.

2. Mix the oil and sugar in a bowl. Add the eggs and beat well. Stir in the flour, baking powder, salt, and extracts.

3. Add the almonds and coconut and mix thoroughly.

4. Divide the dough into fourths. Shape each section into a long roll approximately 2¹/₂-inches wide. Place 5 inches apart on the prepared cookie sheets. Bake for 18 to 20 minutes. Remove from the oven.

5. Slice each strip into ³/₄-inch wide pieces. Separate the pieces so that they do no touch. Sprinkle generously with the cinnamon-sugar mixture, and return the sheets to the oven for 5 to 10 minutes more until the rusks are crunchy. Transfer to racks to cool.

Approximately 4 dozen rusks

ALMOND SHORTBREADS

Almond cake squares crowned with a topping of sugared almond slices.

> 1/2 *cup butter, melted*
> 1 *cup sugar*
> 2 *eggs*
> 1 *cup all-purpose flour*
> 1 *teaspoon almond extract*
> 2/3 *cup sliced almonds*
> 1 *to 2 tablespoons sugar for topping*

1. Preheat the oven to 325°. Generously grease a 9-inch square baking pan.

2. In a bowl, beat together the melted butter and 1 cup sugar. Add the eggs, one at a time, beating well after each addition until batter is light and fluffy. Blend in the flour and almond extract.

3. Pour the batter into the prepared pan. Coat the top with the almond slices. Sprinkle generously with 1 to 2 tablespoons sugar.

4. Bake for 25 to 30 minutes. The cake should be slightly moist. Remove to a rack to cool completely before cutting.

9 large shortbreads

JAM BUTTONS

Buttery thumbprint cookies with a raspberry center. These are a special favorite of my daughter.

> 1 cup unsalted butter
> 1 cup sugar
> 1/2 teaspoon salt
> 2 teaspoons vanilla extract
> 2 egg yolks
> 2 2/3 cups all-purpose flour
> raspberry preserves

1. Preheat the oven to 350°.

2. Cream the butter and sugar together until light and fluffy. Beat in the salt, vanilla, and egg yolks. Add the flour and work evenly into the batter.

3. Using approximately 1 tablespoon of dough, roll into balls. Impress each ball with your thumb, making a deep imprint in the middle of each cookie. Fill the centers with 1/4 teaspoon of jam.

4. Place the cookies on ungreased cookie sheets, and bake for 15 minutes, or until lightly golden. Remove to racks to cool.

4 dozen cookies

BLONDIES

Light and cakelike, butterscotch flavored bars chock full of macadamia nuts.

1/2 cup butter
1 1/4 cups light brown sugar, firmly packed
2 eggs
1 teaspoon vanilla extract
1 cup all-purpose flour
1 teaspoon baking powder
1/2 teaspoon salt
1 cup coarsely chopped macadamia nuts

1. Preheat the oven to 350°. Grease a 9-inch square baking pan.

2. Cream the butter with the sugar until light and fluffy. Add the eggs and vanilla, and beat well.

3. Sift together the dry ingredients and add these to the batter; blend thoroughly. Fold in the chopped nuts.

4. Turn the batter into the prepared pan. Bake for 25 minutes. Remove to a rack to cool completely before cutting into squares.

25 squares

LINZER TEA SQUARES

Modeled after the famous torte—a rich and delicious crunchy short-bread base covered with raspberry preserves and sliced almonds.

Pastry:
1/2 cup butter
1/2 cup sugar
1 teaspoon cinnamon
1 cup flour

Topping:
1 cup raspberry preserves
1/2 cup sliced almonds

confectioners' sugar

1. Preheat the oven to 350°. Generously grease the bottom and sides of a 9-inch square pan.

2. In a bowl, cream the butter and sugar. Add the cinnamon and flour and mix well.

3. Pat the dough into the pan.

4. Spread the preserves evenly over the pastry. Sprinkle the almonds over the layer of jam.

5. Bake for 50 minutes. Remove the pan to a rack to cool. While warm, run a knife around the edges to release the jam from sticking to the pan. When cool, dust the top with confectioners' sugar. Cut into squares and serve.

20 squares

GLAZED VIENNESE CRESCENTS

Horns of cream cheese pastry filled with apricot preserves and glazed with a sugary icing.

Dough:
1 cup butter
1/2 pound cream cheese, at room temperature
1 tablespoon sugar
2 egg yolks, beaten
2 cups sifted cake flour

1. Cream the butter, cream cheese, and sugar together until fluffy. Add the egg yolks.

2. Gradually work in the flour. When the dough is smooth, divide it into four equal parts. Form each piece into a ball and wrap each ball with plastic wrap.

3. Refrigerate the dough overnight.

Filling:
1/4 cup sugar mixed with 1 teaspoon cinnamon
apricot preserves

1. When you are ready to bake the crescents, preheat the oven to 350°. Grease two cookie sheets generously.

2. Place one ball of dough on a floured pastry board. Roll the ball out into a 12-inch circle (it is all right if the edges are not perfect). Keep the remaining dough in the refrigerator until ready to use.

3. Sprinkle 1/4 of the cinnamon-sugar mixture over the circle of dough.

4. With a sharp knife, cut the dough into 8 pie-shaped wedges. Place a scant teaspoon of preserves on the outer edge of each of the wedges.

5. Carefully roll each wedge jelly-roll fashion from the outside towards the center point. Place each crescent point-side down on the prepared cookie sheets. Repeat with the remaining dough and filling.

6. Bake for 18 to 20 minutes. When the pastry comes out of the oven, paint the glaze over the crescents while they are still warm. Then remove the pastry to racks to cool.

Glaze:

2 cups confectioners' sugar
2 to 3 tablespoons boiling water

1. Combine the confectioners' sugar with the boiling water, stirring until smooth and creamy.

2. Use the icing immediately, as it hardens upon standing. If you make the crescents in two batches, make only 1/2 the amount of glaze at one time; for 16 crescents, combine 1 cup of confectioners' sugar with 1 to 1 1/2 tablespoons of boiling water.

32 crescents

GINGER CRISPS

Large, crunchy, and chewy old-fashioned gingersnaps.

3/4 cup butter, melted
1 cup sugar
1/4 cup molasses
1 egg, beaten
2 cups all-purpose flour
2 teaspoons baking soda
1/2 teaspoon salt
1 teaspoon cinnamon
1/2 teaspoon ground cloves
1 teaspoon ground ginger
sugar for topping

1. Add 1 cup of sugar and molasses to the butter, and mix well. Add the egg to the butter mixture, beating until smooth and thick.

2. Sift together the flour, baking soda, salt, and spices. Add the dry ingredients to the batter and blend thoroughly. Cover and chill the dough 2 hours, or as much as overnight.

3. Preheat the oven to 350°. Line two cookie sheets with foil.

4. Remove the chilled dough from the refrigerator. Form it into small balls, using 1 tablespoon of dough for each cookie. Dip each ball in the sugar, coating only one side, and place sugared side up at least 2 inches apart on the prepared baking sheets. Dipping the dough into the sugar gives the cookies a crisp topping.

5. Bake 10 to 12 minutes until the cookies are a dark, golden brown. While baking, these cookies will first puff up, and then flatten. They are not baked until they have flattened. Remove from the oven and let cool about 2 minutes on the baking sheets before removing to a wire rack to cool completely.

3 dozen crisps

LEMON NUT COOKIES

Dainty, buttery, and crunchy lemon cookies. A perfect tea-time snack.

1 cup unsalted butter
3/4 cup confectioners' sugar
1 tablespoon finely grated lemon peel
2 cups all-purpose flour
1/2 cup finely ground walnuts
additional confectioners' sugar for garnish

1. Preheat the oven to 350°.

2. Cream the butter and sugar together until fluffy. Stir in the lemon peel. Add the flour and mix thoroughly. Mix in the ground walnuts.

3. Form the dough into 3/4-inch balls. Place the balls on ungreased cookie sheets and flatten them to form circles about 1 1/2 inches in diameter.

4. Bake for 8 to 10 minutes or until the cookies are just lightly brown around the edges. Remove to racks. While still warm, dust the cookies generously with confectioners' sugar; let cool.

Approximately 4 dozen cookies

MACAROON WAFERS

NOTATIONS

Chewy almond-flavored coconut thins.

1/2 cup butter
1 cup sugar
1 egg
1 teaspoon almond extract
1/8 teaspoon salt
1/2 cup all-purpose flour
1 cup sweetened, flaked coconut

1. Preheat the oven to 350°. Grease two cookie sheets.

2. Cream the butter with the sugar until light and fluffy. Add the egg, extract, and salt and mix well. Stir in the flour, and blend thoroughly. Mix in the coconut.

3. Drop the dough by rounded teaspoonfuls onto the cookie sheets, spacing them about 3 inches apart. Bake for 8 to 10 minutes until golden brown. The cookies will puff up and then flatten during baking, and are not done until they have flattened. Let the cookies cool on the cookie sheet for 1 minute before removing them to racks to cool completely.

3 dozen wafers

OATMEAL DATE COOKIES

A crispy, yet chewy, homespun cookie that's sure to be a crowd pleaser.

1 cup butter
1 cup light brown sugar
1 teaspoon vanilla
1 cup flour mixed with 1 teaspoon baking soda
2 cups quick oats
1/2 cup chopped dates

1. Preheat the oven to 350°. Grease two cookie sheets.

2. In a bowl, cream the butter and sugar until fluffy. Add the vanilla and the flour mixture.

3. Stir in the oats and dates and mix well.

4. Form the dough into walnut-size balls. Flatten the dough and place the cookies 2 inches apart on the cookie sheets.

5. Bake for 10 minutes. Let the cookies cool on the baking sheets for 2 minutes before removing them to racks to cool completely.

3½ dozen cookies

PINE NUT COOKIES

Pignoli nuts, or more commonly called pine nuts, are actually the seeds of the pine tree. They're small, smooth, and have a slightly oily flavor. These cookies are reminiscent of the heavenly pine nut cookies sold in the Italian bakeries in Boston's North End. An almond paste batter is encrusted with pignoli nuts and baked until chewy.

> 7 ounce tube or can of almond paste
> 3/4 cup sugar
> 3 egg whites (from extra-large eggs)
> 1/2 teaspoon almond extract
> 1/2 cup flour
> 1/3 cup pine nuts

1. Preheat the oven to 325°. Line two baking sheets with foil. Grease the foil.

2. In the bowl of a food processor, put the almond paste, sugar, egg whites, extract, and flour. Pulse until batter is smooth and creamy.

3. Drop by heaping tablespoons onto the prepared cookie sheets 2 inches apart. Sprinkle with the pine nuts.

4. Bake about 20 minutes until golden around the edges. Remove the foil from the pan to a rack. Let the cookies cool completely before peeling them from the foil.

24 cookies

OVERNIGHT MERINGUES

Melts in the mouth—light and crispy meringues, studded with chocolate chips. Do not attempt to make meringues in humid weather; they never dry out completely and will be sticky.

>   *3 egg whites (from extra-large eggs)*
>   *1¹/₂ teaspoons vanilla extract*
>   *³/₄ cup sugar*
>   *1 cup semi-sweet chocolate chips*

1. Preheat the oven to 375°. Grease several cookie sheets.

2. In the bowl of an electric mixer, combine the egg whites with the vanilla. Beat the whites until frothy, then gradually add the sugar. Continue to beat on high until the whites are stiff and glossy, approximately 7 to 8 minutes. Fold in the chocolate chips.

3. Drop the batter by rounded teaspoonfuls about 1¹/₂ inches apart onto the prepared cookie sheets.

4. Place the cookie sheets in the oven, and immediately turn off the heat. Leave the meringues in the oven for at least 4 hours, and as much as overnight, without opening the door. Remove from the oven and transfer to serving plates.

6 dozen meringues

STRUDEL

A flaky pastry spread with apricot preserves, wrapped around a spiced fruit and nut filling. Prepare the pastry a day in advance.

Pastry:
1 cup butter
1/2 pint (1 cup) vanilla ice cream, softened
2 cups all-purpose flour

1. Cream the butter with the ice cream in a bowl. Work the flour into the softened butter until it is evenly incorporated and the dough is smooth.

2. Divide the dough into four equal portions and wrap each one separately. Refrigerate overnight.

Filling:
12 ounces apricot preserves
1/2 cup brown sugar
1 cup chopped walnuts
1/2 cup golden raisins
1/2 cup sweetened, flaked coconut
1 tablespoon cinnamon
1/2 teaspoon finely grated orange peel

confectioners' sugar

1. When you are ready to bake the strudel, preheat the oven to 325°. Grease two cookie sheets.

2. Remove the dough from the refrigerator. On a floured board, roll each portion into a large rectangle so that the dough is 1/8-inch thick.

3. Spread 1/4 of the apricot preserves over each portion of dough to within 1 inch of the edges.

4. In a small bowl, combine the brown sugar, walnuts, raisins, coconut, cinnamon, and orange peel and mix well. Divide the filling into fourths, and sprinkle 1/4 of it on each piece of dough covering the jam.

5. Fold the long sides of each rectangle toward the middle of the roll, overlapping the flaps of dough. Tuck the open ends under, and place the rolls seam side down on the prepared cookie sheets.

6. Bake for 1 hour. Remove the strudel to wire racks to cool. When cool, sprinkle with confectioners' sugar. Cut each roll on the diagonal into 10 pieces.

40 pieces of strudel

PRALINE SQUARES

Almost like eating mini-pecan pies—a buttery pastry base encrusted with a pecan and brown sugar topping.

Crust:
1 cup butter
1/2 cup sugar
2 cups all-purpose flour

1. Preheat the oven to 375°. Grease a 10 x 15-inch jelly roll pan.

2. Cream the butter with the sugar in a mixing bowl. Add the flour and mix the dough until it is crumbly. Press the dough onto the bottom of the prepared pan.

3. Bake for 15 minutes until lightly browned. Remove from the oven.

Topping:
1/3 cup butter
3/4 cup firmly packed dark brown sugar
3 eggs
1/2 cup dark corn syrup
3 cups coarsely chopped pecan meats
1 teaspoon vanilla extract
1/8 teaspoon salt

1. Cream together the butter and brown sugar until fluffy. Add the eggs, one at a time, beating well after each addition. Stir in the corn syrup, pecans, vanilla, and salt, and mix well.

2. Pour the pecan topping over the freshly baked pastry base. Return the pan to the oven and bake for an additional 18 to 20 minutes. Run a knife around the edges of the pan while still hot to release the topping from the sides of the pan. Cool in the pan before cutting into squares.

40 to 48 squares

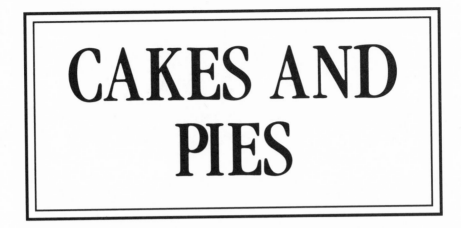

CAKES AND PIES

APPLE STREUSEL CAKE

A moist, buttery tube cake rippled with an apple, cinnamon, and nut streusel.

> 1 cup butter
> 2 cups sugar
> 4 eggs
> 1/4 cup apple juice
> 2 1/2 teaspoons vanilla extract
> 3 cups sifted all-purpose flour
> 1 tablespoon baking powder
> 1 teaspoon salt
> Apple Streusel (recipe follows)
> confectioners' sugar

1. Preheat the oven to 350°. Grease a 10-inch bundt pan and set aside.

2. In the bowl of an electric mixer, cream the butter with the sugar until fluffy. Add the eggs, apple juice, and vanilla and beat well.

3. Sift together the flour, baking powder, and salt. Add the dry ingredients to the batter.

4. Pour 1/2 of the batter into the prepared pan. Cover with 1/2 of the apple streusel. Pour the remainder of the batter over the apples, and top with the rest of the streusel. Gently swirl with a knife.

5. Bake for 60 to 65 minutes, until a tester inserted in the center comes out clean. Remove from the oven and cool in the pan for 30 minutes. Remove from the pan to a rack to cool completely. Sprinkle with confectioners' sugar before serving.

10 to 12 portions

> ### Apple Streusel:
> 3 1/2 cups apples, peeled and cut into 1/2-inch cubes (MacIntosh or
>   Cortlands)
> 1/2 cup chopped pecans
> 1/2 cup raisins
> 1/2 cup light brown sugar
> 4 tablespoons butter, cut into small cubes
> 2 teaspoons cinnamon
> pinch nutmeg and cloves

Combine all of the ingredients and mix well.

APPLE TORTE

A simple and delicious apple presentation that always receives raves. Even more special when crowned with a scoop of vanilla ice cream or a dollop of whipped cream. In the summertime, I often substitute 2 cups of big blueberries or 2 to 3 peeled and sliced peaches for the apples for seasonal indulgences.

1/2 cup butter
1 cup sugar
2 eggs
1 teaspoon vanilla
1 cup flour
1 teaspoon baking powder
1/4 teaspoon salt
3 medium-size apples, peeled, cored and sliced into 1/4-inch wedges
cinnamon-sugar mixture for topping

1. Preheat the oven to 350°. Grease a 9-inch springform pan.

2. In a mixing bowl, cream the butter and the sugar until light and fluffy. Add the eggs and vanilla, and mix well.

3. Sift together the flour, baking powder, and salt, and add the dry ingredients to the batter.

4. Spread the dough in the prepared pan. Layer the apple slices over the dough in concentric circles, overlapping each row. Sprinkle the cinnamon-sugar mixture very generously over the top.

5. Bake for 50 to 60 minutes until a tester inserted in the middle comes out clean. Remove to a rack to cool, or serve hot out of the oven.

6 to 8 portions

CRUMB CAKE

My family's favorite—a Viennese-style vanilla cake with a butter crumb topping.

1/3 cup butter
11/2 cups sugar
13/4 cups all-purpose flour
2 teaspoons baking powder
1/2 teaspoon salt
3/4 cup milk
2 eggs, separated
11/2 teaspoons vanilla extract

1. Preheat the oven to 350°. Grease a 9-inch springform pan.

2. In the bowl of an electric mixer, cream the butter with the sugar until the texture of coarse cornmeal.

3. Sift together the flour, baking powder, and salt. Add the dry ingredients to the sugar mixture, beating only until incorporated. Take out 1/2 cup of the crumb mixture and reserve it for the topping.

4. Add the milk, egg yolks, and vanilla to the mixing bowl; blend gently until smooth.

5. In a separate bowl, beat the egg whites until stiff. Gently fold them into the cake batter, being careful not to overbeat the batter.

6. Pour the mixture into the prepared pan. Sprinkle the reserved crumbs over the top of the cake. Bake for 50 minutes or until a cake tester inserted in the middle of the cake comes out clean.

7. Remove to a rack to cool. When cooled, remove the cake from the springform to a serving plate. The cake may be frozen if it's not devoured first!

8 portions

FRENCH CARROT CAKE

An exquisite cake of grated carrots flavored with cinnamon and ground walnuts spread with a Grand Marnier butter crème frosting.

1 cup butter
1 1/2 cups sugar
1/2 cup firmly packed dark brown sugar
4 eggs
2 teaspoons vanilla extract
2 cups all-purpose flour
2 teaspoons baking soda
1 teaspoon salt
2 teaspoons cinnamon
3 cups coarsely grated carrots
1 cup finely ground walnuts
Butter Crème Frosting (recipe follows)
1 to 2 tablespoons chopped walnuts for garnish

1. Preheat the oven to 350°. Grease two 9-inch round cake pans.

2. In the bowl of an electric mixer, cream the butter with the sugars. Add the eggs and vanilla and beat until the mixture is light and fluffy.

3. Sift together the flour, baking soda, salt, and cinnamon. Add these ingredients to the batter; mix well. Fold in the carrots and walnuts.

4. Pour the batter evenly into the prepared pans and bake for 40 to 45 minutes, until a tester inserted in the center comes out clean. Remove from the oven to racks, and cool completely before frosting. (Up to this point may be prepared in advance and placed in the freezer. Defrost and decorate with the frosting before serving.)

5. Ice the tops of the layers and then assemble the cake. Frost the sides with the remaining frosting. Sprinkle the top with the chopped walnuts and serve.

10 to 12 portions

Butter Crème Frosting:

¹/₂ cup butter
1¹/₂ cups packed confectioners' sugar
2 tablespoons Grand Marnier

1. Place all of the ingredients in the bowl of an electric mixer and beat on medium speed until mixture is smooth and creamy.

2. Spread the frosting on the cake layers and enjoy.

Frosting for one double-layer cake

COFFEE-RASPBERRY TORTE

Layers of vanilla cake spread with raspberry preserves and coffee cream.

> 3 eggs, separated
> 2/3 cup sugar
> 1 1/2 teaspoons vanilla extract
> 3/4 cup sifted all-purpose flour
> pinch of salt
> confectioners' sugar
> 8 tablespoons raspberry preserves
> Coffee Cream (recipe follows)

1. Preheat the oven to 350°. Grease an 11 x 17-inch jelly roll pan and line it with wax paper. Grease the wax paper lining.

2. In the bowl of an electric mixer, beat the egg yolks. Gradually add the sugar and continue beating until pale lemon in color. Add the vanilla and flour.

3. In a separate bowl, beat the egg whites with a pinch of salt until stiff peaks form. Gently fold the beaten whites into the batter.

4. Spread the batter evenly in the prepared pan. Bake for approximately 10 minutes, or until the cake springs back to the touch. Remove the pan from the oven. Dust the cake with confectioners' sugar and cover with wax paper, and then a slightly damp towel. Turn the cake upside down onto the towel and let cool for 15 to 20 minutes. Remove the pan and peel off the wax paper. Transfer to a rack and let the cake cool completely.

5. Cut the cake into fourths.* Spread 2 tablespoons of the preserves on top of each layer. Spread equal amounts of the coffee cream to cover the preserves. Arrange one cake layer on a serving plate. Assemble the remaining three layers on top of one another. Frost the sides of the torte with the remaining coffee cream. Refrigerate until serving time.

1 torte; 12 portions

*

Coffee Cream:

1¹/₂ cups heavy cream
1¹/₂ tablespoons instant coffee
³/₈ cup sugar

1. In a small saucepan, warm ¹/₂ cup of the cream with the instant coffee just to dissolve the coffee granules. Remove from the heat and chill completely.

2. With an electric mixer, whip all of the cream and sugar until stiff. Keep refrigerated until needed.

Cream to generously fill and frost one torte

HAZELNUT TORTE

Fancy party fare—a hazelnut layer cake spread with apricot preserves and covered with a chocolate sour cream frosting.

>   7 eggs, separated
>   1 cup sugar
>   3 tablespoons all-purpose flour
>   1 teaspoon double-acting baking powder
>   1/2 pound skinned, ground hazelnuts*
>   1 cup apricot preserves
>   Sour Cream Chocolate Frosting (recipe follows)
>   2 tablespoons chopped hazelnuts for garnish

1. Preheat the oven to 350°. Grease the bottom and sides of two 9-inch round layer cake pans. Line the bottoms with a circle of wax paper. Grease the paper lightly and dust with flour.

2. In the bowl of an electric mixer, beat the egg yolks until thick and lemon colored. Add the sugar gradually, and continue beating until the eggs are light and fluffy.

3. Combine the flour, baking powder, and ground hazelnuts, and fold this into the egg mixture.

4. In a separate bowl, beat the egg whites until stiff and gently fold them into the batter.

5. Pour the batter evenly into the prepared pans. Bake for 35 to 40 minutes, until the top springs back when lightly touched and the layers barely begin to come away from the sides of the pan. Remove the pans from the oven to racks to cool slightly. Then, carefully remove the cakes from the pans and peel the paper from the layers. Transfer the layers to a rack to cool completely before frosting. (Up to this point may be prepared in advance and stored in the freezer until party time. Defrost and adorn the cake with frosting before serving.)

6. Arrange one cake layer on a platter. Spread the top with 1/2 cup of the apricot preserves. Cover the preserves with a thin coating of the chocolate frosting. Set the second layer on top of this and spread with the rest of the preserves. Cover the top and sides of the cake with the remaining frosting.

7. Decorate the top with a sprinkling of the chopped hazelnuts.

8 to 10 portions

*To skin hazelnuts—spread the nuts on a cookie sheet and toast in a 325° oven for 12 to 15 minutes. Then rub the nuts between your fingers until the skins come off.

Sour Cream Chocolate Frosting:

6 ounces semi-sweet chocolate
2 tablespoons Crème de Cacao liqueur
1 cup sour cream

1. In the top of a double boiler, melt the chocolate, stirring constantly.

2. Remove from the heat and cool slightly. Stir in the Crème de Cacao and sour cream, blending until smooth. Use the frosting while slightly warm.

Enough to frost a double layer cake

GLAZED LEMON POUND CAKE

A rich, buttery, lemon-flavored, sour cream tube cake with an assertive lemon glaze.

>1 cup butter, melted
>2³/4 cups sugar
>6 eggs
>1 tablespoon lemon juice
>finely grated peel of 1 lemon
>3 cups all-purpose flour
>1/4 teaspoon baking soda
>1/2 teaspoon salt
>1 cup sour cream
>Lemon Glaze (recipe follows)

1. Preheat the oven to 325°. Grease and lightly flour a 10-inch bundt pan.

2. In the bowl of an electric mixer, cream the melted butter and the sugar. Beat in the eggs, one at a time. Add the lemon juice and grated peel. Continue beating until the mixture is thick and pale yellow.

3. Sift together the flour, baking soda, and salt. Add the dry ingredients alternately with the sour cream to the batter.

4. Pour the batter into the prepared pan and bake for 1 hour and 15 minutes. Remove from the oven to a rack to cool for 15 to 20 minutes. Remove the cake from the pan to cool an additional 30 minutes before frosting with the warm lemon glaze.

12 portions

Lemon Glaze:
>4 tablespoons butter
>2 cups confectioners' sugar
>2 to 3 tablespoons lemon juice
>finely grated peel of 1 lemon

1. Melt the butter in a saucepan; remove from heat. Sift the confectioners' sugar into the pan, stirring well until the mixture is smooth.

2. Beat in enough lemon juice to make the frosting creamy. Stir in the lemon peel. Pour the warm glaze over the cake, coating it completely.

Enough frosting for a 10-inch bundt cake

STRAWBERRY CHEESECAKE

A moist and feathery light strawberry-rippled cheesecake ornamented with whole strawberries. The cake bakes in an unorthodox fashion, in a low oven for one hour and then remains in the oven for several hours while it cools.

1/3 cup butter, melted
1 1/3 cups crushed butter cookies
1 pound cream cheese, at room temperature
1 pint sour cream
5 large eggs, separated
1 cup sugar
1 teaspoon vanilla extract
2/3 cup strawberry preserves
1 1/2 pints strawberries, hulled

1. Preheat the oven to 300°. Butter a 9-inch springform pan.

2. Combine the melted butter and crushed cookie crumbs in a bowl. Mix well. Pat the crumb mixture onto the bottom and up the sides of the pan to form a crust. Place the pan in the refrigerator while preparing the cheesecake filling.

3. In the bowl of an electric mixer, beat the cream cheese until fluffy. Add the sour cream, egg yolks, and sugar and beat on medium-high setting for 10 minutes. Add the vanilla.

4. In a separate bowl, beat the egg whites until stiff. Gently fold them into the cheesecake batter.

5. Pour the batter into the prepared springform pan. Drop spoonfuls of the jam on the cake. Swirl gently with a knife for a ripple effect.

6. Bake for 1 hour. Turn the oven off and leave the cake in the oven with the door closed until the oven is cold—approximately 4 hours. Refrigerate at least 3 to 4 hours or overnight before serving. (Note—the cake freezes well at this point.) Before serving, adorn the cake with whole berries—stand the berries point end up on the cake in concentric circles.

10 to 12 portions

ORANGE WALNUT CAKE

An orange-flavored cake dotted with chopped walnuts and soaked in a heavenly Grand Marnier syrup.

> 3 eggs
> 1 cup sugar
> 1¹/2 cups all-purpose flour
> 1¹/2 teaspoons baking powder
> ³/4 teaspoon salt
> 1 teaspoon vanilla extract
> 1 tablespoon finely grated orange peel
> ³/4 cup chopped walnuts
> ³/4 cup milk
> 2 tablespoons butter
> Orange Glaze (recipe follows)
> confectioners' sugar

1. Preheat the oven to 350°. Grease and flour a 9-inch tube pan.

2. In the bowl of an electric mixer, beat the eggs until foamy. Add the sugar gradually, continuing to beat until the eggs thicken.

3. Sift the flour with the baking powder and salt. Add the dry ingredients slowly to the batter.

4. Stir in the vanilla, orange peel, and walnuts.

5. Heat the milk and the butter in a small saucepan until hot, being careful not to let the milk boil. Stir the hot milk into the batter.

6. Pour the batter into the prepared tube pan. Bake for 45 to 50 minutes, until a cake tester inserted in the middle comes out clean.

7. While the cake is baking, prepare the orange glaze.

8. When the cake comes out of the oven, pierce it all along the top with a skewer. Spoon the warm syrup onto the cake. Cool the cake in the pan on a rack for 1 hour. Remove the cake from the pan, transfer to a serving plate, and dust with confectioners' sugar before serving.

8 to 10 portions

Orange Glaze:

1/2 cup orange juice
1/2 cup sugar
2 tablespoons butter
1/2 tablespoon lemon juice
2 tablespoons Grand Marnier

Combine the orange juice, sugar, butter, lemon juice, and Grand Marnier in a small saucepan. Simmer for 10 minutes, stirring often, until syrupy.

SOUR CREAM STREUSEL COFFEE CAKE

A moist and rich bundt cake with a brown sugar, nut, and chip streusel. Ideal for Sunday brunch with steaming mugs of coffee.

1¹/2 cups sour cream
1¹/2 teaspoons baking soda
1 cup butter
1¹/2 cups sugar
3 eggs
2 teaspoons vanilla extract
3 cups all-purpose flour
2 teaspoons baking powder
pinch salt
Streusel (recipe follows)

1. Combine the sour cream and baking soda and let stand at room temperature for ¹/2 hour.

2. Preheat the oven to 350°. Grease a 10-inch bundt pan.

3. In the large bowl of an electric mixer, cream the butter with the sugar until fluffy. Add the eggs, vanilla, and sour cream. Mix until the batter is well blended.

4. Combine the flour, baking powder, and salt. Add the dry ingredients to the batter, beating only until the flour is incorporated.

5. Cover the bottom of the prepared pan with a generous layer of the batter. Sprinkle with ¹/3 of the streusel mixture. Add another layer of batter, and then all of the streusel. Spread the remaining batter over the top.

6. Bake for 1 hour or until a tester inserted in the center comes out clean. Remove the cake from the oven and let cool on a rack for 20 to 30 minutes. Then, invert the pan, remove the cake, and cool completely on the wire rack.

12 portions

Streusel:

1/3 cup granulated sugar
1/2 cup firmly packed dark brown sugar
2 teaspoons cinnamon
1/2 cup chopped pecans
1/2 cup semi-sweet chocolate chips

Combine the sugars, cinnamon, nuts, and chips in a bowl and mix well.

SELMA'S SPICE CAKE

A featherlight spice roll filled and frosted with a mocha cream.

6 eggs, separated
1 cup sugar
3/4 cup cake flour
1/2 teaspoon salt
1 teaspoon baking powder
1/2 teaspoon allspice
1 1/2 teaspoons ground cloves
1 1/2 teaspoons cinnamon
Mocha Cream (recipe follows)
confectioners' sugar

1. Preheat the oven to 350°. Grease a 10 x 15-inch jelly roll pan. Line the pan with wax paper and grease the paper.

2. In the bowl of an electric mixer, beat the egg yolks and sugar together until the mixture is pale and fluffy.

3. Sift the flour with the salt, baking powder, and spices. Add the dry ingredients to the batter.

4. In a separate bowl, beat the egg whites until stiff and gently fold them into the batter.

5. Pour the batter into the prepared jelly roll pan. Bake for 20 minutes. Remove from the oven and turn the cake over onto a towel that's been dusted with confectioners' sugar. Lift off the pan and let the cake cool for 10 minutes. Peel off the wax paper from the cake. Carefully roll the cake with the towel, jelly roll fashion, and let the cake remain in this position on a rack for 20 to 30 minutes while it cools completely.

6. When the cake is cooled, unroll to fill. (Note that if the cake is even slightly warm, the whipped cream filling will weep.) Spoon a generous amount of the mocha cream onto the inside of the cake, smoothing it to within 1-inch of all the edges.

7. Roll the cake up to form a log. Place it seam side down on a platter. Spread the remainder of the mocha cream over the roll, frosting it evenly. Run the tines of a fork along the top of the cake roll to create decorative ridges resembling the bark of a tree. Refrigerate the cake roll until serving time. (If you choose to freeze the dessert, wrap it loosely in saran wrap. Defrost for 2 hours in the refrigerator prior to serving.)

10 to 12 portions

Mocha Cream:

1 1/2 pints heavy cream
3 tablespoons instant coffee
3/8 cup sugar
4 1/2 tablespoons sweetened cocoa

1. In a small saucepan, warm 1/2 pint of the cream with the instant coffee just enough to dissolve the coffee. Remove from the heat and chill well.

2. In the bowl of an electric mixer, whip all of the cream, sugar, and cocoa until stiff peaks form. Refrigerate until needed.

Cream to fill and frost one cake roll

STRAWBERRY CREAM ROLL

An almond flavored jelly roll filled with strawberries, ricotta cheese, and apricot preserves.

> 4 eggs, separated
> 3/4 cup sugar
> 1 teaspoon almond extract
> 3/4 cup sifted cake flour
> 1 teaspoon salt
> 3/4 teaspoon baking powder
> confectioners' sugar for garnish
> Strawberry Cream Filling (recipe follows)
> 1 cup sliced strawberries for garnish

1. Preheat the oven to 400°. Grease a 10 x 15-inch jelly roll pan and line it with wax paper. Grease the paper lining.

2. In the bowl of an electric mixer, beat the egg yolks with the sugar until the mixture is light and fluffy. Add the almond extract.

3. Sift together the flour, salt, and baking powder and add the dry ingredients to the batter.

4. In a separate bowl, beat the egg whites until stiff and gently fold them into the batter.

5. Pour the batter into the prepared jelly roll pan and bake for 10 to 13 minutes, or until a tester inserted into the center comes out clean. Turn the cake over onto a towel that has been dusted with confectioners' sugar. Lift off the pan and let the cake cool for 10 minutes. Remove the wax paper. Roll the cake with the towel, jelly roll fashion, and let the cake sit in the rolled position on a rack for 20 minutes while it continues to cool.

6. When the cake has cooled completely, unroll. Spread the inside with the cheese mixture. Spoon the 3 cups of sliced strawberries over the cheese filling. Reroll the cake to form a log and place seam side down on a platter. Dust the top with confectioners' sugar and garnish with the cup of sliced berries. Chill the cake for 1 hour before serving.

8 portions

Strawberry Cream Filling:

1/2 pound ricotta cheese
3 tablespoons apricot preserves
3 tablespoons Amaretto
3 cups sliced strawberries

1. In the bowl of an electric mixer, beat the ricotta cheese until it is light and fluffy.

2. Add the apricot preserves and Amaretto and mix thoroughly.

SOUR CREAM APPLE TART

Apple slices piled high in a deep-dish crust and coated with vanilla cream.

Pie Crust:
2 cups sifted all-purpose flour
2 tablespoons sugar
1/2 teaspoon salt
1/4 teaspoon baking powder
1/2 cup butter

1. Sift together the flour, sugar, salt, and baking powder into a bowl.

2. With a fork or pastry blender, work the butter into the dry ingredients until the texture of cornmeal.

3. Line a 9-inch deep-dish pie pan with the dough, patting it firmly into place.

Filling:
2 pounds apples, peeled, cored, and thinly sliced (I prefer Cortlands or MacIntosh.)
1/2 cup sugar
1 teaspoon cinnamon
2 tablespoons melted butter

1. Preheat the oven to 400°.

2. Arrange the apple slices in concentric circles in the pieshell.

3. Combine the cinnamon and the sugar and sprinkle over the apples. Drizzle the melted butter over the fruit.

4. Bake for 30 minutes. While the pie is baking, prepare the sour cream topping.

Topping:
1 egg
1 teaspoon vanilla extract
2 tablespoons brown sugar
3/4 cup sour cream

1. Mix together the egg, vanilla, brown sugar, and sour cream in a small bowl. Pour the vanilla cream over the partially baked apples. Return the pie to the oven for 25 minutes more.

2. Present the pie hot out of the oven, or let cool to room temperature before serving.

8 portions

COCONUT KEY LIME PIE

Coconut and lime custard topped with a refreshing kiwi garnish and ginger whipped cream.

Graham Pie Crust:
1 tablespoon confectioners' sugar
1/2 teaspoon cinnamon
1 1/4 cups graham cracker crumbs
6 tablespoons melted butter

1. Preheat the oven to 375°.

2. Combine the sugar and cinnamon in a mixing bowl. Stir in the graham crumbs. Add the butter and mix well to moisten the crumb mixture.

3. Press the crumbs onto the bottom and sides of a 9-inch pie pan. Bake for 7 to 10 minutes until lightly browned. Cool the shell on a rack; then refrigerate to set the crumbs before filling.

Filling:
14 ounce can sweetened condensed milk
1/2 cup fresh lime juice
1/2 cup sweetened, shredded coconut
3 kiwis, peeled and sliced into 1/4-inch thick rounds

1. Combine the condensed milk, lime juice, and coconut in a bowl and stir well.

2. Pour the custard into the baked pie shell and refrigerate for at least 3 hours or overnight for the custard to set.

3. Garnish the top with concentric circles of kiwi.

Ginger Cream Topping:
1 cup heavy cream
1/4 cup sugar
1 tablespoon candied ginger, finely chopped

1. When ready to serve, prepare the topping. In the bowl of an electric mixer, whip the cream and sugar until thickened. Add the candied ginger and beat to stiff peaks.

2. Blanket the pie with the ginger cream and present.

Enough topping for one pie.

8 portions

DEEP-DISH PEACH PIE

Peach slices buried under an almond pastry topping.

2^{1}/2 *cups peaches, skinned and sliced into* ^{1}/2*-inch wedges*
3 to 4 tablespoons sugar (amount depends on the sweetness of the fruit)
1 teaspoon cinnamon
^{1}/3 *cup finely ground almonds*
1 cup sugar
1 cup all-purpose flour
^{1}/2 *cup butter, melted*
1 egg
1 teaspoon almond extract

1. Preheat the oven to 350°.
2. Arrange the peach slices in a 9-inch deep-dish pie pan.
3. Combine the 3 to 4 tablespoons sugar, cinnamon, and ground almonds in a mixing bowl. Sprinkle this mixture over the peaches.
4. Beat together the 1 cup sugar, flour, butter, egg, and almond extract until fluffy. Spread this batter over the peaches, covering fruit completely.
5. Bake for 45 minutes. Serve hot, warm, or room temperature— whatever your preference.

6 to 8 portions

THE CHOCOLATE PASSION

Chocolate, chocolate, chocolate—we need only mention the word for images of the dark, sweet, rich dessert and confection to come to mind. Words used to celebrate the popular sweet include: delicious, decadent, divine, delectable, luscious, rich, velvety, and sublime. Chocolate mania is a wide-spread phenomenon. People who have an obsessive passion for chocolate, eat, think, and breathe the heavenly confection. Chocolate lovers will agree that chocolate is one of the most versatile flavorings. All you chocolate devotées take heed—you'll be tempted, teased, and titillated by the unquestionably fabulous treats in store. If you burn with the chocolate fever, you'll find comfort and joy in these recipes. Live your wildest chocolate fantasy and indulge in the ultimate, as chocolate is one of those irresistibles in life!

BEST EVER CHOCOLATE CHIP WAFER

A crispy, yet chewy, version of the unsurpassed all-time American favorite!

1/2 cup butter
1/3 cup brown sugar
1/3 cup granulated sugar
1/4 cup light corn syrup
1 teaspoon vanilla extract
1 egg
11/4 cups sifted all-purpose flour
1/2 teaspoon baking soda
1/8 teaspoon salt
1 cup semi-sweet chocolate chips

1. Preheat the oven to 375°. Grease two cookie sheets.

2. Cream the butter, sugars, and corn syrup together until fluffy. Add the vanilla and the egg and mix well.

3. Sift together the flour, baking soda, and salt and add these ingredients to the batter, mixing until well blended.

4. Stir in the chocolate chips. Drop the batter by rounded tablespoons onto the cookie sheets, 3 inches apart.

5. Bake for 8 to 10 minutes until golden. Let the cookies cool on the baking sheet for 3 minutes before removing them to racks to cool completely.

21/2 dozen wafers

CHOCOLATE MINT SQUARES

A fudgy base covered with a creamy mint liqueur frosting and a bitter chocolate glaze.

Brownie Base:
2 ounces unsweetened chocolate
1/2 cup butter
1 cup sugar
2 eggs, beaten
1/2 cup all-purpose flour
pinch salt

1. Preheat the oven to 325°. Grease a 9-inch square baking pan.

2. Melt together the chocolate and butter in a saucepan, stirring until smooth. Remove from the heat and cool.

3. Combine the sugar, eggs, flour, and salt in a bowl and mix well. Add the cooled chocolate to the batter, blending thoroughly.

4. Pour the chocolate batter into the prepared pan. Bake for 25 minutes. Remove to a rack to cool completely before proceeding further.

Mint Frosting:
3 tablespoons butter
1 1/2 cups confectioners' sugar
2 1/2 tablespoons Crème de Menthe

1. Cream the butter and confectioners' sugar until light and fluffy. Add the Crème de Menthe and beat well.

2. Spread the frosting smoothly over the cooled cookie base. Refrigerate until firm, approximately 1 hour, before covering with the chocolate glaze.

Chocolate Glaze:

1¹/₂ ounces unsweetened chocolate
1¹/₂ tablespoons butter

1. In a small saucepan, melt the chocolate and butter, stirring until very smooth.

2. Pour the hot glaze onto the chilled icing; quickly tilt the pan from side to side to cover the frosting with the glaze. (You will have to work rapidly, as the glaze sets fairly fast.)

3. Refrigerate the pastry about 1 hour until the glaze is set. When ready to serve, cut the cake into small squares using a sharp knife.

36 squares

RUM RAISIN BALLS

Rum, raisins, and pecans team together for a winning combination in these fudgy bon bons.

2 cups finely crushed gingersnaps
1 cup finely ground pecans
1 cup raisins, coarsely chopped
1 cup confectioners' sugar
3 tablespoons Dutch cocoa
2 tablespoons white corn syrup
1/2 cup light rum
large container chocolate sprinkles for coating

1. Combine the gingersnaps, pecans, raisins, confectioners' sugar, cocoa, corn syrup, and rum, and mix well.

2. Using a teaspoon, shape the dough into balls. Roll the bon bons in the chocolate sprinkles to coat completely.

3. Store the bon bons in a tightly covered container at room temperature for 2 days so that the flavors will blend.

45 to 50 bon bons

CREAM CHEESE BROWNIES

No cookbook would be complete without a recipe for brownies. Brownies have been an all-American favorite since the 19th century, but as of late, have taken on more exotic character. These have an almond-flavored chocolate chip cheesecake swirled through a fudgy brownie batter. They're moist, rich, and heavenly.

> 1 cup butter
> 4 ounces unsweetened chocolate
> 2 cups sugar
> 4 eggs
> 2 teaspoons vanilla extract
> 1 cup all-purpose flour
> Cream Cheese Filling (recipe follows)

1. Preheat the oven to 350°. Grease a 9 x 13-inch baking pan.

2. Melt the butter and chocolate in a saucepan over low heat, stirring until smooth. Remove from the heat and let cool. Beat the sugar and the eggs together until fluffy. Add the vanilla. Stir the cooled chocolate mixture into the eggs and mix well.

3. Fold the flour into the batter and blend thoroughly. Pour the batter into the prepared pan.

4. Drop spoonfuls of the cream cheese filling onto the batter. Swirl the cream cheese through the chocolate with a knife until a rippling of the batters is effected.

5. Bake for 30 to 35 minutes. Remove to a rack to cool completely before cutting into pieces.

3 dozen brownies

Cream Cheese Filling:
> 8 ounces cream cheese, at room temperature
> 2 tablespoons butter
> 1/3 cup sugar
> 1 egg
> 1 teaspoon almond extract
> 6 ounces semi-sweet chocolate chips

Beat the cream cheese and butter with an electric mixer. Add the sugar, egg, and almond extract and beat until the cream cheese is fluffy and the ingredients are well blended. Stir in the chocolate chips.

PEANUT BUTTER BON BONS

Balls of crunchy peanut butter coated with a chocolate shell. Especially appreciated by peanut butter fans.

3/4 cup butter
1 pound confectioners' sugar
1 pound 2 ounce jar crunchy peanut butter
1/2 cup mini semi-sweet chocolate chips
1 teaspoon vanilla extract
12 ounces semi-sweet chocolate (not chips)

1. Cream 1/2 cup butter with the confectioners' sugar until smooth and fluffy. Add the peanut butter, chocolate chips, and vanilla and blend well. Place the dough in the refrigerator until firm, about 2 hours.

2. Remove the chilled dough from the refrigerator and roll it into walnut-size balls, using about 1 tablespoon of dough for each bon bon. Set the balls on a sheet of wax paper.

3. When all of the balls have been formed, melt the chocolate with 1/4 cup butter in the top of a double boiler, stirring until the chocolate is smooth.

4. Remove the melted chocolate from the heat. Carefully dip the bon bons into the melted chocolate, rolling them around to coat them evenly. With a spoon, remove the balls to wax paper to set for 1 hour. Refrigerate until needed. (If you find the melted chocolate begins to harden, reheat it in the top of the double boiler until smooth.)

4 to 4 1/2 dozen bon bons

CHOCOLATE TRUFFLES

Decadent, sinfully rich, and delicious! A chocolate-lovers' dream come true.

> 1¹/3 *cups semi-sweet chocolate chips*
> ¹/4 *cup Grand Marnier*
> 2 *tablespoons strong coffee*
> ¹/2 *cup butter, at room temperature*
> ³/4 *cup ground gingersnaps*
> ¹/2 *cup sweetened cocoa*

1. Place the chocolate, Grand Marnier, and coffee in a small saucepan. Heat over a low flame, stirring until the chocolate melts.

2. Remove the pan from the heat and whisk in the butter until smooth. Stir in the ground gingersnaps.

3. Chill the mixture for several hours.

4. With a teaspoon, scoop out chunks of chocolate and form into balls. Roll the truffles in the cocoa.

5. Cover and refrigerate until serving time. Allow truffles to stand at room temperature for 30 minutes before enjoying. (These will keep 2 weeks in the refrigerator, and also freeze well.)

24 to 30 truffles

CHOCOLATE-DIPPED STRAWBERRIES

These always make a beautiful presentation—they lend a special touch to any meal.

45 large strawberries
6 ounces semi-sweet chocolate (not chips)

1. Line a cookie sheet with wax paper.

2. Wash the strawberries well. Leave the stems on the berries and pat dry.

3. Heat the chocolate in the top part of a double boiler until melted, stirring until smooth. Remove from heat.

4. Holding the berries by the stem end, dip the pointed end into the chocolate, coating 2/3 of each berry. Wipe off any excess chocolate against the side of the pan. Place the dipped berries on the wax paper. You will have to work quickly, as the chocolate thickens fairly fast. If it gets too hard, reheat the chocolate briefly over low heat.

5. Chill the berries 30 minutes to set. Keep refrigerated until ready to serve. These are perishable and should be used the same day as made.

6 to 8 portions

CHOCOLATE-GLAZED DRIED FRUITS

For a real treat in the winter, try dipping dried fruits in chocolate—you'll receive accolades!

semi-sweet chocolate (not chips)
dried apricots
dried figs
prunes

1. Melt the chocolate in the top of a double boiler.

2. Remove from heat and dip each piece of fruit, coating only half of it. Place on waxed paper to set.

CHOCOLATE MOUSSE

A rich chocolaty custard doused with Amaretto, and crowned with a dollop of whipped cream.

> *4 ounces unsweetened chocolate*
> *4 ounces semi-sweet chocolate*
> *1/2 cup sweet butter*
> *1/4 cup Amaretto*
> *6 eggs, separated*
> *1 cup plus 1 tablespoon sugar*
> *whipped cream for garnish*

1. In the top part of a double boiler, melt the chocolates and butter together, stirring until smooth. Cool and add the Amaretto.

2. In the bowl of an electric mixer, beat together the egg yolks and 1 cup of sugar until thick and pale yellow in color. Pour the cooled chocolate mixture slowly into the beaten yolks, mixing constantly.

3. In a separate bowl, whip the egg whites to soft peaks. Add 1 tablespoon of sugar and continue beating until stiff. Gently fold the beaten egg whites into the chocolate mixture until no traces of white remain. Pour the custard into 8 to 10 ramekins and refrigerate at least 4 hours, or overnight.

4. When ready to serve, garnish each mousse with a spoonful of whipped cream.

8 to 10 portions

POT DE CREME

A sinfully rich, lusciously chocolaty pudding laced with Crème de Cacao.

> 6 ounces semi-sweet chocolate chips
> 2 tablespoons sugar
> 3/4 cup light cream
> 3 tablespoons Crème de Cacao
> 2 egg yolks
> whipped cream for garnish
> candied violets for garnish, optional (available in gourmet food shops)

1. Heat the chocolate chips, sugar, and cream in a medium-size saucepan over medium heat until the chocolate melts and the mixture just comes to a boil. Remove the chocolate cream from the heat and cool to room temperature.

2. Mix together the Crème de Cacao and the egg yolks. Add to the cooled chocolate in a slow, steady stream, beating constantly, until all the egg is incorporated, and the chocolate is smooth.

3. Pour the crème into 4 custard cups and chill until serving time. This may be done as much as 24 hours in advance.

4. Garnish each pot de crème with a dollop of whipped cream and a candied violet.

4 portions

TORRONE LOAF

Almost fudge-like—a rich, dense, decadent chocolate loaf studded with butter cookie chunks and ground almonds, spiked with rum.

12 ounces semi-sweet chocolate
1/2 cup dark rum
1 cup sweet butter
1/4 cup sugar
4 eggs, separated
1/2 cup finely ground almonds
1/8 teaspoon cream of tartar
11/2 cups crushed butter cookies
whipped cream for garnish

1. Lightly grease a 5 x 9-inch loaf pan. Line the bottom and sides of the pan with plastic wrap.

2. In a saucepan, melt the chocolate with the rum, stirring until smooth; let cool.

3. In the bowl of an electric mixer, cream together the butter and sugar until fluffy. Add the egg yolks, one at a time, blending well after each addition. Beat in the ground almonds and cooled chocolate.

4. In a separate bowl, beat the egg whites with the cream of tartar until stiff, but not dry. Fold the beaten whites into the chocolate mixture.

5. Gently blend the cookie pieces into the batter. Turn the mixture into the prepared loaf pan and chill at least 4 hours. When ready to serve, unmold onto a platter and garnish each portion with a dollop of whipped cream.

Note—This does not freeze well!

12 portions

CHOCOLATE LAYER CAKE

A feather light, moist sour cream chocolate layer cake frosted with a creamy chocolate icing.

> 1 cup sour cream
> 1 teaspoon baking soda
> 3 ounces unsweetened chocolate
> 1 cup butter
> 2 cups sugar
> 5 eggs
> 1 teaspoon vanilla
> 2¹/2 cups cake flour
> Chocolate Frosting (recipe follows)

1. Preheat the oven to 350°. Grease two 9-inch round cake pans.

2. Combine the sour cream and baking soda and let stand at room temperature for ¹/2 hour.

3. In the top of a double boiler, melt the chocolate, stirring until smooth. Let cool.

4. In the bowl of an electric mixer, cream the butter and sugar until fluffy. Add the eggs, one at a time, beating after each addition. Add the vanilla; stir in the cooled, melted chocolate.

5. Sift the cake flour, and add it alternately to the batter with the sour cream, beginning and ending with the flour.

6. Pour the batter into the prepared pans. Set in the oven for 35 minutes. Remove to racks to cool in the pan for 10 minutes. Remove the cake from the pans and cool completely before frosting.

10 to 12 portions

Chocolate Frosting:

4 ounces unsweetened chocolate
6 tablespoons butter
2 cups confectioners' sugar
2 eggs
1/2 cup milk
1 teaspoon vanilla

1. In the top of a double boiler, melt the chocolate with the butter, stirring until smooth. Let cool.

2. Place all of the ingredients in a small mixing bowl and blend well. Put the bowl in a larger bowl of ice and beat on high speed until the frosting is the consistency of whipped cream. (The secret to the fluffy frosting is to beat the ingredients over a bowl of ice.)

3. Frost the tops of the layers and assemble. Spread the remainder of the frosting on the sides of the cake and present.

Frosting for one double layer cake

CHOCOLATE RASPBERRY TORTE

A very elegant dessert—layers of chocolate cake filled with a raspberry-liqueur (Chambord) cream, and glazed with a dark chocolate icing. There is no mistake in the ingredients—this is a flourless cake.

> 1 ounce dark sweet chocolate
> 3 tablespoons instant coffee
> 5 eggs, separated
> 1 cup sugar
> sweetened cocoa
> Chambord Cream (recipe follows)
> Chocolate Icing (recipe follows)
> 1/3 cup sliced, toasted almonds for garnish (see page 273)

1. Preheat the oven to 350°. Butter an 11 x 17-inch jelly roll pan and line it with wax paper. Grease the paper lining.

2. In the top part of a double boiler, melt the chocolate with the instant coffee, stirring until smooth. Remove from the heat to cool.

3. With an electric mixer, beat the egg yolks until light and fluffy. Gradually add the sugar and continue beating until the mixture is very thick and pale in color. Stir in the cooled, melted chocolate.

4. In a separate bowl, beat the egg whites until stiff peaks form. Gently fold the beaten whites into the batter, blending until no traces of the whites remain.

5. Spread the batter evenly in the pan and set in the oven for 15 minutes, or until the cake springs back to the touch. Be careful not to overbake. Remove the pan to a rack and cover the cake with a damp towel for 30 minutes, until it cools. Remove the towel and loosen the cake from the baking sheet; dust the top generously with the cocoa. Turn the cake over onto a sheet of wax paper and carefully remove the paper lining from the bottom. Cut the cake into fourths— and let cool completely before filling and frosting.*

*
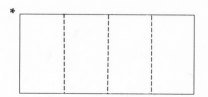

6. Spread equal amounts of the Chambord cream over 3 of the cake layers. Arrange one cake layer on a plate. Assemble one filled layer on top of another, capping them with the plain layer. Pour the warm chocolate glaze over the torte. Work quickly as the icing sets fairly fast. Garnish the top with the sliced almonds. Refrigerate until serving time. This dessert may be frozen. Defrost 2 hours in the refrigerator before presenting to appreciative guests!

1 torte; 12 portions

Chambord Cream:

1 cup heavy cream, well chilled
2 tablespoons confectioners' sugar
3 tablespoons Chambord

1. In the bowl of an electric mixer, beat the cream until thickened.

2. Add the sugar and Chambord and whip until soft peaks form.

Chocolate Icing:

4 ounces dark sweet chocolate
1/3 cup butter
2 teaspoons Chambord

1. Melt the chocolate and butter together in the top part of a double boiler, stirring constantly.

2. Remove the pot from the heat and stir in the Chambord. Spread while warm, glazing the top and sides of the torte.

Enough cream and glaze for one torte

CHOCOLATE ALMOND POUND CAKE

A buttermilk pound cake with old-fashioned goodness—moist, dense, and chocolaty.

> 1^1/$_2$ cups butter
> 3 cups sugar
> 5 eggs
> ^{1}/$_4$ cup Amaretto
> 2 cups flour
> ^{3}/$_4$ cup unsweetened cocoa
> 1 teaspoon salt
> ^{1}/$_4$ teaspoon baking powder
> 1 cup buttermilk
> confectioners' sugar

1. Preheat the oven to 325°. Grease a 10-inch bundt pan.

2. In the bowl of an electric mixer, cream the butter. Gradually add the sugar, beating until light and fluffy.

3. Add the eggs, one at a time, beating well after each addition. Add the Amaretto.

4. Combine the flour, cocoa, salt, and baking powder. Add the dry ingredients alternately with the buttermilk, mixing until evenly blended. Pour into the prepared pan.

5. Bake for 1 hour and 15 to 20 minutes, until a tester inserted in the center comes out clean. Let cake cool in pan for 15 minutes. Remove cake from pan to a rack to cool completely. Dust with confectioners' sugar and serve.

10 to 12 portions

THE GRAND DAME CAKE

An outrageous dessert—a light, moist, fudgy chocolate torte flecked with ground pecans, and finished with a bitter chocolate glaze. It romances the taste buds!

> 12 ounces semi-sweet chocolate (not chips)
> 1 cup butter
> 1 cup sugar
> 5 eggs, separated
> 1 tablespoon vanilla
> 1 cup finely ground pecans
> Bitter Chocolate Glaze (recipe follows)

1. Preheat the oven to 350°. Grease a 9-inch springform pan.

2. Melt the semi-sweet chocolate in the top of a double boiler. Set aside to cool.

3. In the bowl of an electric mixer, cream the butter and sugar until fluffy. Add the egg yolks and beat until thick and pale in color.

4. Mix in the cooled chocolate, vanilla, and ground pecans.

5. In a separate bowl, beat the egg whites to stiff peaks. Gently fold the beaten whites into the batter, until no traces of the whites remain. Spread the batter into the prepared pan. Bake for 1 hour.

6. Remove the cake to a rack to cool completely. Once cooled, remove the cake from the springform before icing.

12 portions

Bitter Chocolate Glaze:
3 ounces unsweetened chocolate
3 tablespoons butter
1 heaping teaspoon instant coffee

1. In a small saucepan over low heat, melt the chocolate, butter, and coffee. Stir to mix well.

2. Pour the glaze over the top of the cake. Spread the chocolate with a spatula, letting the icing run down the sides of the torte.

INDEX

D

INGREDIENTS

for Great Cooking ✦

✦ *The Best Restaurant Cookbooks*

✦ *A Few of Our Classic Cookbooks*

✦ *The Best of Meatless Cooking*

MOOSEWOOD COOKBOOK
Revised & Expanded Edition
by Mollie Katzen

This top-to-bottom revision of our bestselling cookbook retains all the old favorites and adds twenty-five all-new recipes. All recipes are as delicious as ever, and the amounts of high-fat dairy products and eggs now reflect today's lighter tastes. "One of the most attractive, least dogmatic meatless cookbooks printed . . . an engaging blend of hand-lettered care and solid food information."—*The New York Post* $16.95 paper or $19.95 cloth, 256 pages

THE ENCHANTED BROCCOLI FOREST
by Mollie Katzen

Two hundred and fifty more great vegetarian recipes from the author of *Moosewood*. "An imaginative, witty book, a real charmer." —*Library Journal* $16.95 paper or $19.95 cloth, 320 pages

STILL LIFE WITH MENU
by Mollie Katzen

The first major meatless book designed as a menu cookbook, with full-color illustrations. ". . . warm, personal, and inviting . . . with fine color reproductions of Katzen's sumptuous artwork." —*Vegetarian Times* $19.95 paper or $34.95 cloth, 352 pages

THE NEW LAUREL'S KITCHEN
by Laurel Robertson, Carol Flinders, & Brian Ruppenthal

Millions of people have enjoyed this cookbook for its warm tone, lovely art, and, of course, fantastic recipes. This new edition contains updated nutritional information and hundreds of healthful recipes. $24.95 paper or $27.95 cloth, 512 pages.

BREADTIME STORIES
by Susan Jane Cheney

Breads and accompaniments(spreads, soups, etc.) from a former Moosewood restaurant baker. "All the recipes are vegetarian and low in fat and cholesterol . . . the detailed baking instructions and bread recipes are the best part of this book." —*Library Journal* $17.95 paper, 256 pages

FRIENDLY FOODS
by Brother Ron Picarski

Gourmet vegan food—no meat, eggs, or dairy included—from a Franciscan friar and three-time Culinary Olympics medal winner. "When it comes to elegant, dairyless vegetarian cooking, *Friendly Foods* is one of the best books available." —John Robbins, author of *Diet for a New America* $16.95 paper, 288 pages

COYOTE CAFE
by Mark Miller

Exciting, innovative Southwestern cuisine, from the nationally known restaurant, in a beautiful full-color cookbook. "Mark Miller's Coyote Cafe in Santa Fe, in both its design and dishes, is bold and exciting. And his book is all of those qualities combined."—*Washington Post* $25.95 clothbound, 160 pages

THE GREAT CHILE BOOK
by Mark Miller
with John Harrisson

A full-color photographic guide to one hundred varieties of chile—fifty each of fresh and dried, including a brief description, tips for use, and a heat rating. The book also gives a history of the chile in Mexican and Southwestern tradition, and recipes from the Coyote Cafe. $14.95 paper, 128 pages

CHILE PEPPER POSTERS

Created by Mark Miller of the Coyote Cafe, these sumptuous chile identification posters show thirty-one fresh chiles and thirty-five dried ones, with heat ratings and cooking tips for each. A fabulous addition to any wall, kitchen or otherwise. *Fresco* (fresh chiles) $15.00; *Seco* (dried chiles) $15.00; both posters $25.00.

JANOS
by Janos Wilder

Recipes and tales from a celebrated Tucson restaurant whose inventive cuisine mixes classic French cookery with the vibrant tastes of the Southwest. "A splendid and creative assortment of 200 recipes . . . a graceful mix of simplicity and elegance."—*Booklist* $16.95 paper, 240 pages

CAFE BEAUJOLAIS
by Margaret Fox & John Bear

From a beautiful little restaurant in Northern California, a book celebrating fresh ingredients, great food, and country living. In addition to the 132 delicious recipes, *Cafe Beaujolais* offers hints and stories for anyone who's considered starting a restaurant. $16.95 paper or $19.95 cloth, 256 pages

KEO'S THAI CUISINE
by Keo Sananikone

". . . filled with uncomplicated recipes and photographs that manage to be useful and beautiful at the same time."—*Chicago Tribune*

Keo's Thai restaurant is one of the places to visit in Hawaii, and the wonderful recipes in this book prove that its reputation is definitely deserved. Full color throughout. $24.95 clothbound, 192 pages

TEN SPEED PRESS
P. O. Box 7123
Berkeley, California 94707

Available from your local bookstore, or order direct from the publisher. Please include $3.50 shipping and handling for the first book, and 50¢ for each additional book. California residents include local sales tax. Write for our free complete catalog of over 500 books and tapes.